Further praise for *The Marketing Pathfinder*

"In *The Marketing Pathfinder* David Stewart and Michael Saren bring
students a valuable resource for marketing management and strateg
The book views marketers as reflective practitioners – not only do they neea to
access appropriate concepts and frameworks to assess the situation, but also to
have the confidence to make the right decision. Building a capacity for reflective
enquiry, where the art of practice is linked to theories and frameworks becomes
central. This book embraces this concept fully and the book should be considered
as required reading or the basis for a marketing management and strategy course.
I strongly recommend it."

*Professor Rod Brodie, Professor of Marketing, University of Auckland Business
School, New Zealand*

"A highly engaging and accessible read which cuts through the theoretical
technicalities of marketing. Excellent 'live' micro cases, featuring a plethora of
brands and topical issues, offer students a sharp and usable resource for
navigating the pathfinder concepts and undertaking their own research. A
cracking read for those interested in quickly getting to grips with marketing."

*Professor Sally Dibb, Professor of Marketing, Director of Social Marketing,
Open University, Milton Keynes, UK*

"*The Marketing Pathfinder* is unique as it calls for a coherent pluralism of
marketing perspectives rather than claiming the leadership of a particular
marketing perspective. Nor do the authors adopt an overarching integrative
approach or any kind of 'Grand Theory' of marketing. Each micro-case study
enables the student to understand how each theory, necessarily sub-determined,
makes its own contribution to make sense of a situation and to solve marketing
issues."

*Professor Bernard Cova, Professor of Marketing, Kedge Business School,
Marseille, France*

"*The Marketing Pathfinder* suits perfectly both as comprehensive textbook for
teaching purposes as well as an inspirational reading for practitioners. For the
marketing professors and students it offers a balanced combination of
easy-to-perceive concepts and multiple cases illustrating their application in
companies all around the globe. It also helps the marketing practitioners to
structure their experience, obtain a helicopter view of what they are doing and
explore dimensions of possible improvements. Presented in the mind map format
it provides marketing concepts and enhances marketing thinking in a more
convenient and reader-oriented format."

*Professor Margarita Zobnina, Associate Professor of Marketing, National
Research University, Higher School of Economics, Moscow, Russia*

"This is an original, fascinating, and much-needed book by two of the more iconoclastic thinkers in marketing. The approach is novel and engaging, the mix of content is very much in tune with today's environment, and the use of mind maps is an excellent pedagogical tool. This book is going to be extremely useful to instructors in marketing, and very popular with students. The world needs more reflective practitioners in marketing, and this book will help to create them."

Professor Nick Lee, Professor of Sales and Management Science, Loughborough University, School of Business and Economics; Honorary Professor of Marketing and Organizational Research, Aston Business School; Editor in Chief for European Journal of Marketing Research Methods; Section Editor for Journal of Personal Selling and Sales Management

"Written in a lively and interesting style by two senior thought-provoking academics, Stewart and Saren, have written an excellent marketing text that will particularly appeal to marketing students undertaking their placements and internships and marketing practitioners at various levels looking to deepen their marketing and company case knowledge – no reflective marketing practitioner should be without it!"

Professor Paul Baines, Professor of Political Marketing, School of Management, Cranfield University, UK

"Most textbooks fail to inspire but this book captures all the life and excitement of business. Arming you with the latest and most interesting marketing theory, it will put you in the position of real managers making real decisions, about an eclectic and international range of organizations (from Audi to Zapp!). *The Marketing Pathfinder* will engage and challenge you, and make you a better marketer."

Duncan Angwin and Stephen Cummings, co-authors of The Strategy Pathfinder

THE MARKETING
PATHFINDER

KEY CONCEPTS AND CASES FOR MARKETING STRATEGY AND DECISION MAKING

DAVID STEWART – MICHAEL SAREN

SERIES EDITORS:

STEPHEN CUMMINGS – DUNCAN ANGWIN

WILEY

Library of Congress Cataloging-in-Publication Data

Stewart, David, 1948-
  The marketing pathfinder : key concepts and cases for marketing strategy and decision making /
David Stewart and Michael Saren.
     pages cm
  Includes bibliographical references and index.
  ISBN 978-1-119-96176-5 (paperback)
  1. Marketing–Management.   2. Strategic planning.   I. Saren, Michael.   II. Title.
  HF5415.13.S875 2014
  658.8′02–dc23   2014020570

A catalogue record for this book is available from the British Library.

ISBN 978-1-119-96176-5 (paperback), ISBN 978-1-118-75876-2 (ebk)
ISBN 978-1-118-75891-5 (ebk)

Cover design: Cylinder
Cover image: © Shutterstock/Dr Hitch

Set in 11/13.5pt PalatinoLtStd by Laserwords Private Limited, Chennai, India
Printed in Great Britain by TJ International Ltd, Padstow, Cornwall, UK

Contents

Pathways to Marketing

The role of marketing in an organization is becoming increasingly important as the focus is on building long-term customer relationships instead of focusing on short-term profit. Marketing is vital to success but it does not possess a one size fits all solution. Therefore, rather than relying on a prescriptive model to solve problems the marketer must be nimble, able to think on their feet and willing to change. This is even more imperative as each marketing situation is different and context dependent.

As part of the *Pathfinder* series, the book takes a novel approach, building on the work of Donald Schön (1983) by viewing marketers as reflective practitioners. Adopting this concept means that marketers not only need to access appropriate concepts and frameworks to assess each situation but also to have the confidence to make the right decision. Therefore it is not a matter of technical problem solving but the development of reflective enquiry, where the *art of practice* is linked to theories and frameworks to make sense of a situation.

The book is also different in that marketers are positively encouraged to take an eclectic approach to the subject. The book does not build on one perspective alone but instead fuses four different approaches to the marketing discipline which are outlined in Chapter 1. Some more critical perspectives are provided in Chapter 10, for example, about which the reader needs to be reflective regarding the implications.

Another key feature of the Pathfinder Series is that the text covers the main concepts on the topic within each chapter in a format that can be covered in a single module, with room for case discussion. At the end of each chapter a list of references is provided which enables the student to explore areas in detail if they so wish.

In addition to the core concepts the idea is that the micro cases at the end of each chapter allow students to relate these concepts to practice and come to grips with some real-world issues faced by marketers. These micro cases are *"live" case studies* – unlike the traditional case study format, where all the information is detailed in a 20-page document with the primary goal being detailed analysis to solve a problem. Students are encouraged to conduct their own research by obtaining additional information, conducting an Internet search, discussing the issues with colleagues, drawing on past experiences and forming their own opinions, thereby taking ownership of the case.

At the end of the first micro case of each chapter (apart from the last where you are encouraged to take ownership of the case), brief ideas are presented on how the case questions might be answered. This gives the student the opportunity to discuss the ideas and provide alternative views or additional insights. The cases have been prepared for classroom discussion only and are not intended to illustrate effective or ineffective marketing management decisions.

The student will note that some of the cases overlap between chapters. In other words, whilst it may be a pricing case, questions of segmentation may arise, or it may be a brand building case but product innovation and adoption are also relevant issues. This is deliberate as not many marketing problems occur as an isolated topic. Frequently other issues with the market or organization play a part.

A case study mind map is provided. Alongside the name of each micro case is the name of the company. Students are urged to use the mind map dynamically by linking concepts and ideas between cases by drawing lines, thus creating a spider's web. For example, there are linkages regarding modular manufacturing between the Audi AG and the Raleigh bicycle cases.

The questions at the end of each case are for the student to apply concepts and frameworks presented in the chapter. The case will also give rise to other questions, some of which may be borrowed from other cases in the book. By adding your own research and questions, the cases are dynamic rather than static. It is not a matter of looking for the 'right' answer, but rather adding to the conversation, not merely repeating the conversation.

Finally, a chapter mind map is presented showing how the chapters are interrelated. Central to the mind map are the firm and the buyer and the relational exchange that binds the two together. Note the double-headed arrows, indicating that the two parties influence each other. The mind map has a logical flow to it and goes in a clockwise direction. We start the mind map with the organization and how it delivers value. Next is the development of products/services that represent that value. The next chapter concentrates on the buyers and how a marketer can attempt to understand their willingness and ability to partake of an offering, including the price they are prepared to pay. From there the issue of promising is explored and how it relates to the customer experience. Finally, the remaining chapters explore activities the firm can undertake to enhance the relational exchange.

Reference

Schön, D.A. (1983), *The Reflective Practitioner. How Professionals Think in Action*, New York: Basic Books Inc.

FIRM ↔ **Relational Exchange** ↔ **BUYER**

Experience

1. Mobilizing the Marketing Endeavour

Boundary spanning
Four views of marketing
Delivering value
Creating value propositions

2. Developing Products and Services

Product and service typology
Importance of innovation
Product life cycle
Diffusion of innovation
First mover advantage

3. Analysis and Understanding

Demand forecasting
Market analysis
Competitor analysis
Market research

4. Understanding Why They Buy

Influence of culture
Use of neo-tribes
Prosumers
Decision-making process
Means-end chain

5. How Much Are They Prepared to Pay?

Break-even analysis
Price points
Value proposition
Pricing strategies
Revenue management

6. Over-Promising, Ethics, and Sustainability

Role of promises
How & why over-promising occurs
Importance of ethics
Sustainable marketing

7. Successful Brand Building

Strategic brand management
Types of brands
Semiotics
Brand extension
Brand equity

8. Finding the Right Marketing Space

Distribution
Marketing channels
Channel structures
Impact of IT
Role of logistics

9. Communication Heaven

Integrated marketing comms
Communication objectives
Communication mechanisms
Media choices

10. Maverick Marketing

Marketing mavericks
Marketing as practice
Marketing as service
Digital marketing

FIRM ↔ Relational Exchange ↔ BUYER

Experience

1. Mobilizing the Marketing Endeavour

Striding Out (*Cornwall Athletics*)
Are You Being Served? (*Pret a Manger*)
Six Feet Under (*Funeral Services*)
Friend for Life (*Merrythought*)

2. Developing Products and Services

Extended Families (*Audi AG*)
Happy Feet (*Hotter Shoes*)
Three's a Crowd (*Air New Zealand*)
Nighty Night, Sleep Tight (*Megabus*)

3. Analysis and Understanding

Got Fly Buys? (*Loyalty NZ*)
Mind the Gap (*Gap*)
Rugby, Racing, and Beer (*Lion Breweries*)
Mum's the Word (*Mothercare*)

4. Understanding Why They Buy

I Ride Therefore I Belong (*Triumph Motorcycles*)
Hi-de-Hi! (*Pontins*)
Death of the High Street (*High Street Shopping*)
Ship Ahoy (*RNLI*)

5. How Much Are They Prepared to Pay?

The Daily Grind (*Coffee café*)
Take Me Down to the Ball Game (*Red Sox*)
Grape Expectations (*Hunter Valley*)
Auf Wiedersehen Pet (*Deutsche Bahn*)

6. Over-Promising, Ethics, and Sustainability

Horses for Courses (*Horsemeat*)
Rise and Fall (*American Apparel*)
Washes Whiter (*Unilever*)
Foul Play (*Bavaria Beer*)

7. Successful Brand Building

On Yer Bike (*Raleigh*)
One Cool Cat (*Jaguar*)
Loyalty at the Checkout (*Tesco Clubcard*)
Whisky Galore (*Scotch Whisky*)

8. Finding the Right Marketing Space

Keep on Truckin' (*Eddie Stobart*)
Easy to Spread (*Hatuma Lime*)
Cathedrals of Consumption (*Gruen Transfer*)
Give Us Our Daily Bread (*Warburtons*)

9. Communication Heaven

Departing from Platform 9 (*Hornby*)
First Position (*Movitae*)
Black Gold (*Marmite*)
Monkey Business (*Cadbury*)

10. Maverick Marketing

Brave New World (*Zapp*)
Power by the Hour (*Rolls-Royce*)
Organized Chaos (*T-Mobile*)
Different to the Core (*Apple*)

The Marketing Pathfinder Map

1. Mobilizing the Marketing Endeavour

Boundary spanning → Four views of marketing → Delivering value → Creating value propositions

| Striding Out (*Cornwall Athletics*) | Are You Being Served? (*Pret a Manger*) | Six Feet Under (*Funeral Services*) | Friend for Life (*Merrythought*) |

2. Developing Products and Services

Product and service typology → Importance of innovation → Product life cycle → Diffusion of innovation → First mover advantage

| Extended Families (*Audi AG*) | Happy Feet (*Hotter Shoes*) | Three's a Crowd (*Air New Zealand*) | Nighty Night, Sleep Tight (*Megabus*) |

3. Analysis and Understanding

Demand forecasting → Market analysis → Competitor analysis → Market research

| Got Fly Buys? (*Loyalty NZ*) | Mind the Gap (*Gap*) | Rugby, Racing, and Beer (*Lion Breweries*) | Mum's the Word (*Mothercare*) |

4. Understanding Why They Buy

The influence of culture → The rise of neo-tribes → Prosumers → The decision-making process → Means-end chain

| I Ride Therefore I Belong (*Triumph Motorcycles*) | Hi-de-Hi! (*Pontins*) | Death of the High Street (*High Street Shopping*) | Ship Ahoy (*RNLI*) |

5. How Much Are They Prepared to Pay?

Break-even analysis → Price points → Value proposition → Pricing strategies → Revenue management

| The Daily Grind (*Coffee café*) | Take Me Down to the Ball Game (*Red Sox*) | Grape Expectations (*Hunter Valley*) | Auf Wiedersehen Pet (*Deutsche Bahn*) |

6. Over-Promising, Ethics, and Sustainability

The role of promises → How and why over-promising occurs → The importance of ethics → Sustainable marketing

| Horses for Courses (*Horsemeat*) | Rise and Fall (*American Apparel*) | Washes Whiter (*Unilever*) | Foul Play (*Bavaria Beer*) |

7. Successful Brand Building

Strategic brand management → Types of brands → Semiotics → Brand extensions → Brand equity →

| On Yer Bike (*Raleigh*) | One Cool Cat (*Jaguar*) | Loyalty at the Checkout (*Tesco Clubcard*) | Whisky Galore (*Scotch Whisky*) |

8. Finding the Right Marketing Space

Distribution → Marketing channels → Channel structures → Impact of IT → Role of logistics

| Keep on Truckin' (*Eddie Stobart*) | Easy to Spread (*Hatuma Lime*) | Cathedrals of Consumption (*Gruen Transfer*) | Give Us Our Daily Bread (*Warburtons*) |

9. Communication Heaven

Integrated marketing communications → Communication objectives → Communication mechanisms → Media choices

| Departing from Platform 9 (*Hornby*) | First Position (*Movitae*) | Black Gold (*Marmite*) | Monkey Business (*Cadbury*) |

10. Maverick Marketing

Marketing mavericks → Marketing as practice → Marketing as service → Digital marketing

| Brave New World (*Zapp*) | Power by the Hour (*Rolls-Royce*) | Organized Chaos (*T-Mobile*) | Different to the Core (*Apple*) |

About the Authors

David Stewart is a senior lecturer at the Victoria University of Wellington Business School. He teaches on the marketing management and business research courses for the MBA programme and additional post-experience programs. His research interests include the philosophy of social science, marketing strategy and brand management.

Michael Saren is Professor of Marketing at Leicester University, UK. He previously held chairs at the universities of Stirling and Strathclyde and is honorary professor at St Andrews University. His research interests focus on the development of marketing theory, particularly regarding marketing knowledge, consumer culture and issues of creativity and sustainability. He was one of the founding editors of the journal *Marketing Theory* and joint winner of the George Fisk 2012 Macromarketing prize. He was made an honorary fellow and lifetime member of the UK Academy of Marketing in 2007.

This chapter covers the following topics:

▶ Boundary spanning
▶ Four views of marketing
▶ Delivering value
▶ Creating value propositions

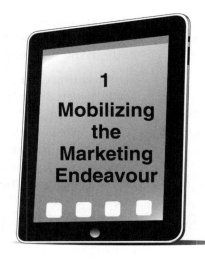

1
Mobilizing the Marketing Endeavour

Border Patrol

Marketing activities take place within the wider contexts of organizations, industries, cultures, and countries. So the marketing endeavour is often viewed as a *boundary-spanning* role between the organization and its environment. Of course the most immediate environment for marketing is the organization in which it takes place, but marketing is considered to extend beyond the marketing department or function itself. This is because, although most organizations nowadays have a function or department labelled "marketing", it is sometimes little more than a sales unit, which delivers advertising, personal selling and promotion activities. Such organizations can be described as "sales oriented". In order to be fully "marketing oriented" however, all the activities of the organization must be centred on the customer; therefore marketing must be undertaken by *all* functions, not just those in the department called "Marketing".

In order to provide something of value to their customers or users outside, the activities and departments involved *inside* the organization each must deliver their part of the process to the other units and functions. For instance, the research department must develop the new system for IT, who must integrate it into existing IT systems for manufacture, which must make the products to order for sales, and the service division must back up sales, etc. In this way, each internal activity can be viewed as having an output and thus a customer *inside* the organization. This is the notion of internal marketing (see Piercy, 1991) where all departments, not just that labelled "marketing", are users of others' output and have "customers" in other functions. And this is why Evert Gummesson (1997) says that everybody in the organization should act as a "part-time marketer".

So marketing can be regarded as the business function located at the boundary between the firm and the outside world. Its role is to manage activities *inside* the firm in order to focus those *outwards*, particularly towards customers. One complication with this view is that the distinction between the organization and its environment is not as clear-cut as this "internal versus external" explanation suggests. For example, many companies contract out large parts of their marketing to other firms, where functions such as market research, advertising and technical research are contracted to outside agencies. They often do this in order to avoid permanently employing lots of specialists and to allow more flexible operations, but are more likely to retain control of overall marketing and core activities like marketing strategy and planning, sales management, in-store promotions, costing and pricing. In practice, many marketing operations span the internal–external divide, making the boundary itself between inside and outside the firm even more unclear. Nevertheless, bearing this qualification in mind it is more helpful to think about and discuss the external aspects of the organization's context separately here in order to then lead on to consider how these boundaries can best be managed by marketing.

The notion of the external environment at its basic level implies that the marketing activities of a company take place between and are crucially determined by other organizations and people in the immediate *micro-environment* such as suppliers, buyers, competitors, etc. The company has some control over these immediate influences through its marketing activities; for example by lowering its price it may encourage buyers to purchase more, but also may encourage competitors to reduce their price. Other factors in the more distant *macro-environment* are also powerful influences, such as technology, cultural norms, economic conditions, etc.

Forces in the macro-environment affect marketing more indirectly by influencing conditions such as the disposable income of customers, the opportunities for new products, the reach and effects of advertising, etc. The organization has little influence over the macro-environment, determined much more by the state of the general economy, social forces, technological advances, government policies, etc. One criticism of the conventional view depicted in Figure 1.1 is that it is too company-centred, not customer-centric. A truly marketing-oriented view of the environment would turn the diagram inside out, situating consumers in the middle and competing companies on the outside because according to the marketing concept the depiction of the marketing environment should be centred

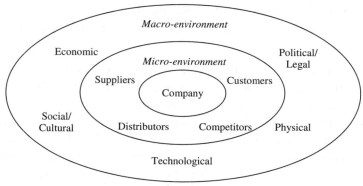

Figure 1.1 The marketing environment. Source: Adapted from Saren, M. (2006) *Marketing Graffiti*: *The View from the Street*. Oxford: Butterworth Heinemann

on the consumer, not the seller. The firm's environment should show the consumer at the centre, with sellers fighting for their custom from the outside and competing for distribution channels, retail space, advertising media, etc.

The role of the external environment is not all encompassing for marketing however, but selective and partial. Companies cannot possibly affect or even engage with *all* of it. Most firms are not even aware of all the macro forces and trends in technology, society, economy, and public policy that may affect them. There are many examples where managers complain that an important external event occurred "out of the blue". Marketers will have their own individual view about which particular external elements are important for their business and will also select a small subset of these to monitor, investigate, or exploit. This is what is called *environmental scanning*, which is systematic information gathering to monitor important trends in the environment.

For example, oil and gas companies undertake regular scanning of oil prices, availability, costs, etc., and forecast future possible scenarios. Also, they constantly monitor key long-term macro-environmental factors such as government stability and national policies in selected countries where they might have or seek exploration licences. Other factors that are assessed include new technologies, regulation of automobiles, transport investments, road infrastructure capacity, and taxation of emissions. In other words, managers in companies such as these *select* to investigate fore-cast and monitor only a small part of all the possible factors that might be or become relevant to their companies' markets and their marketing. They cannot look at everything, nor can they operate and market everywhere. That part of the macro-environment that sellers choose to engage with is called the *enacted environment*. And the part which managers consider relevant is determined by the way they look at their business and the outside world.

In order to manage the firm–environment boundary, marketers also need to gather regular and extensive information. Most obviously, marketers need information about consumers, their wants and needs, and what will satisfy them. Consumer information aids marketing decision-making – pricing decisions, promotion decisions, product decisions, and distribution decisions and so on should all be aimed at satisfying the consumer, so this requires data beyond the basic facts about what they buy, where they shop, their price limits, etc. Marketing also requires knowledge about consumers' fundamental needs, their future preferences, and what determines these. For example, the purpose of loyalty cards in UK retail stores is not just to encourage repeat visits by customers or even to generate "loyalty"; the aim is primarily to generate on a daily basis lots of useful information for the retailer about buyers' purchasing habits. The collection and use of this type of data about consumers' buying behaviour is not sufficient though. Lots of other types of information are needed to aid marketers' decision-making, such as costs, production, competitors, industry; indeed, information about the whole context of the market. Nor is it sufficient to possess and collect information. Marketers also need the ability to integrate and frame such information within the context of their experience, expertise, and judgement.

Whatever Way You Look at It

There are four main approaches to managing marketing's boundaries. These are:

1. Functionalist

2. Managerialist

3. Collaborative

4. Relational

We outline the theoretical and historical bases of these approaches first before moving on to consider how these can be implemented.

1. Functionalist

The functionalist approach studies marketing behaviour as a system and tries to establish ways of making it work better, more efficiently. It is associated with the great marketing theory pioneer Wroe Alderson, writing in the 1950s and 1960s (see Alderson, 1957). Academic study and development of marketing as a separate discipline is essentially a twentieth-century occurrence. It corresponds to the increasing distance of the producer from the final consumers, over whom manufacturers have thus lost control and influence, with distributors, agents and retailers filling the gap.

Figure 1.2 illustrates this shift in market structure and power over the second half of the twentieth century. The rise of marketing was seen by Alderson and others as the solution to this problem for manufacturers. In other words, marketing started to be used by producers of agricultural and manufactured products in order to attempt to wrest knowledge, contact, control, and influence over consumers, back from the various middlemen in the elongated distribution channels. The early editions of the main marketing publication, the *Journal of Marketing*, from 1936 contained papers that used the term "marketing" to mean primarily aspects of distribution as the flow of goods and services from the place of production to the point of consumption. Functionalist marketing utilizes the techniques, tools, and language of systems analysis to acquire the means for producers to directly reach and communicate with customers, who came to be regarded by marketing as the espoused central focus of all business systems.

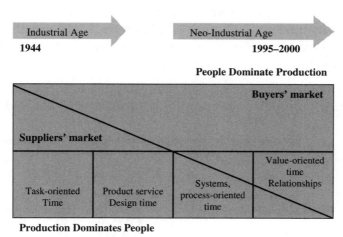

Figure 1.2 Shift from suppliers' market to buyers' market

2. Managerialist

The next development shifts the focus from a functionalist, systems approach to analysing markets to one which focused on managerial and buyer behaviour. The managerial and buyer behaviour view of the 1960s and 1970s studied individual firms and consumers to discover how to control their market behaviour in order to maximize their profit (firms) and satisfaction (consumers). The buyer behaviourist view regarded the consumer as a conditioned organism, open to reconditioning and treated as a "behaving machine", performing cognitive functions within a black box (see Shankar and Horton, 1999). Managerial marketing attempts to influence the behaviour of this "buyer machine" through manipulating the so-called marketing mix or 4Ps of product, place, promotion, and price.

The task for marketers is to develop an optimal marketing mix solution for competing for the preferences of a chosen target segment of consumers, households, or organizational buyers. In order to achieve this they utilize the techniques, tools, and language of market research to acquire the means to understand and analyse buyer preferences, choose a target market, differentiate and position the product in relation to the competing product alternatives, and estimate the customer reactions in terms of attitudes, buying intentions, or sales. The title of Philip Kotler's (1967) classic textbook *Marketing Management*: *analysis, planning and control* epitomizes the managerialist approach to managing the marketing boundaries.

There are several problems with this approach. It prioritizes management interest and values and the role of managers is the main focus, not that of consumers, employees, and other boundary actors – in fact this often represents a minority interest. As Figure 1.3 illustrates, managerialist marketing is mainly concerned with how managers and their firms are perceived in the market, i.e. how *they* look to customers.

As such this approach is highly normative and firm-centric and it assumes that managing complex marketing boundaries can be enacted through a

Marketing Planning Through the Looking Glass

Where are we going?

How do we look?

What do customers think of us?

How do we stand against

competitors?

How can we improve our

performance?

Figure 1.3 Managerialist marketing approach

"how-to", step-by-step guide, rather than by analysing and problematizing the boundary relations and management issues in the first place. Above all, however, although it espouses business as the most important form of boundary relationship and organization, managerialism is surprisingly silent about the organization of marketing activities. It does not contain any theory-based prescriptions for organizing marketing activities. The marketing mix is offered as a decision set or output of marketing, not its organization. A further limitation concerns the absence of attention to strategic issues. Although it covers tactical mix decisions the managerialist view is silent about which specific markets the firm should be in and how to compete in these markets.

The importance of these limitations make all the more surprising the belief that it can also be applied to any other form of non-business activity such as a health service or university education. The recent extension of the application of the managerial view of marketing into almost every aspect of business, public, civil, charitable, social, and even military and scientific activity in modern societies does nevertheless demonstrate that this is indeed what has occurred (see McKenna, 1991).

3. Collaborative

Another view of marketing's boundary management role highlights the fact that buyers and sellers do not only compete with each other for the best deal, they must also often collaborate. This emphasis developed largely due to the wider influence of the business thinking and culture of firms from the Far East and Asia. For example, Japanese business methods and ideas of collaboration, quality control, employee relations, and procurement practices have all had an enormous impact on business methods and thinking in the West. Chinese culture and business also operates with the notion of "guanxi", which is an alternative culture-based value system to the western market basis of legal frameworks, property rights, and contracts. In the West, the concept of trust is nevertheless critical for any marketing collaboration or partnership to work.

As Morgan and Hunt emphasize "commitment and trust are 'key' because they encourage marketers to (1) work at preserving relationship investments by cooperating with exchange partners, (2) resist attractive short-term alternatives in favour of the expected long-term benefits of staying with the existing partners, and (3) view potentially high risk actions as being prudent because of the belief that their partners will not act opportunistically. When commitment and trust – not just one or the other – are present they produce outcomes that promote efficiency, productivity and effectiveness" (Morgan and Hunt, 1994).

Proponents of this approach to managing marketing boundaries agree with Evert Gummesson (1997) that "collaboration in a market economy needs to be treated with the same attention and respect as competition". Three main types of collaborations can be identified, similar to those of competition:

1. Firms collaborate with other firms, even competitors, in alliances and joint ventures. For instance, airlines collaborate to provide global services (e.g. BA, Qantas, Swissair) and IT firms combine with suppliers and business partners to provide a "platform" or whole offering for customers, e.g. Pentium, Intel, IBM. Figure 1.4 illustrates how in the automobile industry various organizations collaborate in supply chains in order to provide a unified offer to customers. Indeed as the diagram shows, they actually collaborate with customers, who themselves become involved in value creation as part of the collaborative network constructed around the leading brand of Ford, Nissan, or Volkswagen.

2. Buyers also collaborate with each other. This can be a formal cooperation, e.g. customer cooperatives, buying clubs, user groups (services,

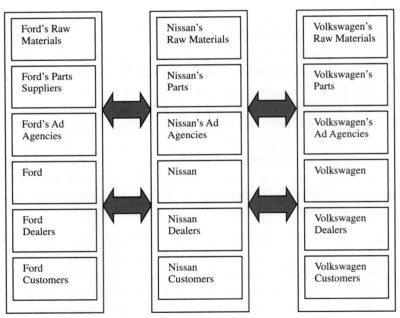

Figure 1.4 Supply chain collaboration in the automotive industry. Source: Adapted from Morgan and Hunt (1994)

gym, health), enthusiast societies (e.g. cars, football supporters). Alternatively, this can be an informal or social arrangement through information sharing, instruction, or friends.

3. Buyers and sellers collaborate. The very act of buying requires information sharing, dialogue, agreement, and trust between the buying and selling parties. Especially in business-to-business (B2B) and service markets, the buyer is often involved with the seller in producing or making together some key aspect of the delivery or transaction or use.

The idea of market as collaboration links to the fields of relationship and network marketing which developed from studies of marketing in B2B and services where collaboration and relationships have been found to be *central* to success. All these relational approaches emphasize long-term collaboration (as opposed to competition and exchange) between market and social actors.

It is actually possible for *all* marketing activities, problems, systems, and behaviour to be conceptualized and conducted by focusing on the collaborations involved to identify best practices, analyse behaviour, and provide solutions. For example, network theory has been applied extensively to industrial marketing by the north European IMP group (see Ford, 1990) which has enabled them to explain the behaviour of marketing systems in terms of networks of relationships and collaboration.

4. Relational

The move towards the relational approach to managing marketing boundaries began to become popular in the early 1990s when some academic researchers and marketing practitioners began to criticize the managerialist marketing mix approach for its essentially product orientation as opposed to customer orientation and for its short-term transactional view of marketing exchange as opposed to a longer-term relational perspective (see Grönroos, 1994). Their focus on relationships obviously relates directly to the management of organization-environment boundaries and it encompasses all marketing relationships including some which can be beyond and independent of markets and commodity exchange, such as those with stakeholders, employees, and the general public (see Webster, 1992; Payne, 2000).

The relational approach to marketing has arisen for a number of reasons: fragmentation of mass markets through information and communication technologies, the ability to collect and analyse more data about individual customers, higher levels of product quality forcing companies to seek competitive advantage in other ways, more demanding customers and rapidly changing customer buying patterns. The relational approach developed from a combination of ideas in business to business marketing, information technology-enabled developments in database and direct marketing, and the wider application of some key characteristics from services marketing (see Möller and Halinen, 2000).

Consequently, by utilizing these developments in technologies and relationship marketing thinking companies have sought new ways of establishing relationships with customers, and ultimately, ways of maintaining these relationships in order to retain customers that they attract. This requires a fundamental shift in marketing from a focus on transactions (i.e. sales) to relationships (i.e. retention) as companies move from short-term transaction-oriented marketing activities to that of long-term relationship-building. The key differences between these approaches are shown in Table 1.1.

The difference in the relational approach to marketing's boundary management is its explicit focus on marketer–supplier relationships and the dynamics of these relationships. It also emphasizes that both the seller and customer can be active participants in these relationships, as opposed to the managerial view which sees the marketer as the active agent and the customer as essentially reactive or passive. The key task for marketing now becomes that of managing these relationships with customers and others, not just the management of products, channels, organizations, or an internal "mix" of marketing variables.

Table 1.1 Transactional vs relationship marketing approaches

Transactional Marketing	Relationship Marketing
Focus on single sales	Focus on customer retention
Orientation to product feature	Orientation to customer value
Short timescale	Long timescale
Little emphasis on customer service	High customer service emphasis
Moderate customer contact	High customer contact
Quality is primarily a concern of production	Quality is the concern of all
Limited customer commitment	High customer commitment

Source: Adapted from Payne (2000)

The approach adopted to managing the marketing boundaries depends on the assumption that managers make about the conceptualization of the environment and the organization's relationship with it.

Increasingly business managers realize that customers are their most important assets and view customer relationships as mutually beneficial exchanges which are all the more important if Vargo and Lusch (2004) are correct that the customer is always a "co-creator of value". The formation and maintenance of relationships with external marketplace entities in a business to customer (B2C) context is typically captured nowadays by the concept of customer relationship management (CRM) (see Srivastava, Shervani, and Fahey, 1999).

The ability to generate and deliver value above and beyond the product or service is critical for CRM. However, it is much less clear how managers can identify what this value is in the eyes of their customers, and how they can develop and mobilize the necessary competencies for generating this value. It is in this task that there is significant potential of CRM in identifying and delivering customer value.

In the past the formula for identifying customer value seems to have been to listen to your customers and learn from previous mistakes. However, rapidly changing and more fluid boundaries and marketing contexts mean that managers are frequently confronting totally new situations, which reduces the value of lessons from the past. Customers can normally only communicate *existing* preferences and needs, providing very few clues or vision for the future which requires new learning cycles for marketers and customers alike. Inter-industry competition with new players reaching across established industry sectors (e.g. supermarkets as banks; AA as insurance; mobile phone as camera) challenges established competitive marketing approaches. In these constantly changing conditions, experience counts for less and managers must always be learning; they must be able, as it were, to remember to forget! The Internet and e-commerce have created a new market space for buying and selling that requires different organizational and marketing competencies. Information technologies have increased customer knowledge and therefore their level of expectations from their suppliers.

These dramatic changes require marketers to reassess their understanding and calculation of what constitutes "value" to their customers and how this value can be produced and delivered. Specifically, this might include detailed attention to customer, shareholder, and employee value; appreciation of the knowledge potential underlying such relationships; mutual understanding and careful positioning of relationships provide the possibilities for firms to re-invent the future with their customers, employees, and shareholders. This is the formula for firms to achieve sustainable competitive advantage for the future that the relationship marketing approach advocates because while products/service can be copied easily by competitors, long-term relationships are difficult to imitate.

Does my Value Look Big in this Proposition?

A value proposition is an implicit promise a company makes to customers to deliver a particular combination of values. The application of this concept has changed the focus of operations of many businesses, i.e. companies such as IBM have shifted the traditional, internally focused functions to customer-oriented, market-driven processes aimed at value delivery. In order to achieve such a shift in marketing thinking and practice marketers need to think in terms of different value propositions and how they can be created and delivered. According to Martinez (1999), these value propositions can then be analysed from three different perspectives – the customer perspective "what customers get?", the marketing perspective "what marketing needs to do?", and the operational perspective "what the company needs to do?"

Norman and Ramirez (1994) argue that there is a danger in paying too much attention to the disaggregating or breaking down of value creation activities. Indeed, they should not be treated as separate activities to be managed but rather as an integrated and seamless process flow. This raises the potential of a role for the consumer in creating value. At a minimum they play a key role in determining the ultimate value of a product or service. Until the customer lets their view be known in the market by offering to pay a given price, the market value of the final product is unknown.

If we take an example of a product which ultimately fails the final market test because the customer will not buy it (or only pays a price beneath cost), what are assumed to be value-adding activities by each firm in the supply chain (e.g. suppliers of raw materials, processing, parts, assembly, manufacture, distributors, retailers) ultimately are found not to actually add the assumed value. Therefore, value creation can only be judged after the market test and it is the customer who has the crucial deciding role in determining final value. If the customer is the focal point of marketing, value creation is only possible when a product or service is consumed. An unsold product has no value, and a service provider without customers cannot produce anything.

Beyond deciding the value of products and services in the marketplace, the role of the consumer in the value creation process is nevertheless far from clear. Norman and Ramirez (1994) go further and contend that value is co-created through the interaction between the firm and the customer. Consumers can play a key role in value creation too, not just firms, and the role of consumption, i.e. the activities, behaviours, and motivations that consumers undertake when making decisions and forming perceptions about products and services, is not just to "use up" or "deplete" value, but is also one of value creation (see also Vargo and Lusch, 2004).

Conclusion

This chapter has taken a view of the marketing endeavour as one which is about managing the boundaries of the organization's relational context, which focuses attention on key relationship learning, retention, and management processes. Within market relationships each party necessarily has a different ability to understand and manage the relationship. This follows from the heterogeneity of organizations, actors, firms, and consumers that operate in and are interconnected with different contexts or networks. Also each party necessarily has different expectations because each party seeks something different from the relationship, but in order to work together, each party must also seek a joint future (see Medlin, 2004).

These distinctions in the way each party seeks the future are important in considering the different sources or capability for each party to create their environment. This occurs because each action shapes the environment of the other party and, through interaction, *also shapes the environment of the acting party*. Therefore, each party's activities at the boundaries affect not only their own enactment and conceptualization of the environment, but also that of the other parties with whom they are collaborating or interacting.

Case 1-1 Striding Out

Included in the rationale used when making the bid for the London 2012 Olympics was that the games would inspire a generation of young people to engage more in sport. The Chairman of the London Olympic Committee, Sir Sebastian Coe, stated, "The greatest driver in participation is what goes on in an elite stadium. When you get that spike [of interest], you have to create that supply of infrastructure, both human and physical, that allows you to absorb that." Overall the objective is to create a culture where playing sport is integral to a person's life.

Sport England, the funding body for organized sport in England, conducts participation surveys in April and October each year. In the latest 2013 survey it was found that a record number of people aged 26 and above were involved in sport but the number of 16 to 25-year-old participants declined by 51,000. This can be partly attributable to young people moving away from traditional, organized sport. One year later, since the initial surge of the Olympics, the overall participation levels have remained steady at 15.5 million. Swimming has the most participants at 2.9 million people, followed by athletics and cycling, with both sports having in excess of 2 million participants each. On the other hand, participation in tennis has declined, despite the success of Andy Murray at Wimbledon (see Table 1-1.1).

Table 1-1.1 Once a week sport participation numbers (16 years and over)

Activity	October 2006	October 2013
Swimming	3,273,800	2,934,200
Athletics	1,353,800	2,016,400
Cycling	1,634,800	2,003,000
Football	2,021,700	1,838,600
Golf	889,100	751,900
Tennis	457,200	406,000
Cricket	195,200	148,300
Rugby Union	185,600	159,900
Netball	111,700	122,200

The task ahead for Sport England is to build on the momentum from the success of the Olympics by increasing sport participation at the elite and local club levels. For Run England, the athletics governing body, the challenge is to retain athletes and secure long-term involvement, as well as grow the sport. Clubs have an important role in achieving the above objectives.

One of the athletic clubs that has steadily increased its membership over the years is the Cornwall Athletic Club. The club was established in 1982 through the amalgamation of the Duchy of Cornwall Athletic Club and the West Cornwall Athletic Club, and caters for athletes from the age of nine to the age of 70 plus. Members include novices, recreational runners, and competitive athletes at the county, national, and international levels. Athletes can participate in a number of disciplines, including track and field, road running, and cross-country. A training session is organized every Tuesday evening at the Carn Brea Leisure Centre, Pool, Redruth, where the track is floodlit in the winter months.

The club has a team of over 20 UK athletics qualified coaches covering the different disciplines. A number of coaches have attained Level Four certification, the top level.

Questions

1. *What insights would be gained if the club were to scan the environment?*
2. *Unpack the club's value proposition from three different perspectives.*
3. *What challenges does the club face?*

◄◄◄ Some Ideas

1. *What insights would be gained if the club were to scan the environment?*

By scanning the environment the club would see factors that might impact upon club membership. One factor is the demographic make-up of the Cornwall catchment area, especially the predicted number of children and teenagers. Also, the general growth trends of the population would be insightful, especially the growth in the number of baby boomers. Another factor is the rise of obesity in the population and the degree to which people are aware of the issue. Also, the economy may impact upon club membership. On the one hand the double-dip recession may affect runners' willingness to pay club fees but on the other hand it may attract potential athletes as running is a relatively low-cost sport to participate in, compared with say skiing or golf.

2. *Unpack the club's value proposition from three different perspectives.*

From the *customer's* perspective the value is in the training sessions, the coaching, and the social aspects of the sport. What *marketing* could do is to liaise with schools to help coach students, organize seminars, produce posters, and write articles for the local newspaper. It could also liaise with triathlon clubs to provide coaching and support for athletes wanting to improve their running. From the *management's* perspective, organizing club nights, running special events, nutritional seminars, and providing opportunities for people who want to tackle being overweight, are possible activities.

3. *What challenges does the club face?*

The club needs to find a way to increase the membership of the 16 to 25-year-old age group. This is a difficult group to motivate as they have social pressures and are either busy at work or attending a tertiary institution, often away from home. Despite this, the club needs to ensure it has a programme that meets this age group's social as well as physical needs.

Another challenge is to increase the qualifications of existing coaches and to enlist new coaches, especially people who are prepared to motivate the "couch potatoes" to join a walking group, and perhaps over time graduate to road running. The club needs to maintain its proposition that it is not only for elite athletes but for all comers.

Case Notes:

Case 1-2 Are You Being Served?

Pret a Manger, meaning ready to eat, is a London-based gourmet food outlet. It was established by Sinclair Beecham and Julian Metcalfe who bought the company from a liquidator. They opened their first shop near Victoria Station, London and in time they were serving 7,000 customers per week. They had spotted a gap in the market as at the time there was no shop selling what they called "proper" sandwiches.

Their offering was based on three main selling points: the food was fresh, tasty, and fast. Their aim is to have customers, who have ordered their food to go, out of the shop in 60 seconds once they had made their choice. Their products contain a lot of natural ingredients without the additives or preservatives normally found in a lot of fast food. The menu includes sandwiches, baguettes, wraps, and cakes as well as hot and cold drinks. Every shop has its own kitchen and food is packaged in paperboard rather than sealed plastic. Pret a Manger customers are mainly office workers who may visit their local shop between 10 and 15 times a week. Shoppers are another segment, along with students.

Currently Pret has 14 outlets in Hong Kong, as well as 46 on the East Coast of the USA and 9 in Chicago. The company has even opened a store in Paris. Within Britain the company has 240 shops, which is small in comparison to McDonalds (1,200), Starbucks (650), and Costa (1,300). Three quarters of Pret's British shops are within the M25 commuter belt and account for 85% of its sales.

Unlike most fast food outlets, Pret is not franchised but has an open line of communication between the outlets and the head office. The aim for each store is to create what is termed the "Pret Buzz", which customers should feel when they enter the shop. Staff are employed for their personality so that customers experience a positive feeling. Staff must be friendly and lively, as well as good humoured by nature. Recruits are told to treat customers like guests in their own home.

Every new recruit is issued with a little book outlining acceptable and unacceptable behaviour. Basically there are three core behaviours that the company wants their staff to exhibit, namely Passion, Clear Talking, and Team Working, and examples of these behaviours in action are outlined (see Table 1-2.1).

A job applicant is assessed on these three core behaviours, then sent for a day's trial at a shop. At the end of the day the rest of the staff in the branch vote whether to accept the new recruit. If the vote is not in favour, the unsuccessful applicant receives £35 for their efforts. If the vote is positive

Table 1-2.1 A selection of expected behaviours of Pret a Manger staff

	Don't Want to See	Want to See	Pret Perfect!
Passion	Blames others	Has initiative. Doesn't wait to be told	Never gives up
	Does things only for show	Takes ownership for their work	Admits their mistakes
Clear Talking	Over complicates ideas	Listens	Paints a clear picture
	Confuses people	Is sincere	Constructively disagrees
Team Working	Moody or bad tempered	Creates a sense of fun	Anticipates others' needs
	Doesn't interact with others	Is genuinely friendly	Goes out of their way to be helpful

the recruit undertakes 10 days of training and tests before becoming a Team Member. Following a further 10 weeks of training in all aspects of the shop's operation the new staff member graduates to become a Team Member Star. Over time there is the opportunity for a Star to graduate to become either a Hot Chef or Barista or to progress to Team Member Training. Further progression is possible to become a Team Leader, followed by an Assistant Manager, then a General Manager.

Pret uses mystery shoppers to ascertain the quality of the service experience. Every shop in visited at least once every week. What is assessed is not the quality of the food, i.e. does it meet the required specifications, but the standard of the experience. If a shop meets the criteria and is deemed to be "outstanding" (usually 86% of stores achieve this), all the shop team receive a bonus of £1 per hour for every hour they worked that week. Unfortunately even if only one member of the team does not meet the standard then there is no payment. If the mystery shopper names an individual in the shop as giving exceptional service, then that individual receives a £50 cash bonus. Finally, if a staff member is promoted, what Pret calls a "Shooting Star", they receive a £50 voucher, not to spend on themselves but to share amongst their colleagues who have helped them attain the position.

The team spirit is enhanced by Friday night drinks once a month, as well as quarterly events with groups of shops, and two big parties for all staff each year. Overall Pret has a high retention rate with a staff turnover figure of 60% in 12 months, with people staying an average of approximately 20 months. This compares favourably with other fast food outlets which tend to have a 100% staff turnover per year.

The food from Pret a Manger does not have a use-by date stamped on it, because at the end of each day the surplus food is distributed to the homeless. In 1995 the Pret Foundation Trust was established to support the daily food runs. The trust also provides funds for an apprenticeship scheme for the homeless and for ex-offenders. To date over 70 people have been hired by the company under this scheme.

Questions

1. *Analyse Pret a Manger's marketing approach. What have been the main contributing factors to their success?*
2. *How has Pret a Manger managed their boundary spanners? How effective do you think this is from the points of view of managers, staff, and customers?*
3. *Critique how Pret a Manger uses "emotional labour".*
4. *What other industries could adopt this approach?*

Case Notes:

Case Study

Case 1-3 Six Feet Under

The New Zealand funeral industry has been professionalized over the years. This is evidenced through the change of language that is used. The undertaker is now a funeral director, the word coffin has been replaced with casket, even though it is still shaped like a coffin and not a casket as in the United States, and wreaths are now referred to as floral tributes. The industry has organized itself with members joining an association and a set of rules for conduct of members has been adopted. Also, tertiary training courses have been established for funeral directing and embalming.

Traditionally the funeral director has taken a transactional approach to conducting business. When a person dies the next-of-kin will contact a funeral director. The choice of funeral director will be primarily based on geographic location, but where two or more companies operate in the same vicinity, the decision will factor in previous experience, word of mouth, or some affiliation through a sport or community club. Upon being contacted, the funeral director will personally visit the next-of-kin to receive instructions.

The funeral director will discuss the venue for the service, whether it will be a burial or cremation, note details of the deceased to register the death, draft a funeral notice for the newspapers, ask the next-of-kin to select a casket, and establish who is to conduct the service. On the day of the service the funeral director will attend the service and ensure proceedings go according to plan. The final act for the funeral director is to send the next-of-kin an invoice. Death's sting can start with the undertaker's bill!

However, the role of the funeral director has changed over the last 20 years, brought about by the secularization of society. The New Zealand 2013 census show 40% of the total population of 4.2 million declare themselves as non-religious, whilst the number of people claiming to affiliate with a Christian church has dropped from over 2 million to less than 1.9 million.

The consequence of the above has impacted upon the types of funeral services being held. Increasingly funerals are being held at venues other than churches, for example, funeral directors' chapels, school halls or sports clubs. The standard Christian service is being replaced by a personalized service, based on the deceased's favourite songs, poetry, their interests and hobbies, with mourners being given the opportunity to speak about the deceased. Such services are conducted by a civil celebrant rather than by a minister or priest.

Technology is playing an important part in the ceremony with the use of digital screens displaying meaningful photos of the deceased, sound and video recordings are played and, in some cases, live webcasts are made. Often the committal is done at the venue saving the mourners the necessity to go the crematorium. This enables the next-of-kin to remain for refreshments, giving them the opportunity to meet the other mourners. Increasingly funeral directors' chapels have an additional space for mourners to gather and the funeral director organizes the catering. In many ways, the traditional role of the undertaker has evolved to become that of an event manager.

Questions

1. Would a funeral director benefit from developing a relationship marketing approach?
2. What would the funeral director need to do to make this happen? What impact would it have on their role?
3. What role does the customer play in the value creation of the service?

Case Notes:

Case Study

Case 1-4 Friend for Life

Stuffed bears were first made in the USA and in Germany in 1902. The name "Teddy" was adopted when the US manufacturer asked President Theodore Roosevelt if the company could use his nickname for the bears. From there on the name "Teddy Bear" has stuck. Teddy bears in Britain are still very popular and are still given as gifts to newborns and are treasured by young children. Favourites are Winnie the Pooh and Paddington Bear, and at some stores it is possible to purchase a teddy bear with your own message recorded on a device which is stitched into the bear.

The sole surviving teddy bear manufacturer in Britain is Merrythought at Ironbridge, Shropshire. The firm was established in 1930 when W.G. Holmes went into partnership with G.H. Laxton to spin raw mohair in a small mill in Yorkshire. The market for mohair yarn fell due to synthetic fibre being developed, but they were fortunate to team up with C.J. Rendle who was working for the Chad Valley toy manufacturer. He brought with him a few workers. One was a woman named Florence Attwood, who was deaf. She had learnt design at the Deaf and Dumb School in Manchester and designed the entire range of bears that were produced in 1931. Some of her designs are still in production today. By 1935 the company was the largest soft toy manufacturer in Britain, employing up to 200 people. Their most famous bear is "Mr Whoppit" who was the mascot for Donald Campbell, the land and water speed record breaker.

Today the company employs 25 staff in a very complex task. Each bear is handmade and takes about one hour to complete. The only piece of technology used in the process is a stuffing machine which was bought in the 1950s. The company made approximately 30,000 bears in 2010, with a retail price of between £50 to £85 each. The projected revenue for 2013 was £1 million.

The bears are sold in Harrods, Hamleys, Fortnum & Mason, Fenwick, and other upmarket shops. The bears are exported, in particular to Japan, where they have achieved cult status. However, half the buyers of Merrythought bears are collectors. Merrythought's Collectors Club has new special offerings, which are limited editions, distinct bears, like "Cheeky Broseley Bear" adorned with a cap, scarf and authentic clay pipe, which sells for £121.

Sarah Holmes, a great granddaughter of the founder, left her PR and recruitment job to join the family firm in 2010. Unfortunately her father, Oliver, died a year later, so she was joined by her sister Hannah, who was working as a chartered surveyor in London, to help run the firm. Sarah and Hannah are joint managing directors but admit they have limited experience in running the company. Whilst they would like to modernize the factory and expand the business, they realize that their brand is a quintessential English teddy bear. They take pride in this attribute and have therefore avoided moving production offshore.

Questions

1. *How can marketing help Merrythought grow their business?*
2. *How might a collaborative approach be used to build the business?*
3. *What specific information might be useful to help the sisters make strategic marketing decisions?*

Case Notes:

References and Further Reading

Alderson, W. (1957) *Dynamic Marketing Behavior: A Functionalist Theory of Marketing*. Homewood, IL: Richard D. Irwin.

Doyle, P. and Stern, P. (2006) *Marketing Management and Strategy*, 4th edn. Harlow, England: Prentice Hall.

Ford, D. (1990) *Understanding Business Markets: Interaction, Relationships, Networks*. London: Academic Press.

Grönroos, C. (1994) Quo Vadis, Marketing? Toward a Relationship Marketing Paradigm, *Journal of Marketing Management*, 10, 347–360.

Gummesson, E. (1997) Relationship Marketing as a Paradigm Shift: Some Conclusions from The 30R Approach, *Management Decision*, 35(4): 267–272.

Kotler, P. (1967) *Marketing Management: Analysis, Planning and Control*. Englewood Cliffs, NJ: Prentice-Hall.

Kotler, P. and Keller, K. (2012) *Marketing Management*, 14th edn. Harlow: Pearson Education.

Martinez V. (1999) *Sustainable Added Value*; Unpublished Master's Thesis in Technology Management, Strathclyde University, Glasgow.

McKenna, R. (1991) Marketing is everything, *Harvard Business Review*, January–February.

Medlin, C. J. (2004) Interaction in Business Relationships: A time perspective, *Industrial Marketing Management*, 33(3): 185–193.

Möller, K. and Halinen, A. (2000) Relationship Marketing Theory: Its roots and directions, *Journal of Marketing Management*, 16(1-3): 29–54.

Morgan, R. M. and Hunt, S. D. (1994) 'The commitment-trust theory of relationship marketing', *Journal of Marketing*, 58(3): 20–38.

Norman R. and Ramirez R. (1994) *Designing Interactive Strategy: from Value Chain to Value Constellation*. Chichester: Wiley.

Payne, A. (1995) *Advances in Relationship Marketing*. London: Kogan Page.

Payne, A. (2000) 'Relationship Marketing: Managing Multiple Markets'. In Cranfield School of Management, *Marketing Management: A Relationship Marketing Perspective*. MacMillan Press Ltd.

Payne A. and Holt S. (2001) Diagnosing Customer Value: Integrating the value process and relationship marketing, *British Journal of Management*, 12, 159–182.

Piercy, N. (1991). *Market-led Strategic Change: Making marketing happen in your organization*. London: Thompson.

Saren, M. (2006) *Marketing Graffiti: The View from the Street*. Oxford: Butterworth Heinemann.

Shankar, A. and Horton, B. (1999) Ambient Media: Advertisings now media opportunity?, *International Journal of Advertising*, 18(3): 305–321.

Srivastava R. K., Shervani T. K., and Fahey L. (1999) Marketing, Business Processes, and Shareholder Value: An organizationally embedded view of marketing activities and the discipline of marketing, *Journal of Marketing*, 63, 168–179.

Vargo, S. and Lusch, R. (2004) Evolving to a New Dominant Logic for Marketing, *Journal of Marketing*, 4, January, 1–17.

Webster F.E. (1992) The Changing Role of Marketing in the Corporation, *Journal of Marketing*, 56, October, 1–17.

Case Acknowledgements

The **Striding Out** case draws on information contained in:

"Athletics participation breaks the two million in 2012", (6 December 2012), *Run England*, retrieved from http://runengland.org/news.asp?itemid=2414 &itemTitle=Athletics+participation+breaks+the+two+million+in+2012 &section=23

"Coe warns on sports funding", by R. Blitz (5 August 2012), *Financial Times*, retrieved from http://www.ft.com/intl/cms/s/0/443c802c-df1f-11e1-97ea -00144feab49a.html#axzz2tujy2Tia

Cornwall Athletic Club website located at www.cornwallac.org.uk

"Funding threat to tennis and football as participation drops", by D. Bond (12 December 2013), *BBC Sport*, retrieved from http://www.bbc.com/sport/0 /olympics/25346493

"Tennis funding at risk as sports suffer big decreases in participation in England", by S. Hart (12 December 2013), *The Telegraph*, retrieved from http://www.telegraph.co.uk/sport/tennis/10513277/Tennis-funding-at-risk -as-sports-suffer-big-decreases-in-participation-in-England.html

Table 1-1.1: Compiled from information contained in "Tennis funding at risk as sports suffer big decreases in participation in England" by S. Hart (12 December 2013), *The Telegraph*

The **Are You Being Served?** case draws on information contained in:

"Pret A Manger chief is stacking up healthy profits in lean times", by R. Smithers (8 October 2010), *The Guardian*, retrieved from http://www.theguardian.com /business/2010/oct/08/clive-schlee-pret-a-manger-interview

"Pret A Manger: A different way of managing fast food workers", by M. Lariviere (11 August 2011), *The Operations Room*, retrieved from http://operationsroom .wordpress.com/2011/08/11/pret-a-manger-a-different-way-of-managing-fast -food-workers/

"Pret A Manger's success is deserved – just hold the mayonnaise, please", by O. Thring (3 April 2012), *The Guardian*, retrieved from http://www.theguardian .com/commentisfree/2012/apr/03/pret-a-manger-success

"Smiley culture: Pret A Manger's secret ingredients", by R. Preston (9 March 2012), *The Telegraph*, retrieved from http://www.telegraph.co.uk/foodanddrink /9129410/Smiley-culture-Pret-A-Mangers-secret-ingredients.html

Table 1-2.1: Compiled from information contained in "Pret Behaviors", (16 July 2011), located on the Pret a Manger website, retrieved from http://web.archive .org/web/2011071683540/http://www.pret.com/us/jobs/pret_behaviors.htm

The **Six Feet Under** case draws on information contained in:

"Census points to non-religious NZ", by B. Heather (11 December 2013), *The Dominion Post*, retrieved from www.stuff.co.nz/national/9501270/Census-points-to-non-religious-NZ

New Zealand Funeral Directors Association website located at www.funeralsnewzealand.co.nz

The **Friend for Life** case draws on information contained in:

"Merrythought sisters battle to protect the British bear", by J. Hurley (3 July 2012), *The Telegraph*, retrieved from http://www.telegraph.co.uk/finance/businessclub/9371070/Merrythought-sisters-battle-to-protect-the-British-bear.html

"A business bearing good news", by A. Haynes (July 2010), *Shropshire Magazine*, retrieved from http://www.shropshiremagazine.com/2010/07/a-business-bearing-good-news/

"Britain's last surviving teddy bear factory", by L. Burton (21 February 2011), *BBC News*, retrieved from http://www.bbc.co.uk/news/business-12523562

This chapter covers the following topics:

▶ Product and service typology
▶ Importance of innovation
▶ Product life cycle
▶ Diffusion of innovation
▶ First mover advantage

**2
Developing
Products
and
Services**

Marketing is concerned with managing the relational exchange between a buyer and a seller, as discussed in Chapter 1. This raises the question as to the nature of the product/service offering that is central to the exchange. A product/service is anything that can be offered to the market for attention, acquisition, use, or consumption; therefore a buyer can attend a movie or concert, acquire a piece of jewellery, spray an insecticide to control weeds in the garden, or consume an ice cream.

A product/service can be broken down into four levels. The first level is about the core benefit being offered in order to satisfy a want or need. For example, the core benefit of a new lawn mower is that the lawn is cut efficiently and effectively. At the next level are tangible aspects of the offering, such as design, price, packaging, and features. The augmented level supports the product offering, for example, after sales service, delivery, guarantees, finance, and warranties. Finally, the last level includes the intangible elements that support the product offering, such as quality perceptions, brand name, corporate image, reputation, and recommendations from other users.

What Counts as What?

The distinction between a product and service can be viewed on a continuum. At one end of the continuum is a pure product, for example, coal. Often products at this end of the continuum are commodities, and as such

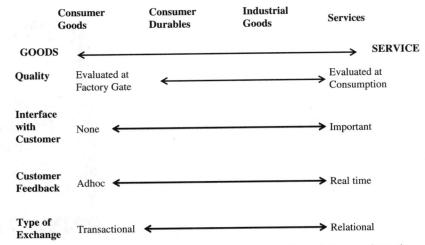

Figure 2.1 Goods – Service Continuum. Source: Adapted from Grönroos (1994)

are bought primarily on price. At the other end of the continuum is a pure service, for example, consultancy. Between these two extremes are offerings that are made up of varying elements of product and services. However, it needs to be noted that most offerings have a degree of service element to them, so therefore it is a matter of degree. Whereas pure products tend to rely on transactional marketing, services attempt to build an ongoing relationship with their customer. Examples of industries and where they lie on the continuum can be seen in Figure 2.1.

Note, however, that whilst the purchase of items of household goods for consumption, the so-called "fast moving consumer goods" category (FMCG), may be seen as transactional, the interaction between the customer and the supermarket is one of relationship, as is the interaction between the manufacturer and the supermarket.

From another perspective, comparisons can be made between a pure product and a pure service, as outlined in Table 2.1.

The Only Constant is Change

Why is innovation an imperative? To answer this question a number of issues need to be explored. First, it needs to be noted that within certain markets, the companies that have the largest research and development spend achieve above average growth and profitability. Notwithstanding the above, a distinction needs to be made between new product/service

Table 2.1 Comparative attributes of product and service

PURE PRODUCT	PURE SERVICE
Tangible Ability to touch, smell, taste, and see. Ownership is transferable	Intangible Physical evidence to indicate servicer capability. No ownership involved.
Standard quality	Variable quality (due to the performance of the service provider)
Evaluated against set specification	Evaluated by experience
Separate exchange Transactions at arm's length	Inseparable exchange Produced and consumed simultaneously so there is a relationship between customer and supplier
Inventory Long storage life so can be sold at a later date	Perishable Cannot be stored so if not sold then the opportunity is lost, e.g. airline seats or consultant time

Source: Adapted from Kotler and Keller (2012)

development and the notion of continuous improvement. Firms entering the market with completely new products can sometimes serve an unknown need or want, and be successful, for example the Sony Walkman. And of course other firms enter the market having done the appropriate market research and they too can be successful. Continuous improvement, on the other hand, is about taking an existing product and improving it, for example the iPhone 4. The two concepts, namely new product/service development and continuous improvement are interrelated as will be shown when exploring the product life cycle, the diffusion of innovation, and the first mover advantage in the following sections.

It will be obvious that the degree of innovation within an organization will be context dependent. Some markets are by their nature innovative. The telecommunication and computer markets are primarily technology driven, with new products being developed at a rapid pace. This is in contrast to products within FMCG categories that have not been developed for decades, apart from a change in package design, for example baked beans. In fact, new appliances have not been developed for kitchen use in the last 30 years, since the introduction of the microwave oven. Dishwashers, toasters, steam irons, and electric kettles have been on the market for over 50 years, but they have been improved in terms of efficiency, and also in style.

Another driving force behind the need for companies to be innovative is competition. Within a competitive market, it is desirable to maintain market share. (*The importance of market share will be explored in Chapter 4, and also in Chapter 5.*) To do this a company needs to innovate to keep ahead of the competition. Being a follower is a risky strategy as it can often mean that the company ends up as a price taker. Instead, the better strategy is to differentiate the product and appeal to a different segment in the market.

Finally, due to the changing nature of the market companies are compelled to innovate with new or improved product offerings. Every market is influenced in varying degrees by different environmental forces. These impact upon the company, and so they need to respond accordingly. For example, demographic shifts, changes in living standards, global warming, global trade and free trade agreements, and technological advancements all impact upon a market. In terms of responding to these environmental forces much depends on the firm's capabilities.

Metamorphosis

The product life cycle (PLC) is a model which describes the pattern of sales of a product over a period of time. The underlying determinant is the amount of growth, positive or negative, that exists in a market. When a product enters a market there is a growth in sales as the product is adopted (see the section on diffusion of innovation later in the chapter).

There are four distinct stages to the model, with different marketing activities associated with each stage (see Figure 2.2). The first stage, Introduction, is where the product is introduced into the market whereby the quality of the product is established and intellectual property is secured, for example, trademarks are registered. Often during this stage there are negative profits as the firm attempts to recoup the sunk costs of research and development as well as the marketing launch costs. The primary communication goal is to build awareness of the product amongst the target market and to educate them regarding the benefits of the product. This can be achieved by offering incentives to trial the product, such as samples and other promotional offers.

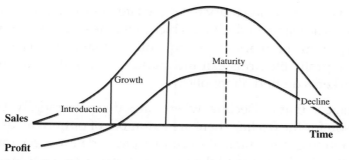

Figure 2.2 The product life cycle. Source: Adapted from Kotler and Keller (2012)

At this stage of the cycle, distribution channels are established, whereby a selective approach is used to choose the right intermediary that will provide the desired exposure. When determining the appropriate pricing strategy, two options are available to the marketer. A skimming strategy is where the product is priced relatively high as the company has a barrier to entry from other firms, for example, patents or manufacturing know-how. Such a strategy is effective if there is inelastic demand for the product. However, the disadvantage of this strategy is that inventory turnover will be low, thereby effecting economies of scale, and it may be necessary to give retailers higher margins to stock the product. Another disadvantage is that the adoption rate will be slow, providing competitors who have noticed the high margins with the opportunity to innovate and consequently leapfrog the first entrant. The other option is to adopt a penetration pricing strategy where the price is set low so as to attract as many customers as possible, thereby increasing market share. This strategy can lead to fast adoption rates, which in turn can create good word of mouth (see First Off the Blocks section). A penetration strategy is utilized by companies when the product appeals to a mass market, is price elastic and economies of scale can be obtained.

The second stage of the PLC is that of Growth. During this stage sales growth increases and an increasing amount of profit is generated. Competition begins to enter the market forcing further product development with added features. The incumbent firm tends to adopt a pricing strategy that prevents competition and builds market share. This also entails increasing the distribution of the product by obtaining more outlets. The communication strategy takes a broader approach, outlining product features and, when necessary, providing incentives for brand switching.

The third stage is that of Maturity where the product is the most profitable. The product is further differentiated and the segments are filled. The pricing strategy is to maintain market share and distribution is increased to cover as many outlets as possible. Product positioning becomes important and incentives may be necessary to keep customers loyal. Towards the end of this stage sales start to decline, which puts pressure on the margins of all the players in the market; consequently a shake-out occurs whereby smaller, less profitable firms exit the market. This partly explains why in mature markets you find oligopolies.

The last stage is that of Decline, where sales decrease rapidly. Depending on the reason for the decline there are a number of options available to the firm. One option is to maintain the product and find new users, for example, Napisan sales declined due to the increased use of disposable nappies, so they targeted everyday wash users by emphasizing the benefit of a brighter, more hygienic wash. Another option is to find a niche market and harvest the product, that is, margins are maintained or enhanced with little support offered in terms of advertising and distribution support, for example, record turntables for DJs. The final option is to discontinue the product. This strategy is often dictated by the nature of technological development in the market, for example, Sony Walkmans being replaced by iPods and MP3 players. Another example is VHS players being replaced by DVDs. When adopting any of the three options outlined above the marketer needs to be aware of the contribution the product makes to fixed costs in relation to the overall business portfolio.

There are a number of problems with the PLC model. First, not all products fit the model. For example, one can ask where greeting cards or carbonated drinks fit within the model as these are products that have been in the market for over a hundred years. Therefore, a distinction needs to be made between the category to which a product belongs, the form it takes, and the brand. A category is a classification of products that fulfil the same customer need, for example, motorcars fulfil the basic need of transport. Form, on the other hand, is a sub-classification of products which fulfils a need of a specific segment of the market, for example, an SUV is a form of motorcar which fulfils a certain segment of the market's lifestyle aspirations. The brand is the name of the supplier of the brand. Whilst some categories have been in the market for some considerable time, the form of the product can have a life cycle depending on environmental or lifestyle characteristics, whereas dominant brands have a life of continuity.

In some industries the product life cycle is not applicable due to manufacturing techniques where shorter runs are possible, thereby serving fragmented markets. These small niches can be serviced by shorter runs due to the reduction of set-up times for complex equipment. Therefore, more customized products are produced serving smaller, well-defined customer groups.

Another problem with the PLC model is that it is not able to predict future sales. The length of the cycle, that is, the time it takes from the introduction stage to the end of the decline stage, varies depending on technological innovation, customer adoption, and competitor reaction. For example, condoms were at the decline stage but due to the AIDS epidemic there was growth in the market.

Spread the Word

The diffusion of innovation is a model that attempts to explain why some innovations are adopted more quickly by the potential market than other innovations. Mirrored to the PLC, the diffusion of innovation model measures the rate of adoption by the target market from the time of introduction to the end of the life cycle. Each stage of the model depicts a typical person, with certain attributes, who is likely to purchase the product.

The first stage of the model is termed "Innovators" and represents, on average, approximately 2.5% of the potential market. Such a group are likely to be young, well-educated with disposable income, risk averse, and have the ability to understand new technology. This group are happy to trial the new product as it is part of their self-image and to discard the product if it is not satisfactory. The group may be outside the mainstream social system but they play an important role as gatekeepers of new ideas.

"Early Adopters" make up the second stage of the model and represent approximately 13.5% of the potential market. This group is more integrated into the social system than the Innovators, so consequently they have the role of opinion leaders thereby serving as a role model for the remainder of the potential market. The Early Adopters are respected for their judgement regarding new ideas and are able to convey a subjective evaluation of new products through interpersonal networks. This is an important group as they act as intermediaries between the Innovators and the rest of the potential market. They wait to see if the Innovators accept the new product, adopt it themselves, and then use their interpersonal skills to influence the remainder of the market.

The third stage of the model is termed "Early Majority", which represents approximately 34% of the potential market. Whilst the group interacts frequently with their peers they are seldom opinion leaders. Making up one third of the potential market the group is important as they provide interconnectedness within the social system. However, they tend to take time in deliberating upon whether to make the purchase.

The "Late Majority" comprises 34% of the potential market and they tend to follow the average trend. Whilst they are cautious and sceptical about the benefit of the new innovation they succumb, over time, to peer pressure. They wait until the product is a norm before making the purchase. Due to their scarce resources the product must be tried and tested before they take the risk to make the purchase.

The "Laggards" are the last group and are reluctant to make the purchase. Many are isolated in the social system and use the past as their point of reference. They tend to be very suspicious of new innovations and are sceptical about the benefits that are being claimed.

An underlying dimension of the model is the concept of time. First, time is involved in the decision process that individuals undertake when deliberating whether to purchase the product (see Chapter 4). Information is sought so that the purchaser can diminish any uncertainty concerning the innovation's expected consequences. Second, time is involved in the relative speed with which the potential purchasers adopt an innovation. The rate of adoption is measured as the number of adopters of the innovation over a given period of time.

Four factors influence the speed of adoption. The first is trialability. The adoption rate will tend to be quicker if the innovation can be trialled, as it will decrease dissonance about the purchase. The second factor is compatibility. If the new innovation is compatible with the values, past experience, or needs of the purchaser, the purchaser will feel comfortable in making the new purchase. The third factor is relative advantage. Purchasers must perceive the new innovation as better than the product it is replacing. The advantage may be based on economic terms, as well as social prestige, convenience, and satisfaction. Also the adoption rate will be quicker if there are no switching difficulties incurred. Finally, observability is an important factor that will influence the rate of adoption. If the new innovation is visible to others, allowing peer discussion regarding the evaluation of the new product, the adoption rate will be influenced.

First Off the Blocks

First mover advantage is the name given to the competitive advantage gained by firms that are first to enter the market with a new innovative product. This advantage is sometimes referred to as pioneer brand or prime mover status. The concept is a contentious issue as there is evidence to support the proposition that an advantage can be gained by a late entrant "leapfrogging" the first entrant. Unfortunately a lot of studies claiming the benefit for the first mover advantage have been based on Profit Impact of Marketing Strategy (PIMS) studies, which are based on self-reports, with a bias towards surviving firms. For many firms with a long history, the respondent in the survey is not able to access the historical company knowledge to determine their order of entry. Also there is confusion within research regarding the measurement of first mover advantage and order of entry effects.

Despite differing research points of view, there are two mutually exclusive questions that can be asked. First, if the firm has invented a new product, do they have the ability to create a defensible pioneering advantage? Second, given that the competitor is entering the market with a new product, is it possible to copy it and improve it in some respect, thereby gaining market leadership? The answer to the above questions will depend on a number of issues. The theory of first mover advantage can be based on two general advantages. The first is a consumer advantage, based on learning theory, which argues that once a consumer trials a product, they then favour it if they are satisfied with the benefits, so do not bother spending the energy to try another brand. Also, by being the first brand in the market the pioneer can set the standard for the product. Finally, a company can lock in buyers where there are high switching costs.

The second advantage is producer-based, where the firm is in a position to exploit benefits based on the supply of the product, which can be based on geographical location or the granting of distribution rights, thereby erecting a barrier to entry. Also, if the product is based on a limited number of suppliers, they can be locked in preventing later entrants gaining supply. In some industries the early entrant can exploit the experience curve, thereby obtaining economies of scale, giving the firm a lower cost structure, which can be used if a price war ensues.

There are a number of reasons why first mover firms either fail or lose their dominant position. First is the free-rider company, which enters the market late with new technology and at a lower cost. Despite patents, information diffusion amongst firms allows other players to gain inside information. This can be achieved by the employment of the competitor's staff, factory tours, and reverse engineering. Second, following on from the above, a late entrant can produce a better product by utilizing superior technology and marketing initiatives. Third, over time consumer tastes may change allowing a late entrant to take advantage of the trend. Fourth, incumbent inertia may hinder the first mover from making the necessary investments and changes required to remain market leader. The pioneer needs to respond to changes in demand, competitive threats, and the environment. Therefore, the pioneer must continually innovate and be prepared to cannibalize sales of their existing product. Finally, a first mover advantage can be lost if the company is unable to commit the necessary resources, financial or otherwise, to maintain their dominant position.

In summary, there is no optimal time to enter a market. If a company decides to be the first mover their judgement must be based on a good understanding of the risks and potential pitfalls, and undertake what is necessary to overcome any obstacles.

Case 2-1 Extended Families

In 1899 August Horch, a 32-year-old engineer, founded the firm A. Horch and Cie. and manufactured his first car two years later. However, in 1909 he fell out with his board of directors and started another company. Unable to use his own name he chose the word Audi, the Latin translation of the German word "hark!" By 1932 four Saxon motor manufacturers – Audi, DKW, Horch, and Wanderer – had merged, forming Auto Union AG. The new firm gained a reputation for motor racing along with the designer Ferdinand Porsche.

After the Second World War, the Auto Union's plants in Saxony were dismantled so Horch and his partners set up a new car company in 1949 called Auto Union GmbH. In 1964 the Volkswagen Group took over Auto Union and the Audi brand was resurrected a year later. See Table 2-1.1 for Volkswagen Group Brands.

In 1980 Audi burst onto the rallying circuit with the introduction of the Audi Quattro, a high performance vehicle with four wheel drive. Audi obtained numerous car and driver titles over the ensuing years; however, in 1986, following a serious accident during the Portugal Rally when Joaquim

Table 2-1.1 Volkswagen group deliveries

Volkswagen Group Deliveries Passenger Cars

Division	2011	2010	2009	2008
Volkswagen Group	8,160,154	7,139,472	6,336,222	6,256,843
Volkswagen Passenger Cars	5,090,849	4,502,832	3,954,454	3,667,843
Skoda	879,184	762,600	684,226	674,530
Bentley	7,003	5,117	4,616	7,604
Audi	1,302,659	1,092,411	949,729	1,003,469
SEAT	350,009	339,501	336,683	368,104
Lamborghini	1,602	1,302	1,515	2,430
Volkswagen Commercial Vehicles	528,810	435,669	361,506	502,265
Bugatti	38	40	–	–
Region	**2011**	**2010**	**2009**	**2008**
South & Central America	933,259	887,867	825,876	803,471
Europe	2,837,213	2,526,819	2,245,745	2,717,527
Germany	1,153,070	1,034,850	1,246,571	1,060,349
North America	666,847	549,238	467,769	503,139
Asia Pacific	2,569,765	2,140,698	1,550,261	1,172,357
Total Revenue (million)	€159,337	€126,875	€105,187	€113,808

Santos lost control of his Ford and plunged into the crowd, Audi pulled out of the World Rally Championship.

In autumn 1986 the company faced a serious problem in America. On 23 November 1986 the *60 Minutes* show presented a documentary titled "Out of Control", which showed compelling evidence that the Audi 5000 had a dangerous propensity to lurch forward, even when the driver's foot was on the brake. The problem, dubbed "sudden acceleration" was said to be responsible for hundreds of accidents. The show was repeated on 13 September 1987. Audi sales plunged sharply after the broadcasts. In 1985 sales had peaked to 74 061 but annual sales in the US from 1991 to 1995 had dropped to 14,000 units, just 19% of the totals prior to the broadcast.

In 1989, the US National Highway Traffic Safety Administration (NHTSA) issued the findings of a two-year study on the problem and found that there were no mechanical issues that directly caused the sudden acceleration of the Audi 5000. On 12 March 1989 *60 Minutes* host, Ed Bradley, presented a short update but fell short of apologizing to Audi by saying that it had made a mistake.

By the 1990s Audi was faced with the task of repositioning its brand. It was forced to forget its past and concentrate on issues surrounding safety and the environment. In 1993 and 1994 the new Audi A6 achieved an outstanding result for a business saloon car in tests conducted by the European New Car Assessment Programme (Euro NCAP). Also in 1994 the A8 was launched with an all-aluminium body, which was a first for a passenger car. By 1996 Audi AG was producing 491,501 vehicles and 620,603 engines, with a workforce of 34,529.

Approximately 20 years following the repositioning of the brand, Audi had a week of festivities to celebrate its 100th birthday (see Table 2-1.2 for Audi Key Figures). The Audi A5 coupe took gold in the highest official design awards in Germany. Audi also launched the TDI clean diesel demonstrating the company's innovation towards the environment. Coupled with this environmental theme there was the launch of one of the most efficient midsized sedans with the Audi A4 2.0 TDIe and test drives of the Audi e-tron, an electric car. In 2010 Audi launched efficiency models of the Audi A3, the luxury Audi A8, as well as the new Audi A1.

Since the 1990s the world automotive manufacturers have increasingly depended on shared platforms, enabling them to reach different market segments whilst recouping significant research and development costs. The term "platform" means that a vehicle's suspension, drive train, and structural components are the same, but the synergies gained are limited to one vehicle class.

Table 2-1.2   Audi key figures

Key Figures	2011	2010	2009	2008	2007
Production	1,365,499	1,150,018	932,260	1,029,041	980,880
Output Engines	1,884,157	1,648,193	1,384,240	1,901,760	1,915,633
Workforce	62,806	59,513	58,011	57,822	53,347
Revenue (Million)	€44,096	€22,410	€29,840	€34,196	€33,617

Building on the traditional platform strategy is the modular system, where engines, transmission, and some electrical components are added to the process. This has meant that the synergies gained can be applied to more than one class of vehicle. Audi, as part of the Volkswagen Group, adopted this type of assembly.

Volkswagen is currently introducing a new assembly system termed the "Tool Kit", whereby the platform is based on four management sectors, namely chassis, body trim, powertrain, and electrical componentry. Within each sector there are 33 component kits, which in turn have 150 modules and each of these contains approximately 1,000 building blocks. The tool kit assembly process has only one fixed dimension, which is from the front axle to the firewall. Therefore, the front, rear overhang, wheelbase width can either shrink or grow. This assembly strategy allows for different vehicles to be assembled on the same factory line, with a typical output of 30 cars per hour, but with the capacity to increase to 60 cars per hour.

The standardization of parts and components has meant a reduction of approximately 20% of the cost of each vehicle. Also, the process has meant that each car will be between 40 and 60 kilograms lighter. Coupled with active cylinder technology, the cars will save between 10 and 20% on fuel economy.

The four tool kits are:

- NSF – new generation small cars
- MQB – modular transverse kit, where the engines are transversely mounted, e.g. Audi A3, Golf, Audi TT, and VW Polo
- MLB – modular longitudinal kit, for example, Audi A4 and S4, Porsche Boxster, Porsche Cayenne, and the VW Touareg
- MSB – modular standard drive train, mainly comprising sportcars in the group, for example, the Audi R8, Bentley, Lamborghini.

It is thought the tool kit assembly process is the most revolutionary step in car assembly since the invention of mass production by Henry Ford.

In the car industry R&D is a significant cost to the manufacturer. For example, the Volkswagen Group spent 5.4% of total revenue on R&D; the BMW Group spent 5.5% of total revenue (see Table 2-1.3 for BMW Group deliveries). Within Audi, major R&D takes place in the Design Studio at Munich. The studio, opened in December 2003, develops creative concepts for the Audi, SEAT, and Lamborghini brands. The building accommodates 20 workplaces for designers, engineers, and trend specialists, as well as 15 modellers working on the vehicle concepts and designs of the brand group's future product generations. Their concept cars debut at international motor shows around the world to solicit feedback from motoring experts and the press. The cars reflect the brand's core values, being sophisticated, progressive, and sporty. The design team has focused on technical engineered design and aesthetic product design, hence the slogan "Vorsprung durch Technik", meaning progress through technology.

Table 2-1.3   BMW group deliveries

BMW Group Production	2011	2010	2009	2008	2007
BMW	1,380,384	1,224,280	1,068,770	1,202,239	1,276,793
Mini	285,060	234,175	216,538	232,425	222,875
Rolls-Royce	3,538	2,711	1,002	1,212	1,010
Workforce	100,306	95,453	96,230	100,041	107,539
Revenues (Million)	€68,821	€60,477	€50,681	€53,197	€56,018

The Audi racing team dominates the World Endurance Championship races. The team has won the Le Mans 24-hour race eleven times over the last twelve years. From 2006 the Audi Team has won the race using a diesel engine in the racing cars, but in 2012 they won using hybrid technology in their R18 e-tron Quattro, diesel powered fly-wheel-based car.

The VW "Group Strategy 2018" aspires to be the global market leader by 2018, by producing more than 10 million cars. It is currently ranked third, behind General Motors and Toyota. The VW Group plans to achieve this goal by being a world leader in innovation and technology, whilst delivering customer satisfaction and quality, and allowing each brand to retain its own identity and to operate independently in the market.

Questions

1. *How has the Volkswagen Group benefited from economies of scale and scope?*
2. *What are the benefits for Audi being part of the Volkswagen Group?*
3. *Compare and contrast VW Group's research and development spend with BMW Group's spend. What are the implications for the BMW Group?*
4. *Why is the Le Mans race important for Audi?*

◀◀◀ Some Ideas

1. *How has the Volkswagen Group benefited from economies of scale and scope?*

The group has benefited from economies of scale by increasing the production of vehicles, which allows them to lower costs. Table 2-1.1 in the case information shows an increase in production of 30.4% from 2008 to 2011, which is considerable growth for a mature industry. This has been achieved by segment filling with different makes, e.g. Audi, Skoda, Bentley, and with different models, e.g. A3, A4, A6, etc.

Economies of scope have been obtained by the use of platforms and modular systems to build four toolkits. Within each toolkit there will be parts that are interchangeable between makes and models, e.g. a light bulb and fitting will be the same for an Audi, SEAT, Volkswagen, and Skoda. Therefore, by increasing the scope of a part, that is, the application over a wide range of makes and models, the number of parts produced increases, thereby increasing economies of scale. Consequently economies of scale and scope are interlinked.

2. *What are the benefits for Audi being part of the Volkswagen Group?*

Audi's slogan "Vorsprung durch Technik" means innovation through technology. Therefore, new product development that takes place in Audi can be passed on to the rest of the VW Group. You will notice in Table 2-1.2 that Audi consistently produces more engines that it produces cars. These engines are "sold" to other marques within the VW Group.

3. *Compare and contrast VW Group's research and development spend with BMW Group's spend. What are the implications for the BMW Group?*

Calculation of the comparative R&D spend of the two groups, as shown in Table 2-1.4, shows that in 2011 the VW Group spent $8.6 million whereas the BMW Group spend was only $3.7 million, which is considerably less. Also VW Group spends $1.05 per car on R&D whereas the BMW spend is $2.27 per car. The implication is that the BMW Group over time will not be able to be the front-runner with technological development. To achieve this position they will need to consolidate with another car manufacturer to gain economies of scale.

Table 2-1.4 Comparative R&D spend

	VW Group	BMW Group
Revenue (€)	159,337,000	68,831,000
R&D (%)	5.4%	5.5%
R&D expenditure (€)	8,604,198	3,785,155
Number of cars	8,160,154	1,668,982
R&D spend per car	$1.05	$2.27

4. *Why is the Le Mans race important for Audi?*

The 24-hour endurance race tests Audi's new technologies, e.g. the diesel engine, under stress conditions. Information and experience gained from these performances enables Audi to apply the technologies to the domestic market. Also, by obtaining successive wins, Audi is able to establish their brand as being reliable, as well as living up to its slogan, thereby firmly positioning itself in the marketing as being technology led.

▶▶▶

Case Notes:

Case 2-2 Happy Feet

Up until the late nineteenth century there were three options for people regarding footwear. They could buy expensive made to measure shoes, wear cast offs (often ill fitting), or wear no shoes at all. However, in a modern consumer society the wearing of shoes has become a necessity. For instance, international airlines insist passengers wear a pair of shoes for boarding and disembarkation. Mass production of shoes has reduced the cost of shoes for everyone but the downside is that retailers have concentrated on volume market sectors by selling the most popular styles, sizes, and fittings, consequently forcing out specialist retailers. As a result people with large feet, either in width and/or length, are poorly served.

The footwear industry consists of four product groups. The first is casual footwear, making up 44% of the market. This group is expected to grow significantly as there is a general trend towards more casual dress. The second biggest product group, at 25%, is formal footwear, for example, shoes for work, but this sector is decreasing. Another large group is sports footwear at 23%; however, this group comprises different types of shoes, such as running shoes, golf shoes, tennis shoes, etc. Finally, evening footwear is the last product group, which represents 7.7% of the market. With a trend towards the smarter style of after-five wear there has been a demand for evening footwear so modest growth is expected in this market.

According to the British Footwear Association, in the UK annual shoe sales total £6.4bn. In the 2000–1 period 63.5% of shoes were imported into the domestic market but this grew to 91.3% in the period 2012–13. In 2008 331 million pairs of shoes were bought equating to 5.4 shoes per capita. The majority of the shoes are imported from low-cost suppliers such as China, India, Thailand, Vietnam, and Poland. The manufacture of shoes in the UK in 2008 was 11 million pairs, which resulted in a decrease in volume by 5.9%. This was due to the industry's slow reaction to imports but there is a view that the UK shoe manufacturing industry is now more competitive. As the choice of shoe is largely by brand name rather than retail outlet, manufacturers have launched advertising campaigns, seized sponsorship opportunities, and gained celebrity endorsements in an effort to build their brands. Another response has been to move the production to low-cost locations, but preferably close to the UK so as to guarantee fast delivery and to respond quickly to seasonal changes in fashion.

Over the years the UK footwear industry has become increasingly concentrated resulting in five main manufacturers. C & J Clark is one of the world's largest manufacturers and distributors of general footwear. Based in Street, Somerset the company is 81% owned by the Clark family and is the 33rd largest private company in the UK. Whilst marketing and design remain in the UK, the shoes are manufactured in Brazil, Cambodia, China, and Vietnam. In 2011 the company had approximately 500 retail shops in the UK.

Dr Martens is a well-known brand, especially in the youth market. The shoes are distinguished by their air-cushioned soles, which make them particularly suitable for working people. However, in the 1960s the boots were adopted by skinheads and in the 1970s by punks. The lead guitarist of The Who, Pete Townshend, enhanced their appeal to the youth culture by wearing the boots. Recently the brand has had a revival due to celebrities like Miley Cyrus and Rihanna wearing the footwear.

Barkers, located in Northampton, the traditional shoe making district with brands such as Church's and Loakes still being made there, has been manufacturing high quality leather footwear since 1880. In 2005 the company launched a sub-brand for men named Barker Black, named after the founder Arthur Black. The shoe is positioned at the high end of the market and has appeared in fashion magazines such as Men's Vogue and GQ.

John Lobb started making shoes and boots for gentlemen in 1866 and in Paris from 1902. In 1976 the company was acquired by the Hermès Group and based the operation in Paris. However, the London bespoke workshop remained in the ownership of the family and still produces shoes at its made-to-order business at their original site in James Street, London. The company caters for the exclusive market with the average price of a bespoke shoe being £2,700. Famous clients have been Queen Victoria, Diana Spencer, and Calvin Klein. The Hermès Group recognized that there was a broader market for the shoe so they launched a ready-to-wear line in Paris in 1990. In 1994 a workshop was opened in Northampton where the ready-to-wear shoe was designed and made, retaining some of the basic qualities of the 190-step bespoke manufacturing process.

Hotter Shoes is a footwear manufacturer based in Skelmersdale, Lancashire, producing over 1.6 million shoes per year, which represents a third of the UK's footwear production. The company targets the over 50-year-olds with comfortable but fashionable shoes. The company started in 1959 by making slippers. When the son of the original owners, Stewart Houlgrave, joined the company in the 1980s he decided to branch into the shoe market. At the time the footwear industry was fighting for survival, with many companies going offshore to compete against cheaper imported shoes. As factories closed Stewart was able to purchase cheap machinery as he had decided to remain in England because he wanted to retain control over costs, product development, and margins. Introducing and testing new product lines to boost sales was easier as many Chinese factories would only take large orders to make it worth their while. Hotter Shoes, on the other hand, was able to do short runs. The factory in Skelmersdale, whilst being antiquated, became a tourist attraction with tours booked out three years in advance. Unfortunately the tours ceased when a new factory facility was opened.

In building the new factory the aim was to build a world-class footwear production facility. However, this was not just a one-off investment as continual re-investment is carried out to keep the factory up-to-date with the latest machinery and processes. Whilst there has been skill depletion due to the number of shoe factories closing, Stewart has retained his experienced staff and developed his own training programme to increase skill levels.

His marketing approach has been unique for the footwear industry as he decided to market directly to customers by mail order. This was to overcome being a hostage to retailers whilst allowing him to build relationships directly with customers. Using a direct response media model he was able to understand what worked and discard what didn't work in gaining sales. When the company had built up sufficient awareness he opened his own stores as customers recognized his shoes. Currently there are 54 Hotter Shoe stores and the company now sells to 200 independent retailers, as well as retaining their direct online sales strategy, making Hotter Shoes a multi-channel marketer.

Questions

1. Why is innovation an imperative in this industry? What aspects should Stewart concentrate on to build the business?
2. How can the Product Life Cycle be applied to the footwear manufacturing business?

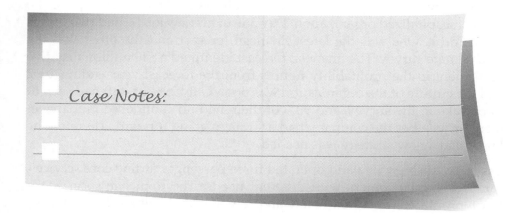

Case Notes:

Case 2-3 Three's a Crowd

Low-cost carriers, known in the airline industry as value-based airlines (VBA), began operating in the 1970s, although prior to this charter airlines had offered low prices to specific holiday destinations. Pioneered by Southwest Airlines in the United States, and easyJet and Ryanair in Europe, VBAs presented a new threat to the traditional airline operators, known as "legacy carriers", as they operate a low-cost strategy. This is achieved by offering a reduced range of services, for example, no pre-booked seating, a single class cabin with food and drink paid for by the passengers on the flight, only flying point to point on short-haul routes between secondary airports, and utilizing the same type of planes. Not providing baggage transfers to other airlines, relying on the internet for sales, and using a ticketless booking system gain additional savings. VBAs are able to cherry pick the profitable routes thereby putting pressure on the legacy carriers who use the profitable routes to cross subsidize other routes within their networks. The response of many of the legacy carriers was to establish their own low-cost subsidiary with the risk that they might be cannibalizing their own sales.

In 2001 Air New Zealand was the dominant airline operator in New Zealand with competition from Qantas New Zealand, which operated as a franchise under the Qantas brand. However, in April 2001 Qantas New Zealand collapsed leaving thousands of domestic travellers seeking alternative flight arrangements. But by July 2002 Jetconnect, a subsidiary of Qantas, was flying between Auckland, Wellington, Rotorua, Christchurch, and Queenstown, under the Qantas brand. At about this time Air New Zealand, following a $1.43 billion annual loss after writing down $1.32 billion from their investment in Ansett Australia, was saved from bankruptcy by the New Zealand government injecting $883 million giving it an 83% shareholding.

In February 2002 Ralph Norris was appointed as Chief Executive of the newly recapitalized organization. Day one in his new job he had two things on his desk. One was the latest financial forecast and the other was the staff climate survey. The financial forecast identified a $40 million negative movement in the profitability figures from the forecast year ending 2002 and the culture of the organization was poor. Only 29% of staff had seen fit to partake in the survey, and 90% of them had no confidence in management or whether the company had a strategy going forward. Therefore he knew that a new strategy was needed.

Basically Air New Zealand operated three passenger airline core services, each serving customers with different needs. The domestic service, the most profitable, operated solely in New Zealand, whereas the Pacific service operated in Australia and the Pacific Islands, and the Long Haul operation consisted of flights over five hours. The decision was made to start restructuring the domestic service by implementing a new business model.

Extensive research revealed that customers did not value all of the in-flight frills that came with Air New Zealand's full service domestic offering and expressed their willingness to trade off some of these for lower fares. As a legacy carrier Air New Zealand realized that it couldn't become a VBA overnight, so a hybrid model was put together to suit the Air New Zealand operation.

The new product for the domestic service was called domestic Express class, which involved making the following changes. The business class seats were removed from the Boeing 737 fleet thereby making a one-class service, enabling the number of seats to increase from 122 to 136. Air New Zealand added a tenth Boeing 737 to expand the main trunk schedule to cope with the anticipated growth in passengers. Meals and drink selections were replaced with a biscuit, tea, coffee, water, and a give-away mug. The number of cabin crew on the Boeing 737 aircraft was reduced from four to three, as their duties did not include meal deliveries. Newspapers were no longer offered, but the inflight magazine was retained. In contrast to VBAs, airport lounges were retained and upgraded as customer research had clearly indicated these aspects of travel were still valued. The fares were lowered and simplified with the removal of advanced purchase or minimum stay conditions. On the main trunk route fares dropped on average 28%, with the cheapest flights on offer dropping by 50%. Frequent flyers could continue to accrue Airpoints (Air New Zealand's frequent flyer programme) on qualifying fares.

To offer travel at as low a cost as possible, Air New Zealand separated the airfare from the cost of distribution and offered its lowest fares online, as this is the channel with the lowest costs. If a passenger booked a domestic fare through a travel agent there would be a $10 surcharge for the use of the Global Distribution System but the travel agents were at liberty to charge their own service fees. Also, commissions to travel agents for selling Express service fares were cut from 5% to zero but incentives for reaching sales targets were retained.

The drive for Internet sales meant that Air New Zealand spent considerable time and effort ensuring that their IT systems and Internet interface could cope with the increased load. Also, the anticipated additional passengers could have resulted in increased costs of extra staff at airports, but again technology had a key part to play. Following on closely from the launch of the Express service Air New Zealand introduced self-service check-in kiosks in main domestic airports allowing customers travelling with electronic tickets to print their own boarding pass. Customers were also able to use the kiosk to select their seats and indicate if they had bags to check in.

The results three years after the introduction of the Express service showed that compound passenger growth was approximately 40%. The passenger load factor had increased from 67.4% to 76.2%. This comprised an increase in capacity, that is, Available Seat per Kilometre (ASK), from 3,638 million to 4,281 million, and an increase in traffic, that is Revenue Passenger per Kilometre (RPK), from 2,453 million to 3,264 million.

On 12 November 2007 Pacific Blue Airlines, a subsidiary of Australian airline Virgin Blue, started operating VBA domestic services in New Zealand with flights between Auckland, Wellington, and Christchurch, flights between Christchurch and Dunedin were added at a later stage. This meant that there were now three operators on the main trunk domestic routes.

In 2009 Qantas replaced its service with their low-cost subsidiary, Jetstar, with up to 16 weekly return domestic flights between Auckland, Wellington, Christchurch, and Queenstown. Jetstar entered the market aggressively by promoting one dollar fares. With the increased competition in the market Pacific Blue announced in August 2010 that it would be withdrawing from the domestic market, with the last flight operating on 18 October 2010.

Since Pacific Blue's withdrawal from the market there have been some modifications of the operations from both Jetstar and Air New Zealand. For example, Air New Zealand added flights between Paraparaumu and Auckland, whereas Jetstar in June 2013 announced it would suspend its year-round service on the Wellington–Queenstown route, just after Air New Zealand announced it would boost capacity on the route by 44%. However Jetstar increased capacity on the Auckland–Queenstown route.

Annual results for the period ending June 2013 make interesting reading. Jetstar has increased its domestic market share over the period from 20.6% to 22.4%. The number of domestic passengers carried increased by 17% to 1.87 million. Over the same period the airline increased its New Zealand capacity by 14% and improved its Revenue Passenger per Kilometre (RPK) by 18% to 1.205 million.

In contrast Air New Zealand passenger capacity increased by 2.8% due to new Airbus A320 aircraft replacing B737-300 aircraft and the addition of an ATR72-600 aircraft. The number of domestic passengers increased from

8.500 million to 8.694 million. Air New Zealand's load factor improved by 1.1% to 82.6% but the yield was reduced by 5.3% as a result of price reductions to stimulate demand. RPK increased from 4.050 to 4.218 million.

Questions

1. *Why did Air New Zealand have to radically change its domestic service offer? What key dimensions of the service were changed?*
2. *How do the four characteristics of a service apply to Air New Zealand?*
3. *How would you measure the "moment of truth" for the domestic service?*
4. *What are some future challenges? How might they be addressed?*

Case Notes:

Case 2-4 Nighty Night, Sleep Tight

Stagecoach Group plc started Megabus in 2003, as a cheap no-frills bus service in competition with National Express. By February 2010 Megabus had 19 bus routes serving 41 destinations in England, Wales, and Scotland. The company advertised fares starting at £1, with a 50p booking fee. These low fares are for people who booked early and are applied to less popular routes. Typically it is only the first six seats that are made available at this price. Tickets can only be bought via their website or by phone. Megabus uses out of town interchanges to save time due to the congestion in urban areas.

In September 2011 Megabus launched a sleeper service between London and Glasgow. The service uses a single-deck articulated "bendy" bus, with 24 beds stacked three high. Curtains screen each bunk, but due to the lack of space, passengers are required to sleep in their clothes. A reading light for each bunk is provided, along with a duvet, eye mask, pillow, and blanket. As much tea, coffee, and water is provided as you want, but there is no on-board catering service. Each bus has a toilet. Two drivers travel on board, swapping at the only stop, which is a motorway service station near Birmingham. The buses depart from the Victoria Coach Station at 23:59 and arrive in Glasgow at 08:05. From Glasgow, the buses depart at 23:15 and arrive in London at 07:20. The fares start at £1 plus booking fee and go up to £40.

National Express is the direct competition to Megabus but they do not have a sleeper service. Offering comparable fares, their Fast Service takes 8 hours 15 minutes. The bus leaves London Victoria Coach Station at 23:00 and arrives at the Buchanan Bus Station, Glasgow at 07:15, whereas the Glasgow service leaves at 22:30 and arrives at the Victoria Coach Station at 06:50. The bus operates seven days a week and calls at Golders Green, Toddington Services, Milton Keynes Coachway, Penrith, Lockerbie, and Abbington Service area.

First ScotRail operates two sleeper train services, known as the *Caledonian*, between London and Scotland using the West Coast mainline. The trains operate six times a week, excluding Saturday night. Fares start at £19, with a Standard fare costing up to £94, but a First Class ticket can cost from £130 plus. The London terminal is Euston, and the trains travel to five Scottish termini, namely Glasgow, Edinburgh, Aberdeen, Fort William, and Inverness.

The *Highland Sleeper* departs as separate trains from Inverness, Fort William (known as the *Deerstalker*), and Aberdeen, which then merge into one train at Edinburgh Waverley Station (where boarding is not possible), before continuing south stopping for passengers to alight at Preston, Crewe, and Watford Junction before arriving at London. From London Euston (departs between 20:00 and 21:15) the front coaches are for Fort William, the middle portion Aberdeen, and the rear coaches are for Inverness.

The Lowland Sleeper operates between London and Edinburgh/Glasgow, departing London Euston between 22:00 and 23:00. The train calls at Watford Junction (for boarding only), Carlisle, and Carstairs (both stops for alighting only). At Carstairs the service separates into two trains, one for Edinburgh and the other for Glasgow Central (also calling at Motherwell). The return journey departs from Glasgow and Edinburgh between 21:00 and 23:00. The two trains form one train at Carstairs, and continue the journey south calling at Carlisle (for boarding only), Watford Junction, and then London Euston the following morning.

There are three classes of travel. The seated sleeper passenger is provided with an airline style seat, with a reading light that can be turned off, but the cabin lights remain on. The Standard Service passenger is provided with an air-conditioned cabin with washbasin, shower point, hand towel, bottled water, and a bar of soap. The standard cabins have two berths so if one person is travelling alone they will have to share. The passengers receive an early morning tea or coffee, with a piece of shortbread. The First Class passenger receives the same service as the Standard passenger but they have a single berth cabin along with a more substantial mini washkit. They also receive either a full breakfast or a continental style breakfast.

Each train has a Lounge Car, which Standard or First Class ticket holders are allowed to use, although at busy times it is restricted to First Class passengers. The Lounge Car makes available meals, snacks, and alcoholic beverages for purchase. There is a buffet service available for seated passengers, and all passengers can take food and beverages back to their seat or cabin.

Apart from driving a car between London and Glasgow, which is 400 miles and can take up to seven hours, one can fly. There are two main operators, as noted in Table 2-4.1:

Table 2-4.1 British Airways and easyJet services between London and Glasgow

Carrier	Airport Departure	Flight Time	Approx Cost
British Airways	Gatwick	1 hr 25m	£45
British Airways	Heathrow	1 hr 25m	£53
British Airways	London City	1 hr 35m	£56
EasyJet	Stanstead	1 hr 15m	£22.19
Easyjet	Luton	1 hr 20m	£24.99
Easyjet	Gatwick	1 hr 30m	£26.99

British Airways operates a full service, including different classes of travel and meals, whereas easyJet is a budget, no frills operation.

Questions

1. *Compare and contrast the service offering of Megabus and ScotRail.*
2. *How can the diffusion of innovation be applied to Megabus?*

Case Notes:

Aaker, D. (2008) *Strategic Market Management*, 8th edn. Hoboken, NJ: Wiley.

Boatwright, P., Cagan, J. and Vogel, C. (2006) Innovate or Else: The new imperative, *Ivey Business Journal*, Jan/Feb, 1–3.

Cahill, D. (1996) Pioneer Advantage: is it real? Does it matter?, *Marketing Intelligence & Planning*, 14(4): 5–8.

Covielle, N., Brodie, R., Danaher, P. and Johnston, W. (2002) How Firms Relate to Their Markets: An Empirical Examination of Contemporary Marketing Practices, *Journal of Marketing*, 66(3): 33–46.

Doyle, P. and Stern, P. (2006) *Marketing Management and Strategy*, 4th edn. Harlow, England: Prentice Hall.

Frawley, T. and Fahy, J. (2006) Revisiting the First-Mover Advantage Theory: A Resource-Based Perspective, *Irish Journal of Management*, 27(1): 273–295.

Golder, P. and Tellis, G. (1993) Pioneer Advantage: Marketing Logic or Marketing Legend?, *Journal of Marketing Research*, 30(2): 158–170.

Grönroos, C. (1994) From Marketing Mix to Relationship Marketing: Towards a Paradigm Shift in Marketing, *Management Decision*, 32(2): 4–20.

Hodock, C. and Adamo, G. (2010) Find the Courage to Attack New Product Innovation, *Marketing Management*, 19(3): 38–41.

Kerin, R., Varadarajan, R. and Peterson, R. (1992) First-Mover Advantage: A Synthesis, *Conceptual Framework, and Research Propositions, Journal of Marketing*, 56, 33–52.

Kotler, P. and Keller, K. (2012) *Marketing Management*, 14th edn. Harlow, England: Pearson Education.

Lieberman, M. and Montgomery, D. (1988) First Mover Advantages, *Strategic Management Journal*, 9, 41–58.

Lindgreen, A., Palmer, R. and Vanhamme, J. (2004) Contemporary Marketing Practice: Theoretical propositions and practical implications, *Marketing Intelligence & Planning*, 22(6): 673–692.

MacVaugh, J. and Schiavone, F. (2010) Limits to the Diffusion of Innovation, A literature Review and Integrative Model, *European Journal of Innovation Management*, 13(3): 197–221.

Perner, L. (2010) 'Diffusion of Innovation', located at www.consumerpsychologist.com.

Rettie, R., Hilliar, S. and Alpert, F. (2002) Pioneer Brand Advantage with UK Consumers, *European Journal of Marketing*, 36(7/8): 895–911.

Schilling, M. and Hill. C. (1998) Managing the New Product Development Process: Strategic imperatives, *The Academy of Management Executive*, 12(3): 67–81.

Skålén, P. and Strandvik, T. (2005) From Prescription to description: A critique and reorientation of service culture, *Managing Service Quality*, 15(3): 230–244.

Case Acknowledgements

The **Extended Families** case draws on information contained in:

"MQB Architecture at Audi and the Volkswagen Group", by J. Vondruska (17 February 2012), *Intel Report*, retrieved from http://fourtitude.com/news /publish/Features/article_7484.shtml

"Volkswagen Is Leading Auto Innovation with the MQB Platform", by I. Labutes (16 March 2012), *Seeking Alpha*, retrieved from http://seekingalpha.com/article /438251-volkswagen-is-leading-auto-innovation-with-the-MQB-platform

DEVELOPING PRODUCTS AND SERVICES

"Audi is first manufacturer to take Le Mans 24 Hours race with hybrid", by G. Richards (17 June 2010), *The Guardian*, retrieved from http://www.guardian.co.uk/sport/2012/jun/17/audi-le-mans-24-hours-race

Table 2-1.1: Compiled from 10-Year Overview statistics, Audi Group Finances 2011

Table 2-1.2: Compiled from Passenger Car and Light Commercial Vehicle Deliveries to Customers by Market statistics, Volkswagen AG Annual Report 2011

Table 2-1.3: Compiled from BMW Group in figures, BMW Group Annual Report 2012

The **Happy Feet** case draws on information contained in:

"The Footwear Market in the United Kingdom", (May 2010), *CBI Market Information Database*, retrieved from http://www.cbi.eu/system/files/marketintel/201020-20footwear20-20United20Kingdom1.pdf

"Hotter Shoes a sole survivor in a dying industry", by J. Hurley (26 June 2012), *The Telegraph*, retrieved from www.telegraph.co.uk/finance/businessclub/9355178/Hotter-Shoes-a-sole-survivor-in-a-dying-industry.html

"Mencyclopaedia – John Lobb", by L. Leitch (1 November 2013), *The Telegraph*, retrieved from http://www.telegraph.co.uk/luxury/mens-style/13577/mencyclopaedia-john-lobb.html

Hotter Shoe website located at www.hottershoes.com

British Footwear Association website located at www.britishfootwearassociation.co.uk

The **Three's A Crowd** case draws on information contained in:

Air New Zealand Annual Financial Results 2013

"Jetstar celebrates four year milestone", (14 June 2013), *Voxy*, retrieved from http://www.voxy.co.nz/lifestyle/jetstar-celebrates-four-year-milestone/5/158385

"Jetstar nibbles into Air NZ's domestic dominance", (29 August 2013), *National Business Review*, retrieved from http://www.nbr.co.nz/article/jetstar-nibbles-air-nzs-domestic-dominance-bd-145091

"Jetstar to suspend year-round Wellington service", by J. Beech (13 June 2013), *Otago Daily Times*, retrieved from http://www.odt.co.nz/news/queenstown-lakes/260830/jetstar-suspend-year-round-wellington-service

Pacific Blue Airlines website located at www.virginaustralia.com

"Red ink too much for Pacific Blue", by R. van den Bergh (17 August 2010), *Business Day*, retrieved from http://www.stuff.co.nz/business/industries/4029883/Red-ink-too-much-for-Pacific-Blue

The **Nighty Night, Sleep Tight** case draws on information contained in:

"Bargain bus is a sleeper hit", by N. Sharpe (19 October 2011), *The Sun*, retrieved from http://www.thesun.co.uk/sol/homepage/news/scottishnews/3880365/Bargain-bus-is-a-sleeper-hit.html

Dalton, A. (2011), "Flat-out to London on the sleeper bus", (9 August 2011), *The Scotsman*, 13

First ScotRail website located at www.scotrail.co.uk

"Megabus gears up for overnight sleeper service", by H. Osborne (2 August 2011), *The Guardian*, retrieved from http://www.guardian.com/money/2011/aug/02/megabus-overnight-coach-sleeper.html

"Megabus sleeper services extended", by T. Sharp (17 April 2012), *Herald Scotland*, retrieved from http://www.heraldscotland.com/news/transport/megabus-sleeper-services-extended.17317833

Megabus website located at www.megabus.com/uk

National Express website located at www.nationalexpress.com/coach

"Stagecoach boss plan 'middle class Megabus'", by N. Thomas (7 July 2012), *The Telegraph*, retrieved from http://www.telegraph.co.uk/finance/newsbysector/transport/9384126/Stagecoach-boss-plans-middle-class-Megabus.html

This chapter covers the following topics:

▶ Demand forecasting
▶ Market analysis
▶ Competitor analysis
▶ Market research

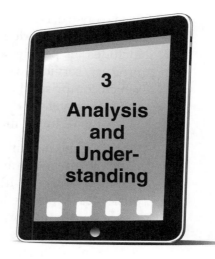

3
Analysis and Under-standing

It's Written in the Stars

One of the central tasks of marketing is to forecast the demand for the product/service. This is an important task because the outcome of the forecast will impact upon the future cash flow of the firm. Predicting sales in terms of units or revenue is difficult given today's dynamic environment. However, not to undertake the task is like playing a game of chance. At best one wants to minimize the risk and narrow the odds in the firm's favour. Another reason to forecast demand is to allow the marketer to take the necessary actions regarding product/service modifications, as well as developing distribution, communication, and pricing strategies. Accurate demand forecasts are also important because of the impact upon other areas of the organization, such as operations and procurement so they can plan capacity, and the finance department so they can plan investment.

The demand for a product/service will be dependent on a customer's willingness and ability to seek a solution to a perceived problem. By seeking, obtaining, and using the product/service the customer is satisfying needs, wants, or desires. Therefore, the role of marketing is to provide solutions to customers, clients, or the general public. However, not all people desire to seek a solution at a specific time. This will be tempered by the situation and the circumstances. Therefore, marketing is interested in managing the demand for a specific product/service based on the willingness and ability of customers (in the generic sense) to seek a solution and partake of the offering.

Two constructs are important when exploring the types of demand, namely potential demand and market penetration. The potential demand includes all people who are willing and able to seek a solution for the product/service. In other words, the potential demand is the total market, which comprises those who are already purchasing the product and those who have yet to do so, for example, the late majority (see Chapter 2 Diffusion of Innovation).

At this stage it is important to make a distinction between the terms category, form, and brand. A category is defined by the group of competing product/services within a market. The product/service will have common attributes which define the category. For example, the cola market comprises competing products which have carbonated water with a distinct caramel taste. However, the category can be defined at different levels thus determining the size and scope of the market. For instance, a more generic category may be all carbonated beverages, and a more extensive category would be all beverages. The scope of the market, whether it is defined as broad or narrow, is an important issue as it will determine the competitors in the market. For example, is the organization operating in the sea ferry market or the transportation market?

Within a specific category there will be different product forms. A form within the cola category is diet cola. Another example is within the motor car category where there are different forms of vehicles such as hatchbacks and SUVs. The final distinction is that of brands. These are the competing products within the form or category, for example, Audi versus BMW.

These distinctions are important for a number of reasons. First, the marketer can estimate the potential demand for their brand. This can be measured by the number of units sold or the revenue gained over a given period, for example, over a year or a purchase cycle. In order to determine the potential demand it is necessary to calculate the market penetration of the category. This will comprise the organization's own market share and also the market share of the competition.

The next issue is to determine if there is any growth in the category. Within any given period the growth will come from two sources. The first is new category users (NCUs) who haven't used the category as yet. For example, in the yoghurt category there may be users who decide to purchase the product for the first time because they have learnt about the health benefits from advertisements and/or friends. Therefore, one of the main tasks for a marketer is to determine the number of NCUs in the market and to develop a campaign to make them trial the product/service. The downside to such a campaign is that the increase of NCUs is often relative to market share, as all players gain from the campaign. In other words, a company may influence people to trial the product/service but at the point of purchase they may select another brand. This is evidenced in the airline industry where cheap flights to European destinations appeal to people who would not normally travel overseas for holidays. Customers have their interest piqued by the advertisement of Airline A, but after a search and evaluation they choose Airline B (The distinction between evoked set and consideration will be explored in the Chapter 4).

The second source for growth within a category is to increase the rate of purchase by customers who are already buying the product/service. In other words, within a purchase cycle it is possible, in some cases, for customers who are already purchasing the product/service to buy more of the product. Taking the yoghurt example, in a week it may be possible to influence a customer, who buys one pottle for lunch on Monday, to buy two or more, so they have yoghurt more than once a week.

In summary, when assessing and forecasting the demand for their product/service the marketer has four distinct objectives that can be addressed with different marketing strategies. The first objective is to ascertain the organization's market penetration and determine the degree of customer loyalty. What strategies can be put in place to increase customer loyalty or minimize their brand switching? The second objective is to ascertain the competitors' market penetration and decide what marketing strategies can be put in place to entice brand switching behaviour. The third objective is to ascertain the amount of NCUs and develop marketing strategies to convince them to trial the category and preferably your brand. The fourth objective is to determine if existing customers can be influenced to increase their rate of purchase over a given period, thereby increasing the potential market.

Not all objectives will be applicable to all organizations. For example, in the soap powder market there will be limited NCUs and it would be difficult to increase the rate of purchase, so brand managers must concentrate on maintaining loyal customers and/or increasing brand switching behaviour. Another example is the national campaign in the UK to vaccinate girls aged 12 to 13 against the human papilloma virus as it can cause cervical cancer, which is the second most common cancer in women under the age of thirty-five. The marketing programme for this campaign is targeting NCUs and through database management it is relatively easy to measure the uptake of vaccinations.

What's Going On Out There?

The previous section outlined four distinct marketing objectives, each requiring different marketing strategies. Before these can be outlined in more detail, it is necessary to conduct a market analysis for the category. To achieve this an organization needs to obtain data, but data itself won't indicate what decisions need to be made. What is needed is the role of interpretation, and this role of judgement plays an important part in determining the course of action. Piercy (1991) uses the concept of market sensing to explain how marketers develop an understanding of the market, which involves the development of simplified models about how the market operates resulting in a shared understanding of the market. However, when this understanding becomes outdated and inflexible, but still adhered to by management, it can lead to problems.

In this digital age, with microprocessors increasing computing capacity, there is a lot of data that an organization can capture. This data can be linked to a company's database and reports can be developed. Therefore, a company needs to design a robust system to capture the data, commonly called a marketing information system (MIS). One problem is that many organizations have developed, over time, task independent databases which don't easily talk to each other. These databases, which in some organizations can be as many as forty, need to be unified and integrated so that the organization has one view of the customer.

The purpose of an MIS is to track trends in the marketplace over a given period of time, whether it be weekly, monthly, or quarterly. The period will be dictated by each company's specific situation, based on the purchase cycle and category spend, and other factors such as competitor activity or obtaining the results of a campaign launch. For example, a company trading in the fast moving consumer goods category (FMCG) is likely to have a weekly MIS report, whereas Boeing Aircraft Corporation is likely to be quarterly.

In designing the MIS the organization needs to think carefully about the information that is required in a timely manner and where the data can be obtained. Table 3.1 contains a list of possible inputs and where such data can be obtained, either within the organization or from external sources.

Once the MIS is up and running the task of the marketer is to track variances. Experience plays a part in determining whether the variance is meaningful or merely an aberration. Therefore it may be useful for the marketer to determine a zone of tolerance for each input. The variances can be colour coded from green (meaning business as usual), yellow (signalling this has potential impact so should be watched carefully, to red (indicates that action is required).

Table 3.1 MIS inputs

Input	Source
Profit, margins, sales	Accounts department
Market share	Sales force, distributors, market research company
Bank orders, inventory	Operations department
Sales trends, competitor's actions	Sales force, distributors
Exchange & interest rates	Bank, online sources
Building permits	Local body
Macro trends	Newspaper, journals, magazines
Customer satisfaction	Social media, including blogs, customer surveys
Innovations	Trade mark registrations, exhibition & trade shows

Source: Adapted from Kotler and Keller (2012)

On occasions it is necessary to solve specific problems regarding customer purchasing patterns, etc., so by utilizing database technology the marketing department can undertake data mining, where buyer behaviour is analysed and solutions created.

Winners and Losers

It is important that competition is analysed for a number of reasons, namely to develop marketing strategies in response to competitor's actions and also to determine where a competitive advantage might reside and marketing's role in developing such an advantage. For example, the competitive advantage may lie in enhancing the existing distribution channel, or by developing the company's differential advantage by building customers' brand knowledge.

There are a number of generic questions that can be used to determine the competition's overall strategy. First, are they pursuing a growth strategy or are they milking the product/service for cash? Following on from this, is there any cross subsidization between one business unit and another? In other words, a competitor may be operating the division at a loss and their operating costs are being subsidized by a more profitable business unit. In such cases, the parent organization will have a long-term strategy for the unit. For example, the industry may be cyclical and so they are waiting for a new growth stage, or the company may want to build market share. Also, the financial situation can be appraised. From the profit and loss account it may be possible to calculate average margins and the debt:equity ratio may give details regarding the competitor's ability to finance further development. In addition, the company's retained earnings will indicate the possibility that finance is available for further market expansion.

The concept of core competency (Prahalad and Hamel, 1990) can be used to determine both the competitor's and your own strengths. A core competency is the way an organization configures its skill set to deliver value to the customer. The skill set must be unique to the organization and is perceived as a strength compared to other competitors within the industry sector. Also, the core competency must be difficult for competitors to copy. In particular, what is of interest is the core competency of the marketing capability within the sector. For example, the Coca-Cola corporation has a core competency in brand management.

Market share is an important concept that has implications for marketing strategy. The Profit Impact of Market Strategy (PIMS) has signalled the importance of market share. PIMS is a database, which has been collecting data from 1972 onwards. Over 3000 companies submit information at the strategic business unit (SBU) level about their financial status, customer profiles, market conditions, and state of competition. Whilst the study indicates that market share is important, there are some caveats. Firstly, the data is weighted towards large corporations so it is questionable if the lessons are applicable to SMEs and entrepreneurial start-ups. Also, it is difficult to determine causal links between variables; for example, does market share determine high profits or is it the reverse? Confounding the issue is the possibility that product quality may be a contributing factor. Finally, self-reporting by companies may lead to bias in the reports, and data from only existing SBUs may lead to "survivor bias". Nonetheless, the PIMS study does signal the importance market share plays in a company's success.

When considering market share there are two important measures that need to be taken into account. The first is absolute market share which is calculated by dividing a company's sales by the total sales in the market and is expressed as a percentage. Note that the share can be calculated by volume (units sold) or by revenue. For example, airlines can use market share compared with capacity share in the sector; in other words, seats sold by the airline divided by the number of seats available (calculated by their own and competitors' available seats) on a given route.

The second measure is that of relative market share, whereby the company's percentage share is divided by the percentage share of the strongest competitor in the market. This means that the market leader will have a ratio greater than one, whilst others in the market will have a ratio less than one. Consequently the relationship is expressed as a ratio, for example the leading brand has 40% market share and a competitor has 20%, therefore the ratio is 2:1.

Another useful concept is that of market concentration, which is a measure of percentage of the market held by a small number of companies. For example, if a large proportion of the market, say 80%, is held by three companies then the market is said to be highly concentrated.

A modified version of Porter's Generic Strategies can be used to understand a company's position regarding market share. Market share has been substituted for competitive advantage on the grid (see Figure 3.1) to explain the dynamics of market share, with a dominant competitor being compared with other competitors. It is debatable as to what counts as a dominant competitor, but it is often assumed that they have market share that is approximately double the nearest rival and three times that of the next competitor. For example, the dominant player has 60%, the nearest competitor 30%, followed by the third player in the market with 20%.

The vertical axis denotes the scope of the competitors' activity. Based on Ansoff's (1968) work, there are four types of scope. The first is product scope, which is a measurement of the extent of the product offering. For example, the product mix can be expanded by adding varieties to the basic offering, as can be seen with Coca-Cola expanding their product mix by adding cherry coke, vanilla coke, and diet coke thereby increasing their product usage by appealing to different segments. The second is industry scope, where a company can move from narrow to broad scope by expanding their business by moving into different categories, for example, banks offering insurance or McDonalds adding McCafé. The third area is that of

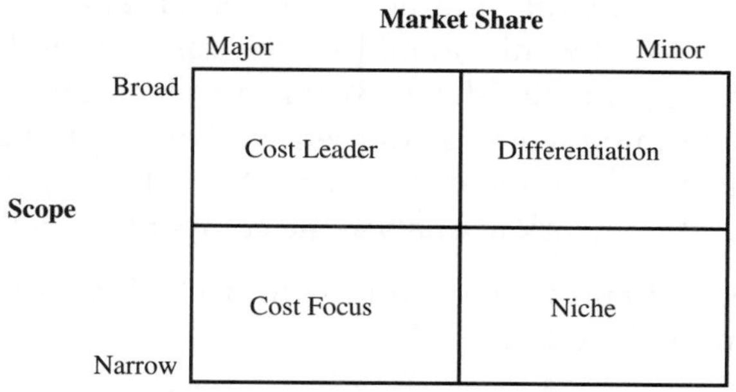

Figure 3.1 Generic Market Share Grid. Source: Adapted from Porter (1980)

geographic scope, for example, Morrisons Supermarket, a predominantly north of England chain, buying Safeway with stores in southern England and Scotland. Finally, a company can broaden its scope through vertical integration by buying either the suppliers and/or buyers within the value chain.

Therefore, it can be seen that an organization with a broad scope and a dominant market share has a cost advantage. This cost advantage can be maintained by utilizing the experience curve, consequently gaining economies of scale and scope. Economies of scale can be gained not only in the scale of production but also other areas such as advertising and distribution.

According to the model, other competitors must differentiate in some way (see Chapter 7) rather than provide just a "me too" product/service. However, it needs to be noted that this does not mean the dominant player does not differentiate its product/service. In fact, by other competitors differentiating their offering, the dominant player is marketing a differentiated product by default. Nor does it mean the other companies do not do all they can to lower costs.

The remaining quadrants, cost focus and niche player, are defined by their narrow scope. For example, many port authorities follow a cost focus strategy as they have a narrow geographic scope. Niche players on the other hand will stay focused on their customer segment offering a narrowly defined product. The Morgan Motor Company is a niche player, producing hand-made sport cars with a waiting list of one to two years. However, niche players are prone to takeover by larger competitors who add the brand to their portfolio of businesses. The main reason the Morgan Motor Company exists as an independent manufacturer, despite receiving offers from other car manufacturers, is that it has been owned by family members since it was founded in 1910.

A number of observations can be made concerning the applicability of Porter's Generic Strategy model. In contrast to Porter's claim that a company cannot sit in the middle, some observers state that there is no imperative as to why this should be the case. Secondly, as noted by Angwin, Cummings, and Smith (2008), it is not clear whether the model is to be used to determine where a competitive advantage may be obtained or used to determine strategic direction. Nonetheless, the model does provide a useful framework to analyse the competitors in the market.

To analyse a market and understand the impact of marketing decisions a simple equation can be utilized.

$$cost + margin = selling\ price$$

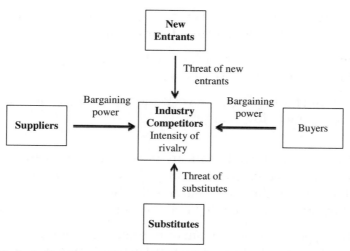

Figure 3.2 Porter's Five Forces. Source: Adapted from Porter (1980)

The equation can be used to understand the dynamics of price increases or conversely cost increases and how they impact on margins, and ultimately profit. By adding the number of units sold (volume) it is possible to calculate total profit.

Keeping the above equation in mind, industry structure can be explored using Porter's Five Forces of Competition (Figure 3.2). The framework was developed to explain how profits can be generated and where an industry can earn more than their cost of capital. The framework can be used to analyse the current situation as well as indicate possible strategic direction.

The degree of rivalry amongst firms will be influenced by the following factors.

- Competitive intensity will increase if the competitors are numerous and/ or they are equal in size and power consequently putting pressure on prices to obtain sales.

- Intensity will increase if there is no growth in the market and thus the only option to increase sales is to build market share.

- If the products are undifferentiated they are commodity products, and by definition, they are sold on price, for example the coal industry.

- Competition will be intense if there is no switching cost so buyers will put pressure on the selling price.

- If economies of scale are significant in the industry companies will want to reap the benefit by attempting to build volume.

- If the product/service is perishable firms will be tempted to reduce prices thereby hopefully reducing their inventory.

- If a business is cyclical there will be, at times, overcapacity so businesses will reduce prices to increase sales.

- When an industry has high exit costs then companies may remain in the market operating at low margins.

If one or more of the above factors are present in an industry competitive intensity will be present. Consequently, there will be pressure on selling prices with corresponding low margins. Obviously, the more factors that are present the more intense will be the competition.

The bargaining power of buyers can put pressure on selling prices and margins. Factors that contribute to an increase in bargaining power will include the number of buyers. If the buyers are concentrated, for instance only one or two buyers, then they will have immense buying power. Another contributing factor is whether switching costs are present. If buyers have a choice between product/service offering without impunity then there will be a pressure on the selling price. To overcome switching behaviour some companies utilize a loyalty scheme to act as a switching cost. Another influence on the bargaining power of buyers is if a product is a significant factor in the overall cost of an item, for example the engine for a leisure boat, then there will be a pressure on the supplier to reduce their price.

The bargaining power of suppliers can be high if they have the ability to raise prices or vary the quantity supplied. The bargaining power also increases if the suppliers are concentrated and/or there are few substitute products.

The risk of new entrants can affect an industry's profit generation. In some markets there are barriers to entry such as tariffs, distribution channels, dominance through high market share, and the existence of a strong brand.

The existence of a substitute product, that is, a product or service that meets the same customer need, will dampen profits within an industry. This also includes new technologies which can affect an industry's profitability, for example DVDs replacing VHS videos.

The Five Forces framework can be criticized for a number of reasons. First, the framework was developed in the 1980s when markets were stable and predictable, which is in contrast to the current turbulent, dynamic global situation where new start-ups and technologies may quickly change the nature of the market. Secondly, the framework is predicated on a perfect market so in regulated markets the framework may be less applicable.

Another problem is that the framework works well in simple market structures, but in some industries the situation is more complex with multiple interrelations and networks. Finally, the framework is based on the view that all companies are acting in a competitive environment and consequently it does not take into account alliances and virtual enterprises.

Despite the above qualifying conditions the framework can give insights into the current market structure and identify areas where further analysis is required.

This analysis of the market and the competition may indicate that more information is required to obtain clarity about a certain issue. It needs to be remembered that information does not guarantee success, but at best improves the odds of making the right decision and so is a form of risk reduction. Therefore, it may be necessary to conduct market research, which can be implemented either by the organization or through a marketing research consultancy firm.

We're Listening

There are a number of typical issues which marketing research can help to address. First, marketing research can help identify a potential need or want so that a marketing strategy can be developed to provide the necessary solution. If the marketing research confirms the existence of an opportunity, the organization can put in place the necessary R&D to develop an appropriate solution (see Chapter 1). Once the prototype has been developed, marketing research can test the new product in the appropriate market and evaluate the results prior to a general introduction into the marketplace. A key question in these product/service tests is the customer's intention to buy.

Second, market research can help select and refine target markets. In other words, the research will determine the type and characteristics of customers that are likely to purchase the product/service. Third, marketing research can help position the product by ascertaining the most important differentiating attributes of a product/service.

Fourth, marketing research can substantiate the demand figures established in the MIS, and from this marketing objectives can be established. Following on from the types of demand outlined at the beginning of the chapter, marketing research can be used to establish the number of NCUs in the marketplace, the likelihood of increasing the purchasing rate, or the degree of brand switching in the marketplace.

Finally, marketing research can help develop specific marketing strategies. For example, pricing research can determine buyer response rates at different price points, which may be of help to judge the degree of brand switching. Distribution research can test distributors' sales against the organization's own sales staff and compare the results. Also, market research can test the in-store environment. This aspect is important in shopping malls where the marketer may wish to determine the effect of the servicescape.

Advertising effectiveness can be measured by marketing research. Research can test alternative executions to determine which ads are the most effective in delivering the product's message. Also, advertising research can help determine how well a specific advertisement is being processed by consumers. The first step is to establish ad cut-through by asking the respondent if they have seen an advertisement for a specific category in media such as television or newspapers. If the answer is yes and they can also name the brand then brand cut-through has been established. This is the ultimate aim of an advertising campaign. If no cut-through is established the next step is to determine the degree of ad recall. This can be achieved by using the brand name as a stimulus and asking the respondent to recall if they have seen an ad for the specific brand. If the respondent cannot recall the ad then brand recognition can be established whereby the specific ad is played or shown and the respondent is asked if they have seen or heard the ad.

The first step in conducting market research is to define the problem. This is an important step as it will dictate the type of questions that are asked and consequently the quality of the information being sought. Clarification of the problem can be obtained by gathering secondary data. In other words, getting information from sources that have already been published, for example, newspapers, the Internet, government reports, articles from trade and business associations and bank updates, including economic forecasts. When using secondary data it is important that the marketer distinguishes between opinion and evidence-based knowledge. Also, the credibility of the source needs to be established. Is the author an expert and is he/she sanctioned by some governing body pertinent to the issue? Finally, the date of the published material needs to be verified. Whilst magazines and newspapers contain their date of publication, this is not necessarily the case with articles or blogs published on the Internet.

During the secondary data search the problem may be solved. In other words, by investigating and reading the material a reason or set of reasons can be derived which explains the phenomenon under investigation. If the problem is not solved, further information will need to be obtained from primary sources.

Primary sources will involve collecting data from people who have been identified as being able to give insights or explanations as to why a certain phenomenon exists, thus solving the problem. Such people, usually referred to as respondents, may be experts in their field or a group of consumers who have inherent knowledge of the buying situation. Conducting this type of research is called empirical research.

Broadly speaking there are two ways to undertake research, namely by conducting quantitative research or by conducting qualitative research. The general aim of quantitative research is to establish causal connections thus enabling predictions to be made, for example, predicting coupon redemption rates based on coupon face value and purchase quality. Such research will involve surveying a large number of respondents and the data will be analysed using a statistical package, with the aim of establishing a correlation between dependent and independent variables. Surveys can be undertaken by using the methods outlined in Table 3.2.

There are a number of sampling techniques that can be utilized. Probability sampling involves the random selection of respondents; consequently any member of the population has an equal chance of being selected for the study. Another probability sampling technique is that of cluster sampling, where the population is divided into sub-groups; for example, farmers in different English counties. Finally, stratified probability sampling is when the population is divided into smaller groups, for instance age, gender, race, or common interests, and the respondents are randomly selected from each group thus ensuring a representative sample of the whole population.

Non-probability sampling on the other hand does not involve random selection. One technique is to use a quota system where a prescribed number of respondents is required in each of several categories. Judgement is another non-probability sampling technique when the interviewer selects respondents on the basis of who would seem to be a good prospect, whereas convenience sampling is where respondents are selected on the basis of who is most accessible at the time of sampling. Finally, snowballing is where respondents are asked to make use of their social networks and refer the researcher to other potential respondents. This method is often used to obtain recruits from "hidden populations", that is, groups where access has proven to be difficult.

It is important that data collected using a quantitative method is accurate. Therefore a number of tests are used to verify the accuracy of the research. The first is that of reliability, which is concerned with the consistency of the measurement and lack of biases. Is the same type of information being collected each time the survey is administered? The notion of replication, that

Table 3.2 Research methods

Method	Advantage	Disadvantage
Mail survey	Low cost, ability to show graphics, anonymous (increase in truthfulness)	Slow, low response rate
Telephone survey	Less time consuming, less expensive	Limited number of questions, low response rate
Online survey	Quick, immediate	Limited to people with access to computers, accuracy, easy to delete therefore low response rate
In-depth interviews	Establish rapport and gain co-operation, high response rate, in-depth questions where insights can be obtained, less rigid than surveys	Limited sample size, expensive, lack of generalizability
Observation, either human or utilizing technology, e.g. cameras	Accurate account of behaviour (compared to self-reports) thereby eliminating bias	Expensive, time consuming (down-time waiting), limited to behaviour so cannot obtain information on attitudes, motivations, etc.
Focus groups	Small groups of 4–12 people, flexible with prompts, gain insights through rich discussion	Expensive, social influence can effect responses, unable to generalize

Source: Adapted from Kotler and Keller (2012)

is, whether the same results are able to be duplicated over a period of time, is an important element of the quantitative research method. Within the issue of reliability the degree of internal consistency of the survey is important. In other words, do different questions measure the same characteristic, which can be tested by correlation or other statistical methods? Validity on the other hand is concerned with the collection of the right information to meet the objective of the research: is the research really measuring what it states to be measuring? In other words, validity is concerned with the accuracy of the measurement.

Quantitative research contrasts with qualitative research, where the aim is to obtain insight and understanding of consumer's opinions, attitudes, beliefs, and purchase intentions. Such information can be explored by conducting in-depth interviews by asking "why" or "would" type questions. Often the questions are open-ended so that comprehensive information is obtained. Unlike quantitative research, this type of research is inductive so it does not develop a hypothesis to start the research. Rather, qualitative research begins by observation, and patterns are detected during the analysis of the data.

The tests for qualitative research are different from those applied to quantitative research. Instead of reliability the qualitative researcher is concerned with dependability, and validity is replaced by the notion of credibility. Whereas quantitative research is concerned with generalizability, the qualitative researcher is interested in transferability, that is, the applicability of the research findings to other contexts.

ANALYSIS AND UNDERSTANDING

Case 3-1 Got Fly Buys?

Every day, shop assistants throughout New Zealand can be heard asking customers if they have their Fly Buys card with them. Fly Buys is a loyalty programme offering over 1500 different rewards, ranging from flights to appliances to perfume. Savvy shoppers know value when they see it, and being rewarded for household spending, be it groceries, petrol, or power, has high appeal. The retail value of rewards redeemed by members in 2013 was $80 million.

Loyalty New Zealand initiated the reward scheme in 1996 with the following four companies: Bank of New Zealand, New World, Shell Oil, and State Insurance. Consumers apply for a free card and use it with various businesses involved in the programme so as to collect points every time they spend a pre-set minimum amount of money (usually about $20). The application form asks for name, date of birth, age, gender, and address. Rewards can be claimed online, by text, or by telephoning the Fly Buys 50-seat call centre.

Since its launch Fly Buys has grown significantly, so that there are now 1.4 million active accounts, representing 2.55 million cardholders. It has 100% brand recognition in New Zealand and at 72%, it has the highest active household penetration in the world for any loyalty programme. The basic tenet of the programme is to ask members not to spend more, but to be rewarded for where they spend.

Companies join Fly Buys for two reasons. The first is to reduce marketing costs based on the reasoning that it costs more – five to eight times more – to recruit new customers than to retain existing ones. It is estimated that companies can increase their profits by almost 100% by increasing their retention rate by 5%. Also, participating members can share the costs of marketing programmes. The second reason is to gain access to information collated from customer transactions. However, the retailers cannot access Fly Buys members' names and addresses as these are held by Loyalty New Zealand. By utilizing the database, member companies can test marketing initiatives to see if consumers respond to offers. If the reaction is positive then the companies would market on a wider scale.

Fly Buys has companies represented across a broad spectrum, including travel, petrol, home and contents insurance, banking, electronics, building, cars, supermarkets, electricity, fashion, and sports retailing. This amounts to more than 50 different brands/companies with a combined total of over 3000 outlets. However, Fly Buys has been careful to select sector leaders as members of the consortium. In other words, Fly Buys avoids joining up companies that do business in the same sector. Fly Buys has introduced business and travel insurance programmes, environmentally friendly loyalty cards, online music stores, and an e-store. While Fly Buys has been lucrative for participating retailers, it has been better for some than others. In particular, it has worked well for big ticket retailers, and those offering similar goods and prices as their competitors.

With the growth of social networking media and the number of Fly Buys members, Fly Buys introduced the online Fly Buys communities, a forum allowing Fly Buys members to discuss and review general topics such as driving and parenting. Fly Buys is active on Facebook and Twitter and its quarterly reward catalogues are posted electronically as well as in hard copy.

Over the last decade there has been a phenomenal increase in the number of reward programmes. Almost every credit card has a loyalty programme attached to it and there are frequent flyer programmes, supermarket schemes, such as Progressive's Onecard, and the AA Rewards programme. It is believed that the average household is a member of three different loyalty schemes.

Questions

1. *How much growth is in the market?*
2. *What information can a member company use, and from what sources?*
3. *Compare and contrast the Fly Buys scheme with a company-owned loyalty programme.*
4. *What is the difference between a reward programme and a loyalty programme?*

◀◀◀ **Some Ideas**

1. *How much growth is in the market?*

   With 100% brand recognition and 72% of householders possessing a card, it would seem that there is little growth potential. With shoppers being asked "Got Fly Buys" as a reminder to have their card swiped at point of purchase, households who have not bothered to obtain a card by now, after the card being in the market for over 17 years, are unlikely to do so. Competition from other companies' cards, e.g. Onecard, has had an impact on card usage. Also, in terms of gaining suppliers, this is problematic as there are suppliers covering a vast range of categories.

2. *What information can a member company use, and from what sources?*

A supplier can gain access not only to data – including demographics – from buyers of their own products but also purchases of other suppliers' products. This allows suppliers to look at trends in the marketplace. The supplier, through Fly Buys, can also conduct marketing surveys as well as segmented price offers to increase demand for a product or service. This is a valuable marketing insight.

3. *Compare and contrast the Fly Buys scheme with a company-owned loyalty programme.*

The database is owned by Fly Buys and can only be accessed through them, whereas with a company scheme the company owns the database so it is easier to interrogate the data. Secondly, Fly Buys customers only receive points for each dollar purchased, for example, $20 = 1 point, $100 = 5 points. With loyalty schemes, such as Lancome or United Airlines Mileage Plus, customers receive extra privileges the more they spend. Therefore such a scheme makes it more attractive to stay loyal to gain a new status level, in addition to the standard rewards. Additionally, the company loyalty programmes can build a one-to-one relationship with their customers.

4. *What is the difference between a reward programme and a loyalty programme?*

With a reward programme, such as a coffee card, the customer accrues a certain number of points per purchase and the reward is gained after a set number of purchases; for example, one free coffee once 10 coffees have been purchased. Usually there is no database kept with customer or purchase details. With a loyalty programme, customer details are recorded on a database – what was purchased and when – and different benefits, depending on the level of purchase, can be given. The company can use the database to build a relationship with the customer.

▶▶▶

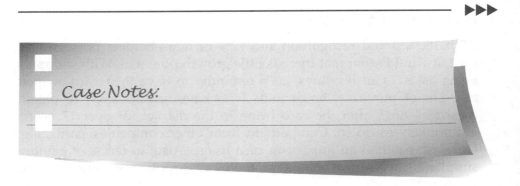

Case Notes:

Brand logos are a visual representation of the company's brand proposition, and as such they are a link to the brand promise. Customers use the symbol as a cue regarding purchasing decisions, and over time, build positive or negative associations with the brand and hence the logo. Companies sometimes modify their brand logo, either to keep up-to-date with modern graphic design or to signal a new marketing strategy.

Shell Oil, for example, started in 1897 by Marcus Samuel, an antiques, curios, and oriental seashell dealer in London, has modified its logo over the last one hundred years. Samuel formed the Shell Transport and Trading Company with the purpose of shipping kerosene to the Far East. In 1904 a pecten seashell emblem was used as the company logo to give visual emphasis to the Shell Company. Although the tankers carrying kerosene to the Far East were named after different types of shells, the pecten, or scallop shell, was chosen following the suggestion by Mr Graham, the importer of kerosene into India and a director of the company.

Over the last century the shell design has changed dramatically, with the colours red and yellow added in 1915, when the company wanted bright colours to compete in the Californian market. Yellow and red were chosen so as to identify with California's Spanish connections. The shell logo is continually being appraised and upgraded so that it is up-to-date with modern graphic design. Heinz is another company that makes subtle changes to its logo, thus keeping the design modern.

However, not all logo changes are readily accepted by the public. In 1997 British Airways replaced the Union Jack on their planes' tail fins with colourful ethnic designs but not everybody was impressed, including Lady Thatcher. The oil company BP, in 2000, replaced the green shield with a green, white, and yellow shaped design at a cost of $4.5 million, which included the cost of research and support for the implementation of the change. A new slogan, "beyond petroleum", was also adopted. The new logo was greeted with derision, especially by environmentalists who believed that the money would have been better spent on renewable energy. Since the logo change there has been a certain amount of online activity corrupting the logo. In 2009 Tropicana changed the famous orange and straw illustration on their packaging to a picture of a glass of orange juice, but after complaints and criticism from their customers, the new owners, Pepsi, relented and brought back the old design.

Gap is another company that attempted to change its logo. Gap is an American clothing and accessories retailer, based in San Francisco, founded in

1969 by Donald Fisher and Doris Fisher, who started selling blue jeans and white cotton t-shirts, and later expanded their product range. The target was the younger generation, hence the company name being derived from the notion of a generation gap. The company currently has stores in the US, Canada, UK, France, Ireland, Korea, Japan, and China, with franchisees in many other countries. In 2010 the company was ranked on the top 100 list of global brands by Interbrand, with a brand image valued at $4 billion. However, recently sales have been eroded by the efforts of specialty stores such as Abercrombie and Fitch, and cheap chic retailers like H&M.

On 6 October 2010 Gap placed the redesigned logo on their website. The iconic white serif type on navy blue background was replaced with a black helvetica font on white background, with a small blue square on the right hand corner, jutting out from the P of the word Gap. The reason for the change was that it was meant to be a more contemporary, modern expression. Marka Hansen, the CEO of Gap, defended the change by saying, "We chose this design as it's more contemporary and current. It honors our heritage through the blue box while still taking it forward."

Within a week of Gap going online with their new logo, there were over 1000 responses on Gap's Facebook page, with comments entirely against the logo, despite 400 responses clicking the "like" button. Gap's response to the criticism was to announce on their Facebook page they were to launch a crowdsourcing site, but the announcement was vague in terms of process.

However, this move by Gap was seen as a cheap marketing stunt and did the brand further damage. A twitter account was set up in protest and received 5,000 followers. One twitter wrote, @superboxmonkey – "New Gap logo looks as if it were done in Microsoft Word." Another twitter user created a site where one could "make your own gap logo", which went viral and generated over 14,000 parody versions.

By 10 October Gap had decided to retain their old logo. "We recognise that we missed the opportunity to engage with the online community. This wasn't the right project at the right time for crowdsourcing. There may be a time to evolve our logo, but if and when that time comes, we'll handle it in a different way." (Hansen, 2010)

Questions

1. *Why did Gap want to change its logo?*
2. *Why did the public act so quickly to the proposed change?*
3. *What are the pros and cons of crowdsourcing?*
4. *How could Gap have handled the launch of the new logo better?*

Case 3-3 Rugby, Racing, and Beer

In the 1950s and early 60s New Zealand's culture was defined by the slogan "Rugby, Racing and Beer". These described New Zealanders' popular pastimes. Whilst rugby is still the national game, with the country going into mourning if the All Blacks lose a World Cup match, horse racing has witnessed a steady decline, with many small-town racing clubs going out of existence. The drinking of alcohol is still a regular activity but beer is starting to take a back seat to the wine industry, now world famous for its Sauvignon Blanc and Pinot Noir wines. Refer to Tables 3-3.1 and 3-3.2 for alcohol consumption in New Zealand.

Table 3-3.1 Volume of alcohol available for consumption (*million litres*)

Year	Wine	Beer	Spirit-based Drinks	Spirits
2007	92.112	312.205	56.733	9.290
2008	94.220	322.490	59.193	10.487
2009	95.295	306.181	59.135	10.498
2010	102.614	299.348	59.485	12.592
2011	97.888	299.794	61.928	12.809
2012	102.218	279.934	62.006	12.885

Table 3-3.2 Volume of beer available for consumption by alcohol content (*million litres*)

Year	Up to 1.150%	1.151%– 2.500%	2.501%– 4.350%	4.351%– 5.000%	More than 5.000%
2007	0.010	3.578	204.483	94.200	9.934
2008	0.029	3.289	206.683	103.404	9.086
2009	0.120	2.922	192.503	103.669	6.967
2010	0.253	2.726	176.059	111.543	8.767
2011	0.341	2.643	172.188	115.666	8.956
2012	0.318	2.021	157.048	106.079	14.468

The New Zealand beer industry has been dominated over the last 80 years by two companies, namely Lion Breweries (Lion) and Dominion Breweries (DB). Lion started brewing in Auckland in 1914. The company Lion Nathan was formed in 1988 when L.D. Nathan, a retailer, merged with Lion Breweries. In 2009 a takeover by Japanese brewing fir took place and merged Australian National Foods, which Kirin ow form Lion Nathan National Foods with its head office in Australi. consortium has two breweries in New Zealand, namely The Pride in Tamaki, Auckland and the Speights Brewery in Dunedin.

In 2010 Lion built a new plant in East Tamaki, Auckland, finally movi. from their original historic plant in Khyber Pass Road. The new plant wa a "greenfields" development meaning the plant was built on underdevel- oped land. At a cost of $250 million, a state of the art factory was built. Equipment was imported from Krones AG, Germany, and a membrane fil- tration system was installed. The new plant recycles waste products and rain water is stored to flush toilets and irrigate native plants. By installing efficient light fittings and control systems the company has reduced energy consumption by 10%.

DB was formed in 1930 when Sir Henry Kelliher purchased Levers & Co and the Waitemata Brewery in Otahuhu, Auckland, then owned by W. J. Coutts. Coutts' son, Morton W. Coutts, became a director in 1946. Their most popular brands are Steinlager, Speights, Macs, and Lion Red. In 1994 the company invested $12 million in plant to meet brewing standards to enable Heineken beer to be sold locally. In the same year the com- pany exited the spirit market and closed Allied Liquor Merchants. Two years later Asia Pacific Brewing, a Malaysia-based joint venture between Heineken and Fraser & Neave, increased their shareholding in DB to 77%. At the same point in time they sold their liquor outlet Liquorland to Foodstuffs, a dominant supermarket chain.

DB mostly produces pale lager and operates four breweries in New Zealand, namely the Waitemata Brewery in Otahuhu, Auckland, the Tui Brewery in Mangatainoka, the Mainland Brewery in Timaru, and the Monteiths Brewery in Greymouth. Their most popular brands are DB Draught, Export Gold, Monteiths, and Tui.

The Sale of Liquor Act (1989) enabled wine to be sold in supermarkets, and an amendment in 1999 allowed Sunday trading and the sale of beer in supermarkets and grocery outlets. In addition, the minimum legal drinking age was lowered from 20 to 18 years.

The two main breweries account for 90% of beer production in New Zealand with Lion accounting for approximately 47% of the total volume. The trend is for consumers to want premium beers, especially domestic premium lagers and imported premium lagers. Craft beer, on the other hand, accounts for only 2% of the volume, but such beers are gaining pop- ularity as consumers start to enjoy the new flavour, aroma, and personality of the different craft beers, and this makes it harder for the small brewers to build brand loyalty. Between 2008 and 2011 there was a growth of 42% in small- and medium- sized craft brewing companies.

Four main ingredients are used to make beer, namely water, yeast, hops, and malt. Hops, which give beer stability and provide flavour, are obtained from the Nelson region, whereas Lion obtains malt from a subsidiary company called Maltexo. Bottles are supplied by the Associated Bottling Company, which is jointly owned by DB and Lion. While DB uses a continuous fermentation process developed by Morton Coutts, Lion brew their beer using a batch method.

Lion bottles, markets, and distributes under licence Guinness, Stella Artois, and Becks beers. Lion also distributes under licence Corona and the Budweiser group of brands. The new plant can also bottle cider and wine. As well as distributing beer, Lion has the agencies to import and distribute a range of spirits, including Baileys, Coruba Rum, Johnnie Walker whisky, Glenmorangie whisky, Smirnoff vodka, Tanqueray gin, and Canadian Club.

Lion distribute their beer through the two main supermarket chains in New Zealand, and in pubs throughout the country. Also, their wine from the Wither Hills vineyard in Marlborough, New Zealand and their vineyards in Australia is sold through pubs, supermarkets, and their own retail outlets branded as Liquor King. It is through this chain, as well as pubs, that Lion can sell their selection of spirits, which they import under licence.

Questions

1. *Use Porter's Five Forces framework to analyse the New Zealand market. What are your conclusions?*
2. *Compare and contrast the two marketing strategies of DB and Lion.*
3. *Where is the growth in the New Zealand beer market?*

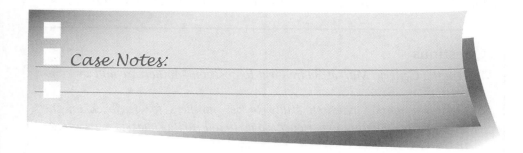

Case Notes:

ANALYSIS AND UNDERSTANDING

Case 3-4 Mum's the Word

Mothercare UK is a retailer of baby-related goods and has been in business for over 50 years. Recently it could be accused of losing the plot, with two CEOs departing within two years. The 2013 Christmas season was very poor, with heavy discounting and weak toy sales affecting profit. The share price dropped which meant the company's market value decreased by £112 million.

Mothercare had expanded overseas with 1028 stores operating in 58 countries (compared with the 311 stores in Britain), although most overseas stores are franchises. In 2011 international sales rose 16% compared to a fall of 6.3% in Britain. However, overseas stores had total sales of £206 million, which is small compared to the £587 million of sales in Britain.

Analysts agree that the Mothercare shops in Britain offer no reason to shop there as there is no point of difference. Unfortunately, Mothercare is squeezed in the middle between supermarkets who offer the same line of products more cheaply, and, at the high end, niche specialist baby stores. There is plenty of competition in the market, for example Next sells baby items both online and at their retail outlets and they are taking customers from Mothercare.

Research has indicated that 200 Mothercare stores are profitable, with two-thirds of the population living within 30 minutes of them, so it has been decided to close the remaining 111 stores to eliminate losses. This will mean 730 retail assistants will lose their jobs, and there will be 98 redundancies in Head Office.

As Mothercare is a strong brand, the company needs to adopt a turnaround strategy by building their international stores, concentrating on making their High Street stores profitable, and developing their online presence.

Many mothers have greater spending power than ever before, with 44% more first-time mothers over the age of 35 than there were a decade ago. It needs to be remembered that it is mothers who market to mothers.

Questions

1. Use the Generic Market Share Grid to position Mothercare and its competitors.
2. Design a market research study to ask mothers for feedback on the Mothercare shopping experience, so as to aid further marketing strategy in the UK.

References and Further Reading

Aaker, D. (2008) *Strategic Market Management*, 8th edn. Hoboken, NJ: Wiley.

Angwin, D., Cummings, S. and Smith, C. (2008) *The Strategy Pathfinder*, 2nd edn. Chichester: Wiley.

Ansoff, H. (1968) *Corporate Strategy: An analytic approach to business policy for growth and expansion*. Harmondsworth: Penguin.

Chakravarthy, B. (1997) A New Strategy Framework for Coping with Turbulence, *Sloan Management Review*, Winter.

Daniel, E., Wilson, H. and McDonald, M. (2001) Towards a Map of Marketing Information Systems: An inductive study, *European Journal of Marketing*, 37(5/6): 821–847.

Doyle, P. and Stern, P. (2006) *Marketing Management and Strategy*, 4th edn. Harlow, England: Prentice Hall.

Farris, P.W. and Moore, M.J. (2004) *The Profit Impact of Marketing Strategy Project: Retrospect and Prospects*. Cambridge: Cambridge University Press.

Guiltinan, J., Paul, G. and Madden, T. (1997) *Marketing Management: Strategies and Programs*. New York: McGraw-Hill.

Hauser, W. (2007) Marketing Analytics: The evolution of marketing research in the twenty-first century, *Direct Marketing: An International Journal* 1(1): 38–54.

Kotler, P. and Keller, K. (2012) *Marketing Management*, 14th edn. Harlow, England: Pearson Education.

Krishna, A. and Shoemaker, R.W. (1992) Estimating the Effects of Higher Coupon Face Values on the Timing of Redemptions, the Mix of Coupon Redeemers, and Purchase Quality, *Psychology and Marketing*, 9(6): 453–467.

Piercy, N. (1991) *Market-Led Strategic Change*. Oxford: Butterworth-Heinemann.

Porter, M. (1980) *Competitive Strategy*. New York: The Free Press.

Porter, M. (1985) *Competitive Advantage*. New York: The Free Press.

Prahalad, C.K. and Hamel, G. (1990) The Core Competence of the Corporation, *Harvard Business Review*, May/June, 79–91.

Wee, T. (2001) The Use of Marketing Research and Intelligence in Strategic Planning: Key issues and future trends, *Marketing Intelligence and Planning* 19(4): 245–253.

Zikmund, W., Ward, S., Winzar, B. and Babin, B. (2011) *Marketing Research*. Melbourne: Cangage Learning.

Case Acknowledgements

The **Got Fly Buys**? case draws on information contained in:

Fly Buys New Zealand website located at www.flybuys.co.nz

"Kiwis flock to use Fly Buys points for grocery gift cards", (5 December 2013), *Loyalty NZ*, retrieved from https://www.loyalty.co.nz/kiwis-flock-to-use-fly-buys-points-for-grocery-gift-cards/

"Loyalty NZ, Fly Buys operator, posts 3% profit growth", (10 October 2013), *Scoop*, retrieved from http://www.scoop.co.nz/stories/print.html?path=BU1310/S00380/loyalty-nz-fly-buys-operator-posts-3-profit-growth.htm

"What we Do – Fly Buys", *Loyalty NZ*, retrieved from https://www.loyalty.co.nz/whatwedo/flybuys/

The **Mind the Gap** case draws on information contained in:

Gap Facebook post (6 October 2010), retrieved from https://www.facebook.com /gap/posts/159977040694165

"Gap logo changes: renaissance or mistake?", by E. Fuller (8 October 2010), *The Christian Science Monitor*, retrieved from http://www.csmonitor.com/Business /new-economy/2010/1008/Gap-logo-changes-renaissance-or-mistake

"Gap's Logo Change Adding Brand Damage (GPS)", by J. Ogg (8 October 2010), *24/7 Wall St*, retrieved from http://247wallst.com/2010/10/08/gaps-logo -change-adding-brand-damage-gps/

"Gap's Logo Redesign Snafu Snowballs with Social-Media Blunder", by A. Picchi (8 October 2010), *Daily Finance*, retrieved from http://www.dailyfinance.com /2010/10/08/gaps-logo-redesign-snafu-snowballs-with-social-media-blunder/

"Gap scraps logo redesign after protests on Facebook and Twitter", by J. Halliday (12 October 2010), *The Guardian*, retrieved from http://www.guardian.co.uk /media/2010/oct/12/gap-logo-redesign

Hansen, M. (11 October 2010), "Gap listens to customers and will keep classic blue box logo", statement from the President of Gap Brand North America, retrieved from http://www.gapinc.com/content/gapinc/html/media/pressrelease /2010/med_pr_GapLogoStatement10112010.html

"How NOT To Crowdsource: Lessons Learned From The Gap's Logo Debacle", by D. Williams (15 October 2010), *Forrester Blogs*, retrieved from http://blogs.forrester.com/dwilliams/10-10-15-how_not_to_crowdsource _lessons_learned_from_the_gaps_logo_debacle

"New Gap Logo Hated by Many, Company Turns to Crowdsourcing Tactics", by M. Isaac (7 October 2010), *Forbes*, retrieved from http://www.forbes.com/sites /velocity/2010/10/07/new-gap-logo-hated-by-many-company-turns-to -crowdsourcing-tactics/

"No logo: The Gap's logo change and crowdsourcing tactics draw consumer and online ire", by L. Goldwert (7 October 2010), *Daily News*, retrieved from http://www.nydailynews.com/life-style/fashion/logo-gap-logo-change -crowdsourcing-tactics-draw-consumer-online-ire-article-1.191477

The **Rugby, Racing, and Beer** case draws on information contained in:

"Boutique beer hard market to crack", by C. Adam (16 August 2013), *The New Zealand Herald*, retrieved from http://www.nzherald.co.nz/business/news /article.cfm?c_id=3&objectid=10912970

DB Breweries website located at www.db.co.nz

"Lion Nathan: Inside the Pride", by C. Adam (28 December 2010), *The New Zealand Herald*, retrieved from http://www.nzherald.co.nz/nz/news/article.cfm?c_id =1&objectid=10696787

Lion website located at www.lionco.com

"Prime Minister opens Lion Nathan's new manufacturing facility", by J. Walter (11 October 2010), retrieved from http://lionco.com/2010/10/11/pm-opens-lion -nathans-new-manufacturing-facility/

Tables 3-3.1 and 3-3.2: Compiled from "Alcohol Available for Consumption: Year ended December 2012", *Statistics New Zealand*, retrieved from http://www.stats.govt.nz/browse_for_stats/industry_sectors/alcohol_and _tobacco_availability/Alcohol-available-for-consumption_HOTPYeDec12.aspx

The **Mum's the Word** case draws on information contained in

"Can Mothercare be reborn?", by T. Espiner (24 February 2014), *BBC News*, retrieved from http://www.bbc.co.uk/news/business-26324991

"Don't kid mum when selling to children, says Toddlebike founder", by A. White (7 November 2013), *The Telegraph*, retrieved from http://www.telegraph.co.uk /finance/businessclub/10433769/Dont-kid-mum-when-selling-to-children -says-Toddlebike-founder.html

"Mothercare: From baby boom to mid-life crisis", by A. Osborne (12 April 2012), *The Telegraph*, retrieved from http://www.telegraph.co.uk/finance /newsbysector/retailandconsumer/9201093/Mothercare-From-baby-boom-to -mid-life-crisis.html

"Mothercare to slash prices to win back shoppers", by H. Wallop (24 May 2012), *The Telegraph*, retrieved from http://www.telegraph.co.uk/finance /newsbysector/retailandconsumer/9288088/Mothercare-to-slash-prices-to -win-back-shoppers.html

This chapter covers the following topics:

► The influence of culture
► The rise of the neo-tribes
► Prosumers
► The decision-making process
► The means-end chain

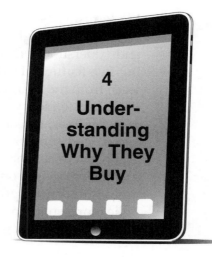

4
Understanding Why They Buy

A central tenet of marketing is customer focus. The role of the marketer is to provide benefits or solutions to customers; consequently, it is important to understand not only consumer buying habits and processes but also what influences a customer's willingness and ability to buy a product/service. How do culture, the macro environment, and personal motivation and circumstances impact on the willingness and ability of a customer to make a purchase? Obviously a person may be willing to make a purchase but not able, and vice versa. For example, a person may wish to go on a Mediterranean cruise but suffer acute seasickness and so be unable, whereas on the other hand, someone else may be able to afford the cruise but is not willing as it is not something they desire to do. Therefore, a marketer needs to explore trends in the marketplace to determine likely events that will impact upon a person's willingness and ability to purchase a product or service, and then make the necessary adjustments to the organization's marketing strategy.

I Think Therefore I Shop

One important factor that influences a consumer's willingness and ability to buy is that of culture. Obviously differences in culture differ from one country to another. A trivial example is that in New Zealand a favourite sweet is Minties, which are difficult to buy in the UK, but conversely Mint Humbugs are near impossible to buy in New Zealand.

Modernism has dominated customer culture over the last century. Building on the age of enlightenment, where reason was championed over tradition and superstition, modernism can be characterized as having the following five features. First, there is progress in thought and consequently we learn from the past. Second, there is a search for universal theories. Third, there is a tendency towards professionalism where there is a separation of disciplines, so consequently there is increasing specialization in intellectual and functional labour. Fourth, there is a split between normative and positive analysis, and finally, there is the general use of mathematical expressions, based on axiomatic and reductionist reasoning, so that science and technology is privileged at the expense of cultural analysis and symbolic representation.

In contrast, postmodernism questions the values and constructs that dominate modernity, and believe that concepts such as self, society, community, reason, values, and history need to be critiqued without the values underlying modernist thinking. Therefore, postmodernism challenges modern values, such as career, office, individual responsibility, bureaucracy, liberal democracy, tolerance, humanism, neutral procedures, impersonal rules, and rationality.

The shift to postmodernism as a cultural phenomenon has meant that appearances have become increasingly important with an emphasis on style, surfaces, and spectacle, as is evidenced by reality television and the increased role of a celebrity culture. Postmodernists believe that society is disintegrating with respect to the old order. Of special significance for marketing discourse, which both Brown (1994, 1999) and Firat et al (1995) have emphasized, are the key concepts of fragmentation, dedifferentiation, hyper-reality, pastiche, and retrospection.

Fragmentation refers to the disintegration of knowledge, language, political and social life, mass market economics, the unified self, and the disconnected array of vivid images generated by the media, with a consequent blurring of entities such as philosophy and literature, and science and religion. As Goulding (2003) notes, fragmentation in the marketing domain takes many forms. There is the fragmentation of markets into smaller segments, accompanied by the increase in the proliferation of products to serve those segments, as well as the fragmentation of media, as witnessed by the increase of television channels, and the growth of the Internet and associated digital media.

De-differentiation comprises the erosion and effacement of established hierarchies such as high and low culture, education and training, politics and show business. Consequently, there is a blurring of what were formerly clear-cut entities; for example, philosophy and literature, author and reader, science and religion, etc.

Hyper-reality, as exemplified by the fantasy worlds of virtual reality and computer games, involves the loss of a sense of authenticity and the substitution of reality by a simulation. Hyper-reality can be seen in the dream worlds of advertising, where new meanings and connotations are attached to mundane products like toothpaste and soap, and also in the make-believe worlds created by theme parks, hotels, airlines, pubs, hotels, and shopping centres.

The term **Pastiche** refers to a juxtaposition of unrelated ideas, consumer experiences, and historical moments. Past styles and symbols are combined in a collage so that symbolic codes are mixed. Such collages are a collection of juxtaposed past styles, which are a paradoxical self-referential mixing of existing codes in diverse areas such as architecture, art, cinema, literature, and music. Pastiche has led to motifs, styles, and themes being recycled with the consequence that there now exists a "society of the spectacle". "Indeed, it is arguable that, despite the undeniable importance of de-differentiation, hyper-reality and the others, pastiche is *the* defining feature of postmodernism. Call it what you will – irony, parody, imitation, medley, quotation, self-referentiality, double coding, in-jokes, the knowing wink, tongue planted permanently in cheek, a refusal to take things seriously, not even taking things seriously – but all of these are characteristic of the pasticheur and nowhere is the pasticheur more prevalent than in marketing" (Brown, 1995: 119).

Retrospection is where there are no boundaries in the sense that fact and fiction are fused and the distinction between theory and practice becomes blurred. In such a state, nostalgia becomes an important force, which can be seen in the rise of retro marketing, with the entry of retro products into the market, for example, the Mini, the VW Beetle, and the Fiat 500. Events can also be linked to the past by attempting to make artefacts look authentic, with the hope that the experience is enhanced, for example, the Guinness factory tour in Dublin.

Come Together, Right Now

The postmodern condition has led to an accent on individualism, where the emphasis is on an individual's freedom to make choices and take responsibility for the outcomes, and by doing so, shape their identity and show their uniqueness. However, due to technological advances the individual has never been so alone; consequently this isolation can lead to narcissism where it is possible to live in a virtual reality. For example, it is possible for someone to conduct their lives entirely from home. This spatial isolation, despite an individual being in virtual touch with the total world, has meant an increased occurrence of individual searching for social links.

These links have taken the form, and led to the creation, of neo-tribes (Cova and Cova, 2002). Whereas traditional tribes were based on a community or village, bounded by physical geography and dialect, neo-tribes are based on a community of shared emotion or passion. The community could be based on shared styles of life, a sense of injustice, consumption patterns, sporting interests, or hobbies. What holds a tribe together is not the modern established norms and traditions but symbolic rituals and cult objects, where the meanings of the symbols are negotiated and interpreted by the members. As such, neo-tribes are unstable and in a constant state of flux, because they exist only for as long as they are deemed to be attractive. What is important for a neo-tribe is not the value derived from the use of the product/service but how it enables consumers to link with other consumers, thereby giving meaning to their existence and reinforcing their identity. Therefore, a product/service has a link value which permits and supports social interaction and an individual's desire to belong.

It is possible for an individual to belong to several different tribes, as the boundaries are conceptual rather than physical. Consequently an individual will wear different masks depending on the occasion. Therefore neo-tribes, having a shorter life span and not being based on a stable set of personality traits and set lifestyle, are different from psychographic segments. This is in line with the postmodern belief that individuals have multiple identities. Also, neo-tribes are different from a brand connection, where the brand is the focus of the relationship with the individual, and the interconnectedness between brand followers is secondary. The brand community is explicitly commercial, with the brand holding the members together, whereas neo-tribes are based on a consumer to consumer relationship, and not necessarily on a single brand. Therefore any loyalty to a product/service will be based on effect. This is in comparison to relationship marketing which is concerned with the development of a relationship between the company and the individual, where loyalty is based on cognition, as is evidenced by the use of such tools as loyalty schemes.

The relationship between a brand and a neo-tribe has to be carefully managed. The brand can provide places or sites for the neo-tribe to meet, for example Nike provides venues for local running events. The brand can also facilitate the joining of new members and help them learn the rituals and the importance of symbols. The brand can help the neo-tribe with communications, whether it be traditional print media or organizing digital media such as Facebook or Twitter. In carrying out these activities the marketer needs to identify the "chiefs" (Mitchell and Imrie, 2011), that is the true believers, much like the opinion leaders of a reference group, who play an important role in maintaining the activities of the neo-tribe.

It is important the marketer's role is that of a member and partner, and not just that of an independent facilitator. In being a member, the marketer must realize that they will lose some control of the brand as the tribe will want to have input into the product/service being offered.

Power to the People

Another trend in postmodern culture is that of the "prosumer". Alvin Tofler coined the term prosumer in his book *Third Wave* (1980), where he claimed that due to the information revolution the consumer would be more demanding and more participative. Due to the advent of mass customization the consumer has become part of the development, production, and delivery of goods/services. In this respect consumers co-create solutions, thereby constructing value for themselves (value-in-use). Also the communication process is enriched with the consumer contributing to the firm's overall message, albeit indirectly via social media.

Therefore the task of the firm is to engage the consumer so that they participate in a positive manner which is beneficial to both parties. If this is achieved the consumer has a positive experience, which leads to a feeling of empowerment.

Notwithstanding the empowerment of consumers, the macro environment will impact upon a consumer's willingness and ability to seek a solution to a perceived problem and purchase the product/service. A useful tool to understand the macro environment is the PESTEL framework (see Table 4.1).

By rating the likelihood of one event happening and then rating the impact on the demand for the product/service, the information can be used in the Opportunities and Threats sections of a SWOT analysis. With further analysis the internal strengths of the organization can be matched with the opportunities, and the internal weaknesses that are deemed important can be turned into strengths. Insights gained from a SWOT analysis can be used to develop marketing strategies.

Table 4.1 PESTEL Framework

Political	Will government legislation effect demand for a product/ service directly or indirectly, e.g. food regulations, safety requirements, labour laws?
Economic	What are the impacts upon a household's disposable or discretionary income: increase in interest rates, the rate of inflation, the fluctuation of the exchange rate?
Social	Do demographic shifts, immigration, unemployment or the ageing population increase or decrease the demand for your product/service?
Technology	How do buyer behaviour patterns change due to technological innovations such as the increase use of social media and applications, the convergence of technologies, including smart phones?
Environment	How do your consumers view the issue of sustainability and related topics such as recyclable packaging, organic produce, carbon emissions?
Legal	What place do trademarks, warranties, and guarantees play in the decision criteria for the product/service?

Source: Adapted from Angwin, Cummings, and Smith (2008)

Decisions, Decisions, Decisions

The processes a potential customer undertakes during the buying process can provide marketing insights regarding the strategies that a marketer can adopt. The degree of intensity concerning the decision can best be seen as being on a continuum. At one end is the routinized buy where the decision is close to automatic so the intensity is very low. This is evident in supermarket shopping where customers place items in their basket with little thought. At the other end of the continuum the customer undergoes extensive problem solving, thereby the decision making is intense. In such cases, as in buying a car, the customer will often have developed a decision criterion, for example, engine size, model, colour, etc.

Often customers use extensive problem solving due to the high price of the item, however other characteristics can also be catalyst, such as potential for harm, anticipated performance issues, or symbolic meanings attached to the purchase, for example, fashion items. Such purchases can also be referred to as high involvement products. When extensive problem solving is involved the customer can pass through five problem solving stages (see Table 4.2). By acknowledging these stages a marketer can influence each stage. Preferably when conducting a search it would be ideal to be in the evoked set, that is, the set that springs to mind when a product category is mentioned. This top of mind awareness is beneficial to the marketer as the customer already knows about the brand before the search for alternatives begins.

Table 4.2 Decision process model

ROLE – Manufacturing Purchase	ROLE – Family Purchase	PROCESS	MARKETER
Initiator e.g. factory manager	Initiator e.g. boy wants mountain bike for Christmas	Problem recognition	Advertise to draw attention
Influencer e.g assistant manager	Influencer Sister knows, in time, she too will get one	Search for alternatives	Internet presence, service directories, point of sale
Decider Group division including finance department	Decider Mum and Dad	Evaluate	Advertise key attributes and benefits so part of decision criteria
Buyer Purchasing Department	Buyer Grandparents	Purchase	Provide purchase facilitation, e.g. finance, convenient location
User Factory floor operator	User Child next door	Post-purchase	0800 number, follow-up brochures. Post purchase dissonance needs to be reduced when products are similar or they are big ticket items

Source: Adapted from Kotler and Keller (2012)

However, it needs to be noted that there are positive and negative brand evaluations, so being in the evoked set is desirable if the customer has a positive attitude towards the brand. If, however, the brand is not in the evoked set, the marketer must influence the decision making during the search phase so the brand is in the consideration set at the time of purchase.

The decision process model implies that there is only one person involved in the decision making. However, within families and in the business sector there are often different buying roles, where each person or group will have input into the decision-making process.

Stairway to Heaven

Means-End Theory explores the drivers of consumer decision making by understanding purchase justifications at different levels of knowledge. The theory is based on a hierarchical organization of consumers' perceptions and knowledge of a product/service, thereby making a chain starting with product attributes, then to consequences regarding the purchase, and finally to values which underline the motivation for the purchase.

The category of product attributes can be broken down to either concrete or abstract attributes which are characteristics of the product observable to the consumer, e.g. price, colour, etc. The consequence, that is, the benefit being sought or the solution that is obtained by the use of the product or service, can either be functional or psychosocial, e.g. save money or spend more time with family. The final end of the chain is values, which can either be instrumental – e.g. security, saving time, family – or terminal – e.g. self-fulfillment, accomplishment, self-esteem.

Laddering is the research method used to elicit responses to develop the means-end chain. Laddering is a technique which attempts to explore the deeper reasons underlying a consumer's motivation for purchasing a product/service. The interviewer begins by asking about the main attributes that persuaded the respondent to make the purchase. Once the significant attributes have been established, which could be concrete and/or abstract, the interview asks why they are important, thereby establishing the consequences of the purchase. The interviewer can then ask why the consequences, be they functional or psychosocial, are important, which leads to a value. The justification of each chain is to maintain cognitive consistency.

There are two laddering methods that can be used to obtain a hierarchical network of meanings. The first is soft laddering which uses the qualitative method to elicit responses; however, this technique is time consuming and costly. There are a number of issues regarding this method, one being that artificial responses can be given as respondents try to find ways to justify their behaviour. Secondly, some respondents may not be honest in their responses as they may not like giving answers to personal questions. Another issue is that the quality of responses can be dependent on the sensibility of the researcher in their ability to recognize differences and similarities amongst the data. Also, the drawing of chains linking the elements can mean that some insights are ignored as they do not fit the imposed pattern.

The second method is hard laddering where a quantitative method is used in terms of a survey. This is a "check the box" approach where the respondent is asked to recognize categories rather than recall their purchase behaviour. Whilst this method is cheaper and less time consuming to administer, it has been criticized due to the lack of respondent involvement in terms of thinking about their behaviour and doubts about the validity and reliability of the method. Also, there is a question regarding the compatibility of results gathered by the hard method with results obtained using the soft method.

Laddering can be used to develop key insights for the development of marketing strategy by tapping into the meanings and associations that consumers have with regard to purchase motivations. By developing different means-end chains from a given population the marketer can develop segmentation strategies (see Table 4.3). Consequently causal benefits of purchasing a product can be developed rather than segmenting on descriptive attributes, such as age, income, or demographics. When segmentation is based on values the competition finds it hard to imitate the approach.

Laddering can also be used to position the product/service in the market. This is particularly the case with parity products, where a brand has functionally equivalent attributes to its competitors, so positioning on attributes does not work. Therefore a company can use either transformational positioning which establishes the link between consequences and values, or informational positioning where the link between attributes and consequences (or benefits) is established. These approaches are also helpful with complex buying situations, for example cars, computers, etc. where consumers tend to simplify the information by categorizing the offer into higher level consequences, such as reliability or value for money.

Table 4.3 Means-end chain – running shoes example

| | Attributes | | Consequences | | | Values | |
	Concrete	Abstract	Functional	Psychosocial	Instrumental	Terminal
Customer 1	Rubber-soled	Colour	Price	Smart Shopper	Save Money	Thriftiness
Customer 2	Air-cushioning	Texture of upper	Injury Free	Feel Better	Fitness	Health

Source: Adapted from Peter and Olson (2008)

94

Case 4-1 I Ride Therefore I Belong

On any Tuesday evening it's possible to see an impressive line-up of motor-cycles outside the Pied Bull pub in Farningham, Kent. It is the informal meeting place of the Bexley Triumph Motor Cycle Club. Formed in 1984 the club organizes club runs, for example in the summer months there's a Wednesday out and back run from their base. Special runs are organized to attend national events; for example, in June 2013 they organized a trip to the Ace Café Ton-Up Day at Brooklands Museum, which is home to the world's first motor racing track. The Ace Café is a former transport café on the North Circular Road, Stonebridge, North-West London and has gained iconic status in the biker community. It was popular for the Ton-Up Boys in the 1950s and the Rockers of the 1960s, and is a venue for bike events, industry reunions, and even weddings!

The Bexley Club is a branch of the Triumph Owners Motor Cycle Club (TOMCC) which was founded in 1949 in South London. All Triumph bike owners are welcome, whether they own old or new bikes, on paying a club membership fee of £20 per year. There are currently 43 branches of the club throughout the UK and the club sells merchandise that can be personal-ized with insignia for each branch or member. The club organizes events for members to attend, with a major event being the National Rally held over a weekend.

Their website allows for small advertisements to be placed and also pro-vides a members' forum, where information and ideas are shared. The site also includes profiles of all the different bikes manufactured over the years, including photographs and specifications. Additionally a dating service is provided for a fee of £5 (or £25 for non-members). By supplying the relevant engine number and frame number, along with any other relevant informa-tion and photographs, the club will provide a Dated Certificate for the bike which can be used for registration and by the government Driver and Vehi-cle Licensing Authority (DVLA).

According to the Motor Cycle Industry Association Limited, there are approximately 1.5 million active motorcyclists in the UK, which represents about 3% of the adult population. This equates to 22 motorcycles per 1,000 people. The number of motorcyclists killed on the road in the UK continues to fall, with the current level being the lowest since records were first kept in 1927.

The appeal of the motorcycle has increased over more recent years, but the market demand trend is for small commuter bikes and bikes with practical applications. The benefit of owning a bike is that it is cheaper than owning a car, and the insurance costs are small, which appeals especially to young people. Additional benefits are that the bikes are cheap to run, have reduced CO_2 emissions, journey times are cut as time is not wasted in congestion, and the bikes are easy to park.

The market in the UK has been dominated by the large manufacturers, namely Honda, Suzuki, Yamaha, and Kawasaki, but in the 2008–11 period the import of motorcycles into the UK fell by 32%. In contrast domestic sales and exports of UK manufactured bikes rose 24.4%. Whilst production of UK bike manufacturers was low in the late 1980s, the production figure for 2011 was 50,000 bikes with Triumph being the major producer, with contributions coming from smaller manufacturers, namely Norton and Cleus Competition Motorcycles (CCM).

Triumph is a well-known brand worldwide with a long history of motorcycle manufacturing. The Triumph Cycle Company was founded by Siegfried Bettman in Coventry in 1887 and by 1905 the company was producing 500 motorcycles per year. Automobiles were added to the assembly line in 1923 but the Triumph Motorcar division was sold off in 1932. After World War II the BSA Group (Birmingham Small Arms Company – then the largest motorcycle manufacturer in the world) bought the Triumph Cycle Company but retained the brand and ran it as a separate concern.

The 1950s and the 1960s were the golden years of British motorcycling where the emphasis shifted from the motorcycle being a workhorse to a leisure toy, used especially by the carefree youth, establishing the motorbike as a symbol of counter-culture and rebellion. Notable brands included BSA, Norton, AJS, Royal Enfield, and Triumph. The status of Triumph was enhanced with their association with celebrities such as Marlon Brando, Bob Dylan, James Dean, Elvis Presley, and Steve McQueen.

The bike which gained icon status was the Triumph Bonneville. Launched in 1959 after the record-breaking ride by Johnny Allen on a T120 at Bonneville Salt Flats, the Bonneville bike is a high performance machine with dual carburetors and a 650cc engine. Production of Triumph Motor Cycles peaked in 1969 at 46,800 units for the year. At about the same time Japanese manufactured motorbikes entered the UK market, led by Honda. The bikes were based on a two-stroke engine, were more stylish, and had key ignition, in contrast to the British kick-start mechanism.

Whilst it was said that UK bikes were easy to work on, with Japanese bikes it wasn't necessary. Not only were they more reliable, they were also cheaper. As a result of the Japanese invasion, and given the problems with component supply and production tooling, Triumph sales plummeted, so much so that by 1973 the government intervened and the BSA Group was merged with Norton Villiers. Later that year it was announced that the Triumph plant was to close which resulted in a workers' sit-in. This action led to the formation of a co-operative which managed the Triumph plant, with the help of a government grant. But by 1983 it went into liquidation.

The intellectual property rights were bought by John Bloor, a property tycoon, but before production could begin again it was deemed necessary to re-engineer the manufacturing process and the bike design. A modular system was utilized so that different types of machines could be built on the one assembly line. A new plant was built in Hinckley, Leicestershire with production of 8–10 bikes per day beginning in 1991. First off the assembly line was the four-cylinder 1200cc Trophy, followed later by the Trident 750 and 900, then the Daytona 750 and 1000 with either three or four-cylinder engines. By 1995 production was approximately 12,000 bikes per year.

By 2011 the company sold 49,000 bikes per year, with 85% of production being sold outside the UK, giving Triumph 6% of the large cubic-capacity motorcycle market. Also in the same period Triumph outsold the Japanese motorbike manufacturers by taking 17% of the market. However, sales started to decline due to the effects of the Eurozone debt crisis. In response Triumph increased their R&D expenditure from £22 million to £24 million and employed an extra 50 people, bringing the total number of employees involved in R&D to 240, which is a high proportion given a total staff number of 2,000. The task is to produce four new models per year as well as update existing models. This strategy of investing during the recession is to position Triumph to take advantage when the economic cycle rebounds.

Questions

1. *In what respect is Triumph a postmodern brand?*
2. *In what respect is Bexley Triumph Motorcycle Club a neo-tribe?*
3. *What are the benefits of belonging to the Triumph Owners Motor Cycle Club?*

◄◄◄ Some Ideas

1. *In what respect is Triumph a postmodern brand?*

Triumph motorbikes can be considered a retro-brand. As such there is a certain nostalgia associated with owning a Triumph bike. Appearances are important in postmodern culture and this is enhanced by Triumph who sell their own merchandise, including jackets and riding gear for bikers. Additionally, there are no clear cut entities, so people who ride Triumphs come from many walks of life, both young and old – they are not all rockers as they were in the 1950s.

2. *In what respect is Bexley Triumph Motorcycle Club a neo-tribe?*

Neo-tribes are based on a shared emotion or passion. Bexley is a local Triumph club allowing people to meet who have a passion for Triumph bikes and what they represent. The bike acts as a link value giving the individual a desire to belong.

3. *What are the benefits of belonging to the Triumph Owners Motor Cycle Club?*

The club organizes outings or rides. These may be to a special event, like a hill climb, where members can test their own bike, and view other bikes as well. Obviously they have the opportunity to swap ideas and stories. The club also organizes an annual weekend where bikers camp over for three nights and participate in organized events.

The club also sells merchandise and provides an online forum for members to discuss issues or problems concerning their bikes. A service is offered by the club whereby old bikes can be identified which makes it easier for registration. Finally, the club offers members a place to belong.

▶▶▶

Case Notes:

Case 4-2 Hi-de-Hi!

During times of an economic downturn, families and individuals are likely to utilize their holiday period by staying at home, commonly termed a stay-cation, in an effort to reduce debt. The trend was confirmed in 2009, when the UK Office for National Statistics announced that visits abroad had fallen by 15%, the biggest drop for some time. The benefits of a staycation are that it is less costly, given that holidaymakers save on travel and accommodation, and it is also less stressful. In 2012 *Forbes* magazine published an article titled "16 Things to do on a Staycation", including going for a bike ride, watching a movie, joining a yoga class and taking a hike.

However, there are risks involved in taking a staycation, as one can be tempted to go to work on the odd occasion. As smartphones give access to emails there is also a temptation to respond to messages and they provide work with the opportunity to make contact. Even without smartphone technology there are people who want to sneak a look at emails on the home computer to avoid missing out. Another temptation is to undertake home projects and other tasks that have been put on the back burner for a while. Unfortunately this can create the feeling that it wasn't a break after all. To overcome these problems it is necessary to have a set of rules and a plan of action to get out of the daily routine. One way to do this is to take a mini-break and spend time and money taking a short holiday close to home – sometimes termed a nearcation.

Parodied by the sitcom Hi-de-Hi, Butlins, a chain of holiday camps in the UK with their famous Red Coats, have reportedly benefited from the staycation trend, with a 62% increase in profits in 2009 to £87.9 million. It is believed the company gained increased sales from short and weekend breaks, but also by their investing in the holiday camps to appeal to a more upmarket clientele. Butlins' competition, Pontins, with their Blue Coats, have not reaped the benefits from the staycation trend due to their down-at-heel image. Pontins was founded in 1946 by the entrepreneur Fred Pontin, who had spotted the trend for self-catering holidays, operating in his heyday 30 holiday villages.

One guest recalls staying at Pontins Southport, in 1994, for a swimming training camp with his teenage children, only to wake up in the morning to water dripping on his son's pillow one inch from his nose. At breakfast the father told the other parents that he would ask for a change of chalets, but their response was not to bother as they all leaked! However, in the mid-90s the holiday camps were refurbished and modernized. In 2008 the company was sold for £46 million with two parks being closed by October

2009, leaving five resorts at Camber Sands, East Sussex; Pontins Southport; Ainsdale, Merseyside; Prestatyn Sands, Denbighshire; Brean Sands, Burnham-on-Sea, Somerset; and Pakefield, Lowestoft, Suffolk.

The camps provide live entertainment, dancing, an amusement arcade, children's activities, restaurants and bars, a convenience store situated in the park, snooker tables, and crazy golf. The parks have indoor heated swimming pools with water slides and an inflatable assault course, with free swimming lessons provided for children by fully trained life guards. Also, different parks have different activities, for example Pontins Southport have added a BMX track and National Cash Bingo is played twice daily at Brean Sands and Pakefield Holiday Parks. Holidaymakers can book either self-catering accommodation or half board that includes breakfast and an evening meal.

In general, three types of accommodation are available. Club apartments are the top of the range either in 1 or 2 bedroom configurations. Free electricity is included, added digital TV channels, allocated car park, a voucher for a free bottle of wine and check in at 2pm. Classic and Popular (Pakefield only has Club and Classic) are cheaper with electricity provided on a metered basis, standard TV, and mostly in 1 or 2 bedroom configurations, with check in at 4pm. In all cases bed linen has to be hired and is cheaper if it is booked in advance. Also, towels are not included but can be purchased on site.

Unfortunately there have been a number of complaints about the accommodation at Pontins. In 2010 the BBC Watchdog highlighted the less than luxurious conditions in chalets, and entries in Trip Advisor have complained of dirty chalets, which in some cases appear not to be cleaned between occupancies. Other complaints have been about the shambles at check-in times, with staff being unable to cope with the number of customers. In the same year Pontins went into administration but fortunately no jobs were lost. The administrators, KPMG, believed that the company had cash flow issues due to a drastic fall in bookings, but believed it could be sold as a going concern.

In 2011 Britannia Hotels bought the holiday parks for an estimated £20 million. The owner of Britannia, Alex Langsham, is an entrepreneur who made his fortune by buying neglected heritage sites, for example, the Adelphi in Liverpool, and positioning the hotels at the cheaper end of the market. He hopes to rebuild Pontins so that it remains a national treasure, where many families over the last 60 years have fond memories of fun holidays. He plans to invest £25 million in the refurbishment of the holiday parks and change the perception of Pontins, so that it is not just for the working class, by providing different offers, such as weekends for bird watchers, and to emulate the fun and excitement of Disney Theme Parks.

Questions

1. *How might culture influence a decision to holiday at Pontins?*
2. *What will affect a family's willingness and ability to purchase a week-long holiday at Pontins?*
3. *Conduct a SWOT analysis for Pontins. What are the marketing implications?*
4. *Develop a means-end chain for two segments of the holiday market. What are the marketing implications?*

Case Notes:

Case 4-3 Death of the High Street

Is the High Street dying? In the United Kingdom alone approximately 1 in 9 shops are closed, with an estimated 271,000 shops surplus to requirements. Dixons, the electrical store, has reduced its stores from 650 to 450, and chains such as Next are moving their stores from the High Street to retail parks. The new tenants of High Street shops are enterprises such as Poundland and charity shops, which attract a distinct clientele. The High Street has become a place for unemployed youth to hang out, which some shoppers find threatening.

In 2011 the British government was concerned about the situation because of the importance of the retail sector to the economy. It employs 6.2 million people, representing 15% of the workforce and accounts for 34% of the nation's turnover. They commissioned Mary Portas, the TV celebrity from "Mary Queen of Shops" to review the situation. Her main recommendations were:

1. Cutting regulations for High Street traders.
2. The launch of a national market day.
3. The High Street to be managed through new "Town Teams" who would be responsible for developing business in the area.
4. The relaxing of licensing rules to allow market stalls to be set up.
5. Axing restrictions on night-time deliveries.
6. Making town centre parking, if not free, at least affordable.

Whilst there has been mixed reviews of her report the government has responded to it by inviting councils to bid for a share of £1.2 million funding to rejuvenate their High Streets. Twelve towns out of 371 applications were selected, namely, Bedford, Croydon, Bedminster, Dartford, Margate, Market Rasen, Nelson, Stockport, Stockton-on-Tees, Wolverhampton, Liskeard, and Newbiggin-by-the-Sea. The government realized that this was not a magic bullet but saw it as a pilot scheme.

Later in 2012 the government released another £1.5 million to the fund. This time the successful councils were Ashford, Berwick, Braintree, London Road in Brighton, Hatfield, Royal Leamington Spa, Lodge Lane in Liverpool, the Cut in Waterloo London, Forest Hills in South London, Chrisp Street, Watney Market, Roman Road in Tower Hamlets, Loughborough, Lowestoft, Morecombe, Rotherham, and Tiverton.

Town councils can play a major role in resurrecting the High Street as a place to shop, as they set business rates, which can be crippling. They can change the licensing rules to allow pop-up shops to take over disused shops for a period of up to two years. They can also re-zone the High Street to allow residential buildings, thereby bringing people into the High Street and they can change their attitude to parking rather than treating it as a revenue resource.

However, the council is only part of the problem. The government's business tax is an issue as it is linked to Britain's above target RPI inflation rate which adds an extra £622 million tax burden on retailers. Also, the double recession has hit consumer spending which has affected shopper numbers visiting the High Street. Another issue is the attitude of some landlords who charge excessive rents and also have restrictive clauses in their lease agreements. Additionally there are landlords who are prepared to leave shops empty as they are happy with the capital gain, which doesn't help occupancy.

The rise of shopping malls, supermarkets, and retail parks is affecting the High Street. Supermarkets currently account for 97% of the grocery spend, which affects the profitability of convenience stores. Malls provide an easy shopping experience under one roof, which is a benefit in inclement weather. Retail parks are a real threat as they are easy to drive to and offer free parking. Positioned on out of town sites they are cheap to build and consequently they currently account for 80% of the planned retail developments.

Another trend is the role of Internet shopping. It is forecast that by 2015 £43 billion sales will be online, representing 14% of retail sales, and this is expected to grow. Half of all CDs and DVDs are now sold online and retailers such as Ocado and Tesco have smartphone apps allowing customers to order groceries whilst being mobile. Internet retailers, being located in relatively cheap warehouses, have lower overhead costs, and companies like Google and Amazon have been accused of paying less tax.

Internet shoppers have taken to show-rooming, where goods are examined in a retail shop, then the same item purchased online at a lower price. This practice is abetted by the use of smartphones and other mobile devices. However, Internet shopping does allow the High Street to develop hubs for the collection of goods. The choice for some customers to visit an interesting store to collect an item is more attractive than standing in a queue at the Post Office.

A problematic issue is that of city centre economies. Large cities, such as London and Manchester, have increased in size over the years with the influx of knowledge-based services, such as banks, financial institutions, and law firms. Therefore employees visit the High Street during the week, whereas medium-sized cities and small towns have lower skilled workers employed in out of town sites with few workers visiting the High Street during the week. This means that a sluggish High Street retail sector is a symptom of a poor city centre economy and not the cause of it.

Finally, is the High Street worth saving? Some commentators believe that people are becoming more isolated in society. Instead of relationships based on kinship, with people being more socially mobile, relationships are based geographically and on friendships. The High Street will play a role in allowing these friendships to develop. Over time the High Street will change by providing not only products but services, both commercial and non-commercial, thereby enhancing experiences of the communal type. This is something the Internet and the mall cannot provide.

Questions

1. *From an independent retailer's point of view use the PESTEL framework to analyse the High Street environment. What conclusions do you make?*
2. *How might a retailer take ownership of the shopping process for potential shoppers?*

Case Notes:

Case 4-4 Ship Ahoy

Case Study

There are approximately 160,000 charities in the UK with a combined income of £37 billion. The charities with an annual income above £10 million represent only 1% of charities, whereas 54% of charities are small, local, volunteer-run organizations with an income of less than £10,000 per annum. Research by the Charities Aid Foundation on charitable activity, which is an estimate of the value of donations and the value of time, indicates that 9% of people account for 66% of charitable activity. What they term the "middle ground" is the 67% of people who account for the remaining 34% of activity. According to this research, 24% of the population do little or no charitable activity.

The Royal National Lifeboat Institute (RNLI) received in 2012 an income of £166.5 million (see Table 4-4.1 for breakdown) and relies on volunteers to man the lifeboats and partake in other activities. Volunteers make up 95% of the RNLI workforce.

Table 4-4.1 RNLI 2012 Income Sources

Income source	Percentage
Legacies	61%
Fundraised voluntary income	31%
Net merchandising and other trading	4%
Net investment income	2%
Lifeguard income	2%

The income raised through fundraising was £51.9 million, which is consistent with previous years, despite the economic climate. Legacies are an important revenue source and 17p in every £1 donated is used to generate more funds.

RNLI has two main activities. The first is the operation of lifeboats. There are 236 lifeboat stations in Great Britain, Ireland, Isle of Man, and the Channel Islands, as well as four on the River Thames, covering 19,000 miles of coastline. In 2013 there were 8304 launches, with an average of 23 per day, 325 lives were saved and 8384 people were rescued (see Table 4-4.2).

The RNLI has 4,700 lifeboat crews, 8% of which are women, and crews are mostly volunteers. They are alerted by pager so they must stop what they are doing and arrive at the lifeboat station within minutes. The crews spend their own time training to become highly effective seafarers in what can

Table 4-4.2   RNLI 2013 lifeboat launches

Lifeboat Launches in Response to	Percentage
Leisure craft users	50%
People ashore	20%
People in the water	12%
Fishing and commercial boats	10%
Other sea users	8%

often be difficult and dangerous conditions. In 2012, 2270 crew members were trained around the coast by the RNLI mobile training units. Also, 398 volunteers undertook competency based training at the RNLI College, Poole, Dorset where there are specialist training facilities, including a wave and capsize pool, a fire simulator, and an engineering workshop.

The other main activity of the RNLI is to provide lifeguards at 183 beaches throughout the UK. The lifeguards are paid by the local town/city councils but the RNLI provides equipment and training. In 2012 the lifeguards attended 19,594 incidents, saved 100 lives, and assisted 24,467 people. The lifeguards operate a fleet of inshore rescue boats, rescue watercraft, and four wheel drive vehicles.

Questions

1. *Outline the decision process a person may undergo when deciding to leave a legacy to the RNLI. How can the RNLI help them through the process?*
2. *What insights can be gained from a PESTEL analysis regarding potential donations?*
3. *Construct a means-end chain for volunteer lifeboat crew and develop a message strategy from your analysis.*

Case Notes:

Aaker, D. (2008) *Strategic Market Management*, 8th edn. Hoboken, NJ: Wiley.

Addis, M. and Podesta, S. (2005) Long Life to Marketing Research: A postmodern view, *European Journal of Marketing*, 39(3/4): 386–412.

Angwin, D., Cummings, S. and Smith, C. (2008) *The Strategy Pathfinder*, 2nd edn. Chichester: Wiley.

Blaiech, R., Charbi, A. and Hamouda, M. (2013) Postmodern Marketing: Towards a Convergence between the Individualistic and the Tribal Approach, *Interdisciplinary Journal of Contemporary Research in Business* 4(9): 1294–1307.

Brodie, R., Saren, M. and Pels, J. (2011) Theorizing about the Service Dominant Logic: The bridging role of middle range theory, *Marketing Theory*, 11(1): 75–91.

Brown, S. (1993) Postmodern Marketing?, *European Journal of Marketing*, 27(4): 19–34.

Brown, S. (1994) Marketing as Multiplex: Screening Postmodernism, *European Journal of Marketing*, 28(8): 27–51.

Brown, S. (1995) *Postmodern Marketing*. London: Routledge.

Brown, S. (1999) Postmodernism: The End of Marketing? In Brownlie, D., Saren, M., Wensley, R. and Whittington, R. (eds), *Rethinking Marketing*. London: Sage Publications.

Cova, B. (1997) Community and Consumption: Towards a definition of the "linking value" of product or services, *European Journal of Marketing*, 31(3/4): 297–316.

Cova, B. and Cova, V. (2002) Tribal Marketing: The tribalisation of society and its impact on the conduct of marketing, *European Journal of Marketing*, 36(5/6): 595–620.

Cova, B. and Dalli, D. (2009) Working Consumers: The next step in marketing theory?, *Marketing Theory*, 9(3): 315–339.

Doyle, P. and Stern, P. (2006) *Marketing Management and Strategy*, 4th edn. Harlow, England: Prentice Hall.

Firat, A. F., Dholakia, N. and Venkatesh, A. (1995) Marketing in a Postmodern World, *European Journal of Marketing*, 29(1): 40–56.

Firat, A. F. and Venkatesh, A. (1995) Liberatory Postmodernism and the Reenchantment of Consumption, *Journal of Consumer Research*, 22, 239–267.

Goulding, C. (2003) Issues in representing the postmodern consumer, *Qualitative Market Research*, 6(3): 152–159.

Goulding, C., Shankar, A. and Canniford, R. (2013) Learning to be Tribal: Facilitating the formation of consumer tribes, *European Journal of Marketing*, 47(5/6): 813–832.

Gummesson, E. (2008) Quality, Service-dominant Logic and Many-to-many Marketing, *The TQM Journal*, 20(2): 143–153.

Kolar, T. (2007) Linking Customers and Products by Means-End Chain Analysis, *Management*, 12(2): 69–83.

Kotler, P. and Keller, K. (2012) *Marketing Management*, 14th edn. Harlow, England: Pearson Education.

Mitchell, C. and Imrie, B. (2011) Consumer Tribes: Membership, consumption and building loyalty, *Asia Pacific Journal of Marketing and Logistics*, 23(1): 39–56.

Peter, J. and Olson, J. (2008) *Consumer Behavior and Marketing Strategy*, 8th edn. Boston: McGraw-Hill.

Phillips, J. M. and Reynolds, T. J. (2009) A Hard Look at Hard Laddering, *Qualitative Market Research: An International Journal*, 12(1): 83–99.

Schembri, S. (2006) Rationalizing Service Logic, or Understanding Services as Experience, *Marketing Theory*, 6(3): 381–392.

Tofler, A. (1980) *The Third Wave*. New York: William Morrow.

Vargo, S. and Lusch, R. (2004) Evolving to a New Dominant Logic for Marketing, *Journal of Marketing*, 68(January): 1–17.

Veludo-de-Oliveira, T.M., Ikeda, A.A. and Campomar, M.C. (2006) Laddering in the Practice of Marketing Research: Barriers and Solutions, *Qualitative Market Research: An International Journal*, 9(3): 297–306.

Wansink, B. (2003) Using Laddering to Understand and Leverage a Brand's Equity, *Qualitative Market Research*, 6(2): 111–118.

Zwick, D., Bonsu, S. and Darmody, A. (2008) Putting Consumers to Work, *Journal of Consumer Culture*, 8(2): 163–196.

Case Acknowledgements

The **I Ride Therefore I Belong** case draws on information contained in:

Bexley Triumph Owners Motorcycle Club website located at www.bexleytriumph.org

"Triumph Motorcycles – A Brief History", retrieved from http://www.collinscycle.com/triumph_motorcycles_history.htm

The **Hi-de-Hi!** case draws on information contained in

"16 Things To Do On A 'Staycation'", by S. Odland (31 May 2012), *Forbes*, retrieved from http://www.forbes.com/sites/steveodland/2012/05/31/16-things-to-do-on-a-staycation/

"Challenge Britannia: to perform some Disney-style magic at faded Pontins", by Z. Wood (18 February 2011), *The Guardian*, retrieved from http://www.theguardian.com/business/2011/feb/18/the-friday-interview-alex-langsam

"Pontin's falls into administration as fond memories fail to save firm", by J. Finch and J. Treanor (13 November 2010), *The Guardian*, retrieved from http://www.theguardian.com/business/2010/nov/13/pontins-administration-holiday-camps

The **Death of the High Street** case draws on information contained in

"Fifteen towns share £1.5m aid to revive High Streets", (25 July 2012), *BBC News*, retrieved from http://www.bbc.co.uk/news/business-18972391

"High Streets to share £1.2m funding", (26 May 2012), *BBC News*, retrieved from http://www.bbc.co.uk/news/uk-18212669

"High Street Blues: The slow death of retail Britain", by P. Bignell and M. Leftly (20 January 2013), *The Independent*, retrieved from http://www.independent.co.uk/news/business/analysis-and-features/high-street-blues-the-slow-death-of-retail-britain-8458766.html

"Is the UK high street facing an inevitable 'death spiral'?", by S. Carey (13 February 2012), *The Guardian*, retrieved from http://www.theguardian.com/local-government-network/2012/feb/13/mary-portas-uk-high-street-facing-death-spiral

"Mary Portas unveils report into High Street revival", (13 December 2011), *BBC News*, retrieved from http://www.bbc.co.uk/news/uk-16153541

"Up to 40% of high street shops 'could close over next five years'", by J. Kollewe (20 March 2012), *The Guardian*, retrieved from http://www.guardian.co.uk /business/2012/mar/20/high-street-shops-close-deloitte

The **Ship Ahoy** case draws on information contained in

"Britain's Civic Core: Who are the people powering Britain's charities?", *Charities Aid Foundation 2013*, retrieved from https://www.cafonline.org/publications /2013-publications/britains-civic-core.aspx

"RNLI Review 2012", retrieved from http://rnli.org/aboutus/aboutthernli/Pages /review-of-the-year.aspx

"The Royal National Lifeboat Institution is the charity that saves lives at sea", (May 2012), *RNLI Fact Sheet*, retrieved from http://rnli.org/aboutus/aboutthernli /Pages/Our-purpose.aspx

This chapter covers the following topics:

- ▶ Break-even analysis
- ▶ Price points
- ▶ Value proposition
- ▶ Pricing strategies
- ▶ Revenue management

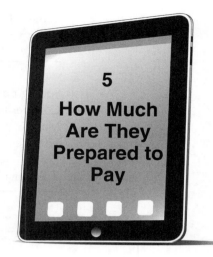

5

How Much Are They Prepared to Pay

Within marketing, pricing is one of the most difficult tasks to get right. Over and above applying such methods as cost-plus pricing, marginal pricing, target return on investment, and demand backward pricing, the price strategy needs to take into consideration a number of factors. First, the price of a product/service communicates a message about the position of the product in relation to the competition. The price also gives an indication of the relative quality of the product/service to the extent that price and quality are often correlated. A high price can signal prestige and exclusivity, resulting in the product being aspirational for some segments.

Not all organizations can set their price, for example, some may need government approval. On the other hand, some industries seek price stability as they don't want peaks and troughs in sales which affect cash flow. This is the case in industries with high fixed costs, for example, the petro-chemical industry. Other products/services are affected by immediate competition, especially so when the product is undifferentiated. Some products/services have the price set by the industry norm, called "pegged" pricing. Examples are candy bars and coffee in cafes. Yet other industries have follow-the-leader pricing, where the dominant company in the market with a large market share sets the price, and the competitors will follow.

The pricing scenario shown in Table 5.1, not unlike the cola market, indicates that Firm A has a cost leader position (see Generic Market Share Grid, Chapter 3, Figure 3.1) and has economies of scale. Therefore, Firm B cannot compete on price, so accepts the price set by Firm A and competes on other dimensions. Notice that Firm A has economies of advertising so consequently has the dominant "share of voice".

Table 5.1 Pricing scenario example

	Firm A	Firm B
	Firm A	Firm B
Selling per unit	9	9
Cost per unit	6	7
Margin	3	2
Volume	7,000	3,000
Profit	21,000	6,000
Advertising @ 50c/unit	3,500	1,500

Making a Buck

However, before price points and price strategies can be developed it is important that a firm understands their cost structure and the price sensitivity of their customers. To understand the organization's cost structure the fixed costs and the variable costs need to be identified. From this, a volume break-even analysis can be developed by utilizing the formula.

$$\text{Units} = \frac{\text{Fixed Cost}}{\text{Contribution Margin}}$$

where contribution margin equals the unit selling price less variable cost per unit. Determining the break-even point can be challenging when fixed costs have to be allocated over a product range. The task then is to split the fixed costs by a pro-rated factor. Obviously a better break-even point can be achieved by actively lowering the fixed and variable costs. Break-even analysis has limitations. Total cost curves are assumed to be linear, which may not be the case. Additionally average variable costs are not always the same at all levels of output. As well, the total revenue line is not necessarily straight as there may be discounts per quantity (see Money Makes the World Go Around later in the chapter).

How sensitive are your customers to price increases or price decreases? To answer this question the concept of price elasticity needs to be explored. Elastic demand means that if prices are increased, the revenue will decrease, and on the other hand, if prices decrease the quantity will increase leading to an increase in revenue.

$$\text{Elastic demand} = \frac{\%\ \text{change in quantity demanded}}{\%\ \text{change in price}}$$

Conversely, inelastic demand means that it is possible to raise prices and revenue will increase, but by dropping the price there will not be enough revenue to make up the shortfall. By calculating the elasticity as per the formula above, it is possible to determine how sensitive a certain product/service is to changes in price. If price elasticity of demand is >1 the product/service is price elastic (sensitive to price change). If price elasticity of demand =1 then demand is unit elastic. If price elasticity of demand is <1 then demand is price inelastic.

In general, a high price sensitivity indicates that if a price goes up consumers will buy less, and when a price goes down, sales will increase. Inelastic demand, on the other hand, indicates that a change in price will have little effect on demand. Certain conditions will make products/services inelastic (that is, not sensitive to a price increase):

- There are no substitute products or competition.
- Buyers are slow to search for lower prices or change their buying habits.
- Buyers think the higher prices are justified due to product improvements or an increase in inflation.
- The proportion of income spent on an item.
- The item cannot be readily stored.

Everything Comes at a Price

A price point is the selling price in a category compared to other products/services being offered by the company and the competition. For example, the price point of a Big Mac is different from the price point for a Quarter Pounder, and is different again from a KFC chicken burger. Setting the price point is not about determining customers' willingness to pay by undertaking conjoint analysis, estimating the likely demand at different price points, then reacting optimally to the best outcome, because customers put different value on the offer depending upon their circumstances, such as when and how they buy. For example, an airline ticket can be purchased three months in advance for a planned holiday, or the day before due to an unscheduled business meeting, and the customer can buy through a travel agent or via the airline's internet site. Any combination of the above scenarios will have different values for the customer so they will be prepared to pay different prices. Therefore value is the benefit gained by purchasing the product or service, or the solution that is received by accepting the marketing offer.

According to Smith and Nagle (2002), there are three types of value. **Use value** is the benefit, either tangible or intangible, that the purchaser receives from using a product. **Economic value** is the monetary value of the benefit received by the buyer compared to a competitor's product or service or a substitute product/service. This type of value is important in the B2B market. The specific value features that customers are willing to pay over and above need to be identified, for example, after sales service or 24/7 monitoring. Finally, **perceived value** is the benefit the buyer believes they are getting from the purchase. It is easy to either overestimate or underestimate a product's or service's value to a customer, therefore perceived value needs to be explored using in-depth interviews. With new interactive products it is tempting to use price discounts to attract new customers but the downside of this is that it may set future price expectations. Also, it is easy to respond to lack of demand due to the cyclical or seasonal nature of the business by reducing the price, but this may drive down industry price levels. As shown in Figure 5.1, dropping the price may negatively impact on the perceived benefits, with the danger that the product/service is seen as a commodity, where price becomes the determining factor.

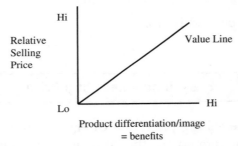

Figure 5.1 Customer values. Source: Adapted from Leszinski and Marn (1997)

Claim to Fame

A value proposition is a promise made by a company to its customers that they will deliver a bundle of benefits. From the customer's perspective the value proposition is the set of experiences provided by the use of the product/service, including value for money. Therefore, perceived value is the trade-off or difference between the perceived benefits, which may be either economic or psychological and the price of the product/service, including the activities of purchasing, transportation, and installation. Consequently price is inextricably linked with value. To understand this dynamic Fifield (cited in Hassan, 2012) formulated the equation:

$$\text{Value Proposition} = \text{Benefits} - \text{Effort} - \text{Risk} - \text{Price}$$

Benefit is the value gained from usage of the product thereby providing a solution to the marketing problem. **Effort** is the exertion required by the customer to seek information regarding the product, including time spent sourcing the product/service. Marketers can make this easier by utilizing e-business, training sales staff, and providing informative communications. Customers may equate **Risk** with financial, personal, or social jeopardy. This can be reduced by offering testimonies, warranties, guarantees, and financing options. **Price** refers to the customer weighing the price of the product/service against the opportunity cost.

Money Makes the World Go Around

Over the last few decades there has been a drive for companies to customize products and this has been matched with customized communication and targeted media tailored to specific audiences resulting in increased perceived value as the customer believes they have a personal relationship with the company. However, the same amount of customization has not happened with pricing, which has meant that companies have missed opportunities.

In a mass market the same price for everyone works well if everyone is homogeneous, but as customers have different needs and desires, then pricing strategy opportunities exist (Berry, 2013). For example, if a company sells a product for £50 with a cost of £30, then the profit would be £20. If they sell 100 units then the total profit is £2,000. However, if they sell 70 units they make a profit of £1,400 but then sell 30 units at £60 (making the margin per unit £30), the profit increases by £900 to a total of £2,300, an increase of 15%. On the other hand, there may be, say 20 customers who cannot afford £50 but will buy a simplified product at £40, giving a margin of £10. This represents an additional £200 profit, increasing the overall profit to £2,500 or an increase of 25%. Therefore, what pricing strategies can be put in place to take advantage of the type of situation described above?

Price lining is where products/services within a category have different price points. The concept is based on the realization that the market comprises a collection of small segments, who seek similar products but of differing quality. Price lining is achieved by offering different features with a product, for example, in the car market customers are offered a standard version, a GT and a LTD version. There is a price/quality trade-off where higher prices equate with better quality. If the product quality is not easily viewed, as is the case, for example, with laptop computers, then price is used as an indicator of quality. However, if customers don't see that the higher price is justified they may disregard the offer and also the brand. The downside to price lining is that when an economic downturn in the economy occurs, the company may be left with high-priced inventory. The benefit for the company is that instead of developing completely different product offerings, they can expand the number of customers by making modifications to an existing product thereby saving communication, inventory, and distribution costs.

Another pricing strategy is multi-dimensional pricing, where two or more price parameters are set based on detailed information regarding customer spend plus the number of times purchased over a given period (Hermann and Dolan, 1998). For example, a visit to a zoo may be priced at £20, but they develop a "friends of the zoo" card at £120 per year allowing unlimited access, with a 10% discount at the café. Aligned with multi-dimensional pricing, another strategy is to offer a discount for the number of units purchased. In other words, this is a non-linear tariff where the price paid is not proportional to the number of units consumed. For example, to encourage the use of the facility, a bowling alley may charge £20 for the first game, £15 for the second, and £10 for the third game. To implement this strategy, a company needs to understand a customer's willingness to pay and also take account of the competition's pricing strategies.

Multi-person pricing is where two or more pay less than full price (Hermann and Dolan, 1998). For example, an airline may offer a business class ticket for £2,000 but offer an accompanying person the same ticket for £1,200. In an industry where marginal costs are minimal, this is an attractive source of revenue when there is inventory available. Multi-person pricing is popular in tourism and sport industries where there are large groups.

For companies entering the market with a new innovation, for example Apple iPhone, there are two distinct pricing strategies that can be followed. Penetration strategy is where the price is set low to gain entry and market share. As market share increases the company exploits the experience curve so over time prices are lowered further so that further market share is gained. This strategy is effective when the market is price sensitive and the experience curve can be exploited by economies of scale, process innovations etc. Skimming, on the other hand, starts with a high price to recoup R&D costs, for example, and over time the price will be lowered.

116

This strategy is effective if there is high demand for the product, the company wants to position the product as superior, and competition is deterred from entering the market, especially if barriers to entry exist, such as patents, technological and production expertise, or exclusive distribution rights have been negotiated.

Finally, pricing bundling is a strategy where two or more products are sold together, based on the premise that a customer's willingness to pay will be transferred to another product. Price bundling is sometimes referred to as product building and is different from a two-for-one deal of the same product as seen with sales promotions. Bundling is where the price for a set of products or services is cheaper than if the items were sold separately, for example, a Sky TV package or fast-food offerings. By bundling, the company is increasing their profit by giving customers a discount. Also, customers may benefit from the joint performance of the product, as well as the simplification of the purchasing process. It is a pricing strategy suitable for high volume products which have high margins, where economies of scale can be gained. From a company's perspective bundling can simplify production and stop customers quibbling over the price of each item. There are two types of bundling strategies. The first is pure bundling where only the bundle is sold, and the second is mixed bundling where individual products are sold as well.

These strategies are an attempt to customize pricing based on the notion that there are differences between small customer segments. The important point is that customers see the difference in price is fair, so the company needs to carefully communicate the different offers, for example, it may be better to offer an off-season discount rather than a high season premium.

Optimized or Just Optimistic?

Revenue management involves matching revenue maximization with optimized inventory allocation. In other words, balancing pricing strategies with inventory control. "It is essentially the process of allocating the right type of capacity to the right customer at the right time at the right price" (Wirtz et al, 2003). Revenue management grew out of the concept of yield management, which was developed in the airline industry. Yield can be calculated for each flight by dividing revenue per seat kilometre by costs per seat kilometre. By using this data yields can be compared and contrasted with routes and also by the date and time of flights. Yield management uses the process of forecasting which in turn allows airlines to overbook flights due to predicted passenger cancellations and no-shows. Also, the practice of discounting seats needed to be managed as capacity needed to be available for late booking, high revenue passengers. A process called *nesting* makes sub-sets of seats available at different discount rates, but automatically ensures that a low value fare is not available when high value fares are closed to additional sales. Each day the fare for a flight is calculated to optimize the inventory. Finally, yield management is used to balance traffic management. Connecting passengers to other flights need to be given priority over and above point-to-point passengers.

Yield management and revenue management are closely related, with the former being viewed as more tactical and the latter as more strategic. Revenue management varies prices over time to reflect demand and dynamically allocates inventory to match demand. By understanding buyer behaviour and price elasticity, sub-segments can be identified. For example, not everyone wants to fly the "red eye". The task, termed optimization, uses statistical packages, based on linear programming or regression analysis, to obtain the highest revenue by matching service offerings with inventory levels and with different price points. Revenue management is ideal for a number of organizations such as airlines, rental car firms, hotels, sports venues such as bowling alleys and golf clubs, and restaurants. It suits organizations with the following characteristics:

- Relatively finite capacity, for example, the number of hotel beds that are available.
- The inventory is perishable and cannot be stored, for example, a passenger seat for a specific time and date.
- The market can experience fluctuating demand, for example, mid-week bowling versus Saturday night bowling, etc.
- The market has sub-segments, such as business travel compared to leisure travel.
- Inventory can be sold in advance allowing the opportunity to adjust future offerings.
- Companies have low variable to fixed cost ratio. For example a golf club has high fixed costs due to the cost of green maintenance etc., but very low variable cost.

One issue that companies need to guard against is that of unfairness. Customers may view different price points for seemingly the same level of service as not being fair, more so if the reference point is difficult to

118

assess. One way to make sure customers understand the different price points it to erect rate fences. These can be physical, for example, tour groups in a separate part of the restaurant, or non-refundable fares, or non-physical such as length of stay or squash court availability. The more restrictions in place, the lower the price point. By erecting price fences the perceived value for the particular offer increases. In some circumstances it may be preferable to set the highest price artificially, thereby making it the reference point and giving the impression of value for lower priced offers, for example, hotel rack rates are set high.

For revenue management to be successful the company must collect and store historical data for inventory, price points, demand, and other causal factors, for example public holiday weekends, which can be analysed to predict future demand, based on the response of different segments at specific times and places. The organization needs to be careful that customers do not view revenue management as opportunistic, which may impact the loyalty of customers. Therefore the company needs to consider the time value of customers. Consequently, revenue management needs to link with customer relationship management. In some organizations this may give rise to problems of integration between property management systems, customer relationship management systems, and revenue management systems.

Case 5-1 The Daily Grind

George has been a barista for a local café in Wellington for the last four years. During this time he has talked to many coffee sales representatives who all reinforced his view that the owning of a café was easy to get into considering that it didn't require any tertiary education or specialist training, although Well Tec offered a sixty-hour evening course on how to become a barista. However, he knew that running a successful café business requires more than just being a good barista. George therefore decided to do some homework before pursuing his dream of operating his own café.

Over 1.4 billion cups of coffee are drunk each day around the world. Over the last two decades New Zealand has developed a strong coffee culture. For instance, in Wellington there is particularly strong demand for various styles of cafés, perhaps due to the idealistic nature of its people.

The growth of coffee consumption in New Zealand can be attributed to the number of local roasters such as Allpress, Atomic, Burton Hollis, Alturas (based in Auckland), and L'Affare and Havana (based in Wellington). There are now approximately 70 roasters in New Zealand. It is thought that a contributing factor to the growth of the café society has been the increasing intolerance of drink driving so people have turned to socializing over a cup of coffee. The overall demand for coffee in cafés has grown over the years. According to Nestle, New Zealanders drink 380 cups each per year. In Tauranga, busy café restaurant Bravo sells about 300 cups of coffee per day, whereas in Wellington the bigger cafés sell over 500 cups of coffee per day.

New Zealanders are particular about their daily cup of coffee be it instant or fresh ground roasted. Many like to have a great café experience as well as good coffee to start their day. Subsequently New Zealanders can be picky about the type of coffee beans used and where these are sourced as fair trade and organic coffee popularity increases. It is therefore important for George to have a good understanding of his potential customers. Successful cafés have done just that and succeed due to a combination of location, foot traffic, and word of mouth about service, and coffee consistency and taste.

Two-thirds of coffee is drunk outside the home. The flat white was invented in Australia or New Zealand, depending on whom you talk to and is the favourite of café goers. Flat whites, lattes, and cappuccinos use 200ml of milk. Based on his experience, George thought that these coffees would appeal to 80% of his customers, with 20% of his market preferring americanos, espressos, and long blacks. Over the years he observed that 50% of his clients used 3-gram sugar sticks, which was not a great cost to the company as they bought them for $33.45 for a box of 2,500. George's research found that 33% of New Zealanders buy a coffee from a café at least once a week, but on the other hand 20% never do.

Instant coffee is the largest selling type of coffee in New Zealand. This incorporates both premium granulated instant coffee and powdered instant coffee as well as the introduction of new flavoured coffee sachets such as Moccona Café Classics. The home market comprises 92% of instant coffee sales but represents 80% of the total market. The total coffee market includes home, work/office, and vending machines. Despite the dominance of instant coffee in the home, market research indicates that 80% of households have plungers. Over a five-year period instant coffee sales have grown from 1.9 million kg to 2.25 million kg. Research shows that 7 out of 10 people drink instant coffee at least once per month and it accounts for 26% of all drinks consumed – hot or cold. Nestle has the largest market share with 59% of the world market with its Nescafe brand. In New Zealand Greggs is the next biggest player with its Greggs and Robert Harris brands, followed by Bushells.

Fresh ground roasted coffee offerings range from café/restaurant coffee to home/office plunger and espresso. Market research figures show super-market sales of fresh roasted coffee rose from 723,726 kg per year in 1998 to 882,638 kg for the year-end April 2004. In 2010, there was a 16% increase in coffee output worldwide with global consumption currently between 130 to 131 million bags of coffee beans a year. However, according to Statistics NZ the total amount of imported coffee beans in 2003 was 6.7 million tonnes although this is lower than the figure imported a decade earlier by approximately 134,000 tonnes. This drop can be attributed to the fact that the multinationals have taken their roasting operations overseas in that period. Wholesale roasted coffee beans sell for between approximately $28 per kg and $32 per kg, depending on the quality and the supplier. Each cup of coffee needs around 10 grams of coffee.

The take-out market has increased over the past decade and this can be attributed to two reasons: first, the smoke-free policy in the workplace has meant people will have a coffee during their "smoko" break. Second, city people in particular seem to be working harder so they want a coffee "on the go". George thought that 40% of his sales would be take-out but realized that there would be an extra 30 cents for a paper cup and lid.

George decided that a great location would be in Cuba Street, somewhere between Ghuznee Street and Vivian Street, as the area was close to student hostels and Victoria University School of Architecture and Design. He also knew that foot traffic was high as many students from Massey University used the route on the way to the city centre. He contacted a local commercial real estate agent and was informed that a retail outlet of 90 square metres at a cost of $500 per square metre per year was on the market. There was an additional cost of electricity at approximately $360 per month.

Unfortunately he had not anticipated the high fit-out cost. He was quoted $90,000, which would include a bar, 5 tables, and 20 chairs and a long bench down one side meaning that the café could seat approximately 30 people. However, he was relieved to learn that the fit-out cost would cover the revamping of the small kitchen area. Included would be a commercial washing machine and fridge, along with a modern bench and cooking facilities plus a Nuova Simonelli espresso machine. He liked this machine as it was a legend in the market and was made by an Italian company that had been making espresso machines since 1936. Also it was the official choice of the World Barista Championship. His preferred model was the Apia, as it was ideal for busy cafés and takeaway coffee environments.

He needed to find some financial backing as his savings account had only grown to $10 000 over the last four years. Given the location and the prices of other cafés in the Wellington CBD, George decided he would sell his black coffees at $4.00 per cup and all others at $4.50 per cup.

Questions
1. *Write a brief analysis of the New Zealand coffee market.*
2. *Prepare a break-even analysis for George.*
3. *Advise George as to the viability of his proposed café.*

◀◀◀ Some Ideas

1. *Write a brief analysis of the New Zealand coffee market.*

   Issues to consider:

   ° There are 70 local roasters, which is considerable given the country has a population of only 4.2 million.

   ° There is a coffee culture, with two-thirds of coffee drunk outside the house.

   ° Instant coffee is the most popular choice, with 92% usage in the home, but it represents 80% of the total market, therefore it is used a lot at work.

° 80% of homes have plungers, but these are only used on special occasions, e.g. when friends visit.

2. *Prepare a break-even analysis for George.*

The following is a break-even calculation, based on these assumptions:

° The café opens six days per week for 50 weeks.

° The open hours are from 7.00am until 3.00pm.

° Staff, including George, get paid $15 per hour.

Coffee Break-even Analysis

Fixed Costs	Annual	Daily	Variable Costs	
Rent	$45,000	$150.00	Coffee	$0.30
Electricity	$2,880	$9.60	Milk	$0.40
Depreciation	$9,000	$30.00	Sugar	$0.01
Interest	$9,600	$32.00	Cups, Lids, etc	$0.12
Labour		$360.00	**Total**	**$0.83**
Total		**$581.60**		
			Contribution	$2.17
Units = FC/$3-VC			**Break-even**	**268**

3. *Advise George as to the viability of his proposed café.*

According to the break-even analysis George would have to sell 268 cups of coffee per day, which is approximately 34 an hour. This may be a hard task as only big coffee shops sell 500 cups a day in Wellington. George needs to get data on foot traffic and also undertake a competitive analysis of other coffee shops in the area. He also needs to take into account that the Design and Architectural Schools are nearby, so demand will decrease outside of term time. He also needs to think about selling food, such as muffins, slices, etc. as these items tend to have a 200% mark-up.

Using all the above information he needs to do some sensitivity analysis on the break-even analysis, e.g. can he increase the price? What items has he missed out, e.g. insurance? The break-even analysis assumes one shot per coffee, but most cafes nowadays use two shots. Once he has undertaken this further analysis, he will then be able to make a decision as to the viability of his café.

Case 5-2 Take Me Down to the Ball Game

Case Study

Sports organizers know it is important to fill a stadium for a number of reasons. A large crowd creates a buzz with such an atmosphere adding to the spectators' positive experience. This is further enhanced if the home team is winning. For many of the big leagues, half the organization's revenue is obtained through media rights, with the other half gained at the stadium through ticket sales and the selling of merchandise. If the stadium is full and the home team is having a winning streak, then the price for future tickets can be increased.

The Red Sox baseball team have been on a winning streak for 820 consecutive games. During the seventh innings of a game, the attendance figures are announced followed by the words "sell out". The club sold 36,605 tickets per game for their Fenway Park Stadium, despite having a capacity of only 34,807 (as at 2003; it has since increased to 37,000). The attendance figures are calculated by National Baseball League rules, which are the official number of tickets sold, not the number of people in attendance.

Red Sox caps the number of season tickets at 22,000 leaving 15,000 to sell. Fans cannot buy more than eight passes for a single game and the club holds back a few hundred to sell on the day. There is a secondary market, commonly called scalpers, who obtain tickets from season pass holders and people who want to exchange their tickets for money. Scalping is illegal in most countries, but in the United States it is banned only in some states, so the scalpers operate outside of those particular states. The scalpers hope to make money over and above the face value of the ticket, but if the team is performing poorly or there is poor weather, then the scalper may end up with spare tickets, thus losing money. It is estimated that between 20 and 30% of tickets are sold in this secondary market.

For Major League Baseball clubs the pricing task involves a pre-season judgement to estimate demand at various price levels versus the finite supply of tickets. This is most important for season ticket passes, which can account for approximately 60% of sales. Data analysis shows that the ticket price ranged from $8.55 per game to $222.58, with a median price of $39.96.

In 2009 three teams used different pricing mechanisms. The Yankees used a traditional method, which requires long range planning, knowing what customers accept as value, and anticipating the reaction to the team's performance. The club made a clarification between premium and non-premium tickets, where the premium tickets sold between $500 and $2,600.

They believed this was justified because of the high demand driven by the performance of the players, which the club had invested in to get the best.

Also, the club had to finance a new stadium and the premium deluxe service was attractive to big-spending corporates and the like. The scalpers' prices for the previous season indicated there was a demand for premium seats. By raising the price it was hoped that the role of the scalpers, who were making markups of 100%, would be diminished.

The Red Sox followed a different pricing strategy by keeping ticket prices at the 2008 level. This was justified as they had less to finance and they had a lower payroll. Also, they had raised prices consistently over the last five years and they had no corporates to attract.

The New York Mets were more innovative, as they lacked team performance and a level of fan support, as well as corporate support. They rarely sold out games and scalpers were only obtaining minimum premiums over ticket face value. Therefore they adopted a Dynamic Ticket Pricing mechanism, where the balance of supply and demand is calculated game by game. It is estimated that in 2013, 17 of the 30 MLB teams had adopted dynamic pricing.

In April 2013, sell-out crowds for the Red Sox ended. They hosted 17 games in a span of just 21 days, with some of their opponents not being big draw cards. The club responded by offering free food for children under 14 if collected before the third innings. Also an offer of "buy one and get one free" was used for hotdogs, and the beer price was dropped from $8.50 to $5.00. Whatever way they do it, the Red Sox know the importance of filling as many of the red and blue seats at Fenway Park as they possibly can.

Questions

1. *What role does the scalper play?*
2. *Compare and contrast the different pricing strategies.*
3. *Under what circumstances could sports clubs, other than baseball clubs, adopt Dynamic Ticket Pricing?*

Case Notes:

Case 5-3 Grape Expectations

The Hunter Valley is Australia's oldest wine growing region and is home to Wyndham Estate, the internationally acclaimed vineyard, which attracts 40,000 visitors per year. Located in New South Wales, the Hunter Valley is about a two-hour drive north of state capital Sydney. Newcastle and Lake Macquarie are the major towns of the region, but there are also numerous communities and townships throughout the area.

Visitors to the Hunter Valley can experience a range of activities, including golf, spa treatments, gardens, and food and wine schools, in addition to sampling the regional produce of wine, craft beer, cheese, and olive oil. Accommodation options in the region range from international resorts, luxury villas, self-contained lodges, cottages, B&Bs, and budget pub rooms. Many are boutique family run businesses, and some are attached to working farms and vineyards.

Carol and Tom moved from Sydney to Mount View in the Hunter Valley after falling in love with the area having attended a friend's wedding at nearby Polkobin. They purchased an old villa with the idea of running a B&B. Tom, a carpenter by trade, has renovated the house, keeping as much of the original character as possible, and it now offers two guest rooms, each with its own en-suite. Carol has worked hard on capturing the history of the area in the villa's furnishing and interior decoration. They have decided that healthy breakfasts, using locally sourced produce, would be served in their newly refurbished conservatory offering lovely views of the Brokenback range.

They have worked with the Hunter Valley Wine & Tourism Association to list their B&B on the Association's official website. The site enables people to plan their visit to the Hunter Valley, check out upcoming events, find the location of tourist attractions, and book accommodation online (which gives instant confirmation and captures payment). Tom and Carol have spent most of their savings getting the villa up to the standard they wanted. With renovations on track, they are planning to open for business to coincide with this year's annual "Opera in the Vineyards" event at Wyndham Estate.

Questions

1. *What information do they need to be able to set the price per room?*
2. *What circumstances would lead them to differ their pricing?*

In 2010 the European Union changed the rules so that anyone with the relevant licence could operate a train within the EU. The German train operator Deutsche Bahn (DB) announced that it would operate a train service from London to Frankfurt and Amsterdam, starting in 2013. So DB will be another challenger to Europe's busiest aviation market. There would be three services a day in each direction, carrying 888 passengers in 16 coaches. At Brussels the train would split, with eight coaches going to Rotterdam and then Amsterdam, with the other eight coaches travelling to Cologne then Frankfurt, the finance capital of Germany. There is the possibility of the train using the high speed terminal at Stratford, East London, which would appeal to the business market at Canary Wharf and in the City.

DB plans to use their Inter City Express series 3, known as the ICE train, which can travel at speeds of up to 200 mph. The train must pass stringent safety tests so that it can use the channel tunnel (chunnel). The train will be 375 metres long with the front and rear doors being able to connect with the central service tunnel for emergency evacuation.

When comparing train travel to air travel most travellers used a cut-off point of three hours. That is, if the journey time by train was longer than three hours it would be better to use air travel. However, with frequent air traffic delays and stringent airport security the cut-off point is now estimated to be four, if not five, hours. DB expects the train trip to take between four and five hours, which competes favourably with the door-to-door air travel time, that includes travel to the airport, check-in time and a one-and-a-half-hour flight. The train has the added advantage of having wifi and power sockets at each seat, allowing passengers to be more productive than if they were flying. Also trains achieve a 90–95% on-time and within 15 minutes departure time, whereas airlines achieve 63–68% on-time departures.

DB hopes to grow the market by 10%, which means adding another four million to the 10 million people who use the chunnel. Currently Eurostar, majority owned by French state railway (SNCF), operates trains between St Pancras Station, London to Paris and Brussels. Eurostar's fares to Brussels are as cheap as £69 standard return. They believe another train operator will not dampen fares because they are already low due to low-cost airlines such as Ryanair and easyJet.

DB have conducted trials with trains going through the chunnel, but they have decided to push back the start date to 2016.

Questions

1. *Why would DB want to push back the start date of the service?*
2. *What pricing strategies should they adopt?*
3. *Outline the essential components to include in a revenue management system.*

Case Notes:

References and Further Reading

Aaker, D. (2008) *Strategic Market Management*, 8th edn. Hoboken, NJ: Wiley.

Berry, T. (2013) "Understanding your pricing choices", (www.mplans.com/articles).

Doyle, P. and Stern, P. (2006) *Marketing Management and Strategy*, 4th edn. Harlow, England: Prentice Hall.

Frow, P. and Payne, A. (2011) A Stakeholder Perspective of the Value Proposition Concept, *European Journal of Marketing*, 45(1/2): 223–240.

Hassan, A. (2012) The Value Proposition Concept in Marketing: How Customers Perceive the Value Delivered by Firms – A Study of Customer Perspectives on Supermarkets in Southampton in the United Kingdom, *International Journal of Marketing Studies*, 4(3): 68–87.

Hermann, S. and Dolan, R. (1998) Price Customization, *Marketing Management*, 7(3): 10–17.

Hogan, J. and Lucke, T. (2006) 'Driving Growth with New Products: Common pricing traps to avoid', *Journal of Business Strategy*, 27(1): 54–58.

Kotler, P. and Keller, K. (2012) *Marketing Management*, 14th edn. Harlow, England: Pearson Education.

Leszinski, R. and Marn, M. (1997) Setting Value, not Price, *McKinsey Quarterly*, February.

Mason, C. and Simmons, J. (2012) Are They Being Served? Linking consumer expectation, evaluation and commitment, *Journal of Services Marketing*, 26(4): 227–237.

Milla, S. and Shoemaker, S. (2007) Three Decades of Revenue Management: What's Next?, *Journal of Revenue and Pricing Management*, 7(1): 110–114.

Murphy, R. and Narkiewicz, V. (2010) Electronic Commerce and the Value Proposition, *The Journal of Human Resource and Adult Learning*, 6(1): 99–105.

Shoemaker, S. (2003) The Future of Pricing in Services, *Journal of Revenue and Pricing Management*, 2(3): 271–279.

Smith, B., Leimkuhler, J. and Darrow, R. (1992) Yield Management at American Airlines, *Interfaces*, 22(1): 8–31.

Smith, G. and Nagle, T. (2002) How Much Are Customers Willing to Pay?, *Marketing Research*, 14(4): 20–25.

Wirtz, J., Kimes, S., Ho Pheng Theng and Patterson, P. (2003) Revenue Management: Resolving Potential Customer Conflicts, *Journal of Revenue and Pricing Management*, 2(3): 216–226.

Case Acknowledgements

The Daily Grind case draws on information contained in:

"Hot Drinks in New Zealand", (April 2010), *Euromonitor*, retrieved from http://www.euromonitor.com/Hot_Drinks_in_New_Zealand

"Turning into a caffeine nation", by I. Chapple (22 May 2004), *The New Zealand Herald*, retrieved from http://www.nzherald.co.nz/business/news/article.cfm?c_id=3&objectid=3567948

"World coffee output seen up 19 pct in 2010/11 -NKG", (20 May 2010), *Reuters*, retrieved from http://uk.reuters.com/article/idUKN1920301420100519

The **Take Me Down to the Ball Game** case draws on information contained in:

"Baseball Ticket Pricing: 3 Teams, 3 Strategies . . . .1 Foul Ball!!!", by R. Thaler (14 May 2009), *Bleacher Report*, retrieved from http://bleacherreport.com/articles /174969-baseball-ticket-pricing-3-teams-3-strategies1-foul-ball

"Everything you ever wanted to know about baseball ticket prices", by D. Yanofsky (2 April 2013), *Quartz*, retrieved from http://qz.com/69086/everything-you -ever-wanted-to-know-about-baseball-ticket-prices/

"Fortunes uncertain, Red Sox offer deals", by A. Benjamin (25 March 2013), *Boston Globe*, retrieved from http://www.boston.com/sports/2013/03/25/red-sox -make-price-cuts-concessions-woo-fans/Rie2F457L2HqHTEWA6RGVL /story.html

"Is Dynamic Ticket Pricing Hurting MLB Attendance?", by L. Igel (8 June 2012), *Forbes*, retrieved from http://www.forbes.com/sites/sportsmoney/2012/06 /08/is-dynamic-ticket-pricing-hurting-mlb-attendance/

"Why Baseball Seats Should be Priced like Airline Tickets", by R. Mohammed (5 April 2013), *HBR Blog Network*, retrieved from http://blogs.hbr.org/2013/04 /why-baseball-tickets-should-be/

The **Grape Expectations** case draws on information contained in:

"Hunter Valley", Tourism Australia website located at http://www.australia.com /explore/states/nsw/hunter-valley.aspx

Hunter Valley Wine & Tourism Association website located at http://www .winecountry.com.au

Wyndham Estate website located at http://www.wyndhamestate.com/Our-Story /History

The **Auf Wiedersehen Pet** case draws on information contained in:

"Auf Wiedersehen jet: London to Frankfurt by train", by D. Milmo (19 September 2010), *The Guardian*, retrieved from http://www.guardian.co.uk/world/2010 /sep/19/london-frankfurt-train-high-speed

"Blitz-speed: Germans finally get the chance to cross the Channel as 200mph Berlin to London service is given the green light", by R. Massey (14 June 2013), *Daily Mail*, retrieved from http://www.dailymail.co.uk/news/article-2341847/Blitz -speed-Germans-finally-chance-cross-Channel-200mph-Berlin-London-service -given-green-light.html

This chapter covers the following topics:

▶ The role of promises
▶ How and why over-promising occurs
▶ The importance of ethics
▶ Sustainable marketing

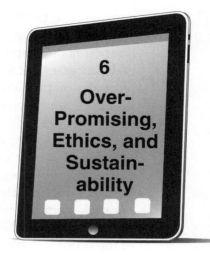

6
Over-Promising, Ethics, and Sustainability

Promises, Promises

Marketing is all about promises according to Grönroos (2009) – making them, meeting them, expectations and perceptions of them. From the customer's perspective it is the quality and delivery of the promises made about the performance or value of a product or service which influence their propensity to purchase and their level of satisfaction. He argues that for standardized products the conventional marketing management approach based on a mix of key variables may in some cases be sufficient to communicate and deliver the firm's promises. More complex, irregular, or intangible offerings present greater difficulties however. Even conventional offerings normally constitute more than the core product, with augmented and intangible elements such as credit, insurance, warranty, and after-sales service for which the promise is an intrinsic element. Levitt explains this as follows:

> When prospective customers can't experience the product in advance they are asked to buy what are essentially promises – promises of satisfaction. Even tangible, testable, feelable, smellable products are, before they are bought, largely just promises. (Levitt, 1981: 96)

Grönroos (2009) defines what he calls "promises management" as the process of "enabling, making and keeping promises", which goes a long way beyond the set of conventional marketing variables such as four or even seven "P" variables, the dominant approach of marketing management textbooks. He does accept that some marketing activities and processes do *aim* at making promises, such as communicating and pricing, but points out importantly that promises are often *kept* by other activities and processes such as order taking, deliveries, repair and maintenance, recovery of problems and mistakes, and call centre advice. Moreover, promises cannot be expected to be successfully kept by the firm unless its employees are willing and motivated to do so, thus enhancing the role of internal marketing activities (Berry, 1981; Ballantyne, 2003) for promise delivery. However, enabling promise delivery also requires more resources than just employees, such as goods, IT systems, physical resources and information, and also external actors such as customers themselves and network partners who have to be developed in ways that support the fulfilment of promises. Thus "enabling promises" becomes an integral part of the process of making and keeping promises.

A further issue is that keeping promises may be complicated by the different perceptions of the promise made by the marketer and the customer and indeed by different customers. This highlights the critical role of expectations in promises management which may vary from person to person and from situation to situation. This has been well documented in services marketing research (e.g. Bitner, 1995) where for example customers may have implicit expectations as well explicit ones or "silent" expectations which do not transform into explicit ones until customers experience the product. Also, some expectations are actually unrealistic therefore some customers are bound to become disappointed. So, it is not the promises made themselves that should be kept, but the individual customers' expectations that are created by these promises.

For these reasons authors such as Colonius (1983) and Grönroos (2009) regard the promise concept as central to value creation as the goal for marketing, including promise making and promise keeping and as a prerequisite for the enabling of promises. Expectations that are created by promises must subsequently be realized and delivered by providing resources and processes – goods, services, information and people, systems, infrastructures, physical resources, and interactions between the customer and these resources and processes as well as by mobilizing customers as a resource in the purchasing and usage processes. Customers must be able to use goods and services and information as well as to handle systems and infrastructures in order to create value and fulfil their expectations created by the original promise. This approach can be contrasted with the conventional marketing mix management focus on a list of variables for decision making. Promises management is a process in which there are "no specified marketing variables" (Grönroos, 2009: 352). Any list such as the 4Ps will eventually be rendered obsolete and tends to turn into a fixed guideline. On the contrary, promise management has no list of variables; it prescribes what should be planned and implemented in the marketing effort as any resource, system, or activity that supports customers' value creation processes by making promises, enabling these processes, and fulfilling expectations created by them.

So anything can be a marketing resource as long as it influences the customers' willingness to buy and their perception of how value is created in their processes. This will vary from industry to industry, from customer to customer, and one single organizational function cannot take responsibility for all of the promises made in the management process. Making promises can sometimes be handled by one single function but keeping promises will normally be the responsibility of several functions. Therefore, many organizational departments have to take a customer focus and take responsibility for marketing when it is viewed as promise management.

So, promises management is first and foremost a holistic organization-wide process which extends beyond the functional department labelled "marketing" involving the entire organization. But there is evidence that this idealistic picture of marketing organization and management is rarely achieved in practice. This is illustrated by Brown's (2005) findings regarding top managers' comments on the importance of the customer to the firm. He reports that marketing and sales seem to have a major role in making promises to customers and generating new business, whereas the keeping of promises and building customer loyalty is "typically considered the responsibility of others in the enterprise" (Brown, 2005: 3). If this represents top business attitudes and behaviour more generally, the implication is that marketers are given or accept responsibility for tactical tasks of persuading customers to buy, including promising making, but the tasks involved in meeting and delivering promises to customers is assigned to other organizational functions. It is clear how this split in responsibly for the promise management process can easily lead to circumstances where from the customer point of view the organization as a whole fails to deliver on the promises made by the marketing department – in other words "over-promising".

The Truth is Out There

One reason for over-promising has been discussed already, i.e. when managerial responsibility for promise management is unclear and/or there is a lack of organizational integration which results in a split in the promise management process between the making of promises and their delivery. But there may also be other causes of excessive promising which are consequences of particular modern marketing activities. Often consumer marketing, in particular in promotions and events, aims to add excitement and glamour to everyday products and stimulate desire in jaded consumers. In doing so however there are several ways in which enthusiastic marketing activities can result in unrealistic customer expectations or over-promising. These include examples such as the following.

1. Many industries with "fast moving consumer goods" are built on customers' continual dissatisfaction with the old, such as entertainment, fashion, and clothing. One marketing strategy for these firms is to attempt to make consumers *dissatisfied* with existing products, then to instil a desire for stimulation of the new and thus create demand for new products. Familiarity breeds discontent. The result is potentially to create continually rising expectations as to the superiority of the new over the old which it replaces and to which it can be directly compared by the customers.

2. The hundreds of adverts, pop-ups, clichés, and product placements to which consumers are exposed every day can cease to amuse, become repetitious and tedious, or just not noticed at all. Some advertisers therefore try vying for consumers' attention by presenting more and more outrageous claims for their products and services. Although many of these claims are deliberately ridiculous, humorous, or ironic and not meant to be taken seriously, not all consumers may get the joke. The message may not be taken seriously but because the information about the product is inflated or unclear, for some of the audience this may serve to raise expectations as to what will be delivered when the product is purchased.

3. Products are becoming increasingly standardized in design, manufacturing, raw materials, supply sourcing, and components. For example VAG manufacture Volkswagen, Skoda, Audi, and SEAT marques in which most parts and components are interchangeable; only the brands and the prices differ for the "target segments". This means that consumer experiences too are becoming more and more standardized (Ritzer, 1998) despite apparent competition and choice in most markets. Within a given product class there is little to differentiate offerings except the brand, perhaps explaining the increased role of branding in consumer marketing in recent years. If the brand itself constitutes the major difference, it may promise more symbolic differentiation from

the competition than the very similar tangible product can deliver, thus creating unrealizable expectations for consumers.

4. Consumers normally expect that having purchased a product the benefit will be delivered to them without much effort on their part. Recently, however, more work has been required on the part of consumers themselves in order for them to realize or "co-create" the value from the products and services they purchase (Vargo and Lusch, 2008). In some cases consumption has become more like work involving effort, decisions, transport, queuing, and taking up valuable free time (Zwick, Bonsu, and Darmody, 2008). With this extended consumer role in self-service, DIY, "shadow" work co-creation, and co-production, it is not surprising that consumers' expectations are not met if they do not realize their role or are not prepared to contribute sufficiently to the value creation process.

5. Along with products and services, consumers are bombarded with opportunities for social interactivity of various types, like brand communities, online forums, twiteratti exchanges, value co-creation, and media relations. They are encouraged to join, get involved, engage, co-create, communicate, dialogue, and participate. These exhortations and invitations can convey the promise of engaging post-purchase social involvement with other consumers as well as identifying with the brand. However, many such online networks, brand communities, and consumer tribes are not real tribes or communities in any original ethnographic or sociological sense. And by no means all are consumer initiated social phenomena or communities. Indeed, most are artificially created for marketing purposes, not as social movements; therefore some consumers may feel disappointed or let down by the promise of exciting post-purchase interaction with other consumers.

So what happens when consumers' promises are not met? According to Hirschman (1970) they have two main choices – to complain or to switch their custom elsewhere. She provided a theoretical foundation known as the "exit, voice and loyalty framework" which when applied to the case of promises which are not met challenges the traditional view that consumers will simply switch from one supplier to one offering higher quality. Hirschman discovered that the dissatisfied customer does not always exit the brand but instead uses "voice" to articulate their dissatisfaction and feed this back to the supplier. As a result, exit and voice are viewed as the methods by which wayward organizations are made aware of customer complaints such as non-delivery of promises, and can amend their product and service operations accordingly.

Singh's (1990) study supports Hirschman's notion that customers would not exit if they could be assured their voice would bring about the desired results. When customers voice their complaints, management has the opportunity to recover the customer's goodwill and many customers have unsuccessfully complained prior to deciding to exit. This implies that the management of customer complaints by the company, and how it is perceived by customers, can be a critical element of the promise management process which if implemented successfully can potentially recover customers' loyalty even following cases of failure to deliver on promises. This application of the exit voice loyalty framework to promise management is only a second best remedial solution. It is far better for the firm not to over-promise in the first place and to ensure that their delivery process ensures that promises to customers are kept.

The next section will examine the importance of ethics in marketing as an over-arching framework or philosophy which can mitigate against mal-practices which can mislead or over-promise to customers.

Honest Guv!

Ethics is the branch of moral philosophy that deals with moral judgements, standards, and rules of conduct and it involves perceptions and attitudes regarding right and wrong. After more than 60 years as a professional and academic discipline it can be now argued that the ethical basis of marketing theory and practice is moving towards more complex modes of analysis and understanding. Even traditional marketing textbooks such as Kotler's (1967) original *Marketing Management, Planning and Control* take into account a wider set of alternative values beyond the utilitarian, free-market, consumer choice bases for ethical decisions. One of the first seminal articles on marketing ethics was a review by Murphy and Laczniak (1981) who nevertheless concluded that "the function within business firms most often charged with ethical abuse is marketing". More recently, as commentators still remind us, marketing continues to have a bad name. In common parlance it is often used as a byword for deception and exploitation and many see it as an engine driving forward materialism and excess consumption (Barber, 2007).

Most early work in this area studied ethics from a normative perspective, meaning that they were concerned with "constructing and justifying the moral standards and codes that one ought to follow" (Hunt and Vitell, 1986). Chonko and Hunt (1985) looked at both the nature and extent

136

of marketers' ethical problems and examined the effectiveness of top management actions and codes of ethics in promoting ethical behaviour. They found that bribery, fairness, honesty, price, product, personnel, confidentiality, advertising, manipulation of data, and purchasing were the major ethical issues facing marketers. Later Gaski (1999) conducted a survey to identify the normative ethical frameworks from a review of the previous twenty-five years of marketing literature and found that there were surprisingly few distinct ethical recommendations stipulated in such codes. He concludes that most so-called ethical guidelines for marketers are mere restatements of other principles or bland legalistic definitions or statements of economic self-interest; there is a " ... total redundancy and superfluity of marketing ethics ... a vacant construct, representing nothing beyond what is already contained elsewhere" (Gaski, 1999).

Laczniak and Murphy (2008) take a different ethical perspective than the normative framework by examining distributive justice in marketing by employing Rawls' (1999) notion of fairness to ask the question: whose conception of fairness should be used to settle competing marketing claims? The model which has been applied most extensively is the Hunt-Vitell (1986) "general theory" of marketing ethics in which both deontological (ethical rules) and teleological (end results) arguments were used to ground their theory.

It's Not Easy Being Green

There is widespread criticism of the traditional, managerial, anthropocentric, and consumerist marketing, which many argue is fatally implicated in the waste, destruction, and excess that many environmentalists see as the consequence of the modern market and consumption system. The traditional language of marketing employs the grammar of the mechanistic world, where matter is regarded as inert and mute, passive and exploitable (Kajzer-Mitchell and Saren, 2000). It speaks the language of material possession, individuality, and newness, of the assumption of unlimited growth and the accumulation of waste. The key to success is through growth in sales and material output and the primary purpose of marketing is to design strategic plans and sales forecasts to support this goal. Traditional marketing theory is predicated on the central role of the product in the exchange process and the notion of the "product concept" as a distinct entity and object of exchange. This has led to fragmentation of elements in the environment and treating resources as if they consisted of separate parts, to be exploited by different interest groups (Capra, 1983).

Books such as Fuller's *Sustainable Marketing: Managerial-Ecological Issues* (1999) have begun to introduce notions of sustainability into marketing. Fuller argues that sustainability is "a logical extension of contemporary marketing … sustainable marketing is structured around the traditional '4Ps' of marketing and explains how marketing mix decisions can and do influence environmental outcomes". In this respect he appears to think that managers can simply "bolt on", as it were, a "green extension" to the basic marketing concept and the traditional 4Ps approach to marketing and thereby achieve sustainability. However a truly sustainable approach to marketing requires more than just making products "green" or environmentally "friendly". It requires a completely new way of thinking about the role of marketing and the ethical framework and basis for marketing decision making.

For more radical advocates of sustainable marketing such as Kilbourne, McDonagh, and Prothero (1997), nothing short of a revolutionary reassessment of basic marketing ideas, techniques, orientation, and practice is required to achieve the undeniably radical goal of sustainability. Senge and Carstedt (2001) argue that it was the metaphor of the machine that marketers employed in the industrial age whereas it is the image of living systems that are required in order to inspire a truly sustainable "post-industrial" marketing. In this new age the roles of people, society, and technologies all have to change fundamentally. Firms must also be increasingly flexible and creative in finding new ways of doing business, which are consistent with an uncertain world and the need for a commitment towards sustainable development. In some ways change may be seen as a measure of sustainability and organizations in the future will need to embrace change and uncertainty as a vital management function.

Thus, a fully sustainable view of marketing not only has to take into account the ecological management of resources in meeting customers and firm needs, but also must pay greater attention to organizational–environmental configurations that are dynamic, flexible, and provide space for dealing with uncertainty. Sustainable marketing requires a critical re-examination of the concept of the marketing and environment interface, and the components that make it up. In light of contemporary – and future – environmental problems and marketing's contribution to them, there is a need for marketing to account for the wider context of its relationship with the natural environment of which it is a part. One way to reconsider this is by examining the nature and characteristics of living ecological systems, from disciplines such as ecology and biology, popular science, environmental management, environmental philosophy, and design (Tsui, 1999). Thus one essential requirement of a more sustainable approach to marketing not only concerns efficient resource management, but also learning to think in new ways; generating a new more adaptable marketing mindset that thrives in uncertain and complex conditions.

This chapter has discussed the phenomenon of over-promising in marketing and related this to marketing ethics and contemporary issues of sustainability. All these considerations point to the need for a new dynamic approach to re-conceptualizing and reorienting marketing activities that alters the way marketing theory and practice look at products, brands, consumption, consumers, and relationships, built upon ecological principles, that is informed by a strong set of ethical values.

Case 6-1 Horses for Courses

In January 2013, Irish food inspectors found traces of horsemeat in frozen beef burgers sold by Tesco, Iceland, and Lidl supermarkets. During the following few months more testing was carried out and more products labelled as beef were removed from the supermarket shelves. In some cases, products were found to contain 100% horsemeat. More brands became affected, including Asda, Burger King, and Birds Eye. The supermarket Aldi too found horsemeat in their products, blaming their French supplier Comigel. Findus Foods, whose product was sourced from France, was found to have 100% horsemeat in their frozen meals. The scandal also affected schools, hospitals, takeaways, and catering firms.

Following the news of the scandal, burger sales decreased by 41% of volume and frozen meals fell to 15% by April 2013. The Food Standards Agency began an investigation but found that the supply chain, where the labelling takes place, included up to 40 different suppliers. The supply chain is highly valuable, multinational, and lightly regulated making it easy for criminal activity to take place. Horsemeat, when produced as pet food, fetches £1 per kilogram; but if it is relabelled as fit for human consumption, the figure is £4 per kilogram.

During the investigation the leading players have shifted the blame around so there have been no criminal proceedings. The supermarkets have apologized but have mitigated responsibility by saying they didn't know. However, they have promised to make significant changes.

Questions

1. *Should customers trust the supermarkets' promise? What do they need to do?*
2. *How does the power of the supermarkets affect regulation in the industry?*
3. *How could independent butchers respond?*

◄◄◄ Some Ideas

1. *Should customers trust the supermarkets' promise? What do they need to do?*

Essential to the notion of a promise is trust. Some argue that trust is an essential component of a strong brand, so the question arises as to whether the consumer trusts supermarkets. Certainly trust has to be rebuilt. The best possible scenario would be for supermarkets to offer a money back guarantee. This would mean that they would have to implement stringent controls. On the other hand, the supermarket may not want to incur the expense of testing the product and choose to pass this cost on to the supplier. However, the relationship is between the supermarket and the consumer so there is an obligation to own the problem.

2. *How does the power of the supermarkets affect regulation in the industry?*

Supermarkets put pressure on suppliers to provide products at the cheapest rate because they want to position themselves as being competitive. The suppliers need the supermarkets as in many cases it is their only source of distribution therefore supermarkets have high bargaining power. Also, if the government puts pressure on supermarkets to test products, the supermarkets respond by saying they will increase prices. The last thing a government wants is inflation directly impacting households.

3. *How could independent butchers respond?*

Independent butchers should advertise that they can guarantee the source of their meat. By going to Smithfield, or the equivalent, to purchase their meat they know what farm the animal comes from. They are in a position to market this aspect in terms of quality assurance. For some customers having this peace of mind is worth paying extra.

▶▶▶

Case Notes:

American Apparel took the humble T-shirt, a basic clothing item, and transformed it into a fashion icon. The company grew by making cotton basics and currently produces 55,000 different products, manufacturing approximately a million pieces a week.

An important brand attribute is that the products are manufactured in the USA. The CEO has resisted moving production off-shore to a low-cost location, which makes the CEO a hero in many people's eyes. The manufacturing warehouse is in downtown Los Angeles where the majority of the workers are immigrants who are paid twice the minimum wage, offered full family healthcare, and are allowed free international telephone calls, which can be made in work time.

The marketing campaigns have also added to the brand essence. The ads capture young models in casual situations, in moments of "vulnerable sensuality". Unlike a lot of fashion photographs these have not been airbrushed but have a raw edge to them. The ads have added to the debate in the fashion industry as to what counts as too sexy.

The CEO, Dov Charney, is a Canadian who founded the company. His image is part of the brand's DNA. He is known to walk through the factory in his underpants and attend meetings in a thong. At times he wears only a sock, which is not worn on his foot. Charney is an exhibitionist, which you may expect in the fashion industry, but his carnality is sometimes over the top. Recently three employees have filed sexual harassment lawsuits against him, but none have ended up in court.

The other side to Charney is that he is a progressive social libertine. He wants to liberalize immigration and believes in workers' rights. He insists on paying fair wages and refuses to outsource manufacturing. He sees American Apparel as a heritage brand, which stands for everything American: liberty, property, and the pursuit of happiness.

In 2010 the auditor of American Apparel, Deloitte and Touche, resigned their position due to "material weaknesses" in the company accounts. This action nearly put American Apparel into bankruptcy. The company lost money for three years after an immigration investigation in 2009 found 2,000 workers did not have proper documentation. The company was fined $38,000 and 2,000 workers were dismissed, which led to poor production.

Questions

1. *Is Dov's behaviour acceptable?*
2. *Do CEOs have to behave in accordance with a code of ethics?*

Case Notes:

Case 6-3 Washes Whiter

Unilever is an Anglo/Dutch multinational that sells consumer goods in 170 countries. The company's brands include Dove Soap, Ben & Jerry's ice cream, Flora margarine, Hellmann's mayonnaise, Vaseline, Persil, Marmite, PG Tips, Pot Noodles, and Colman's mustard. It is estimated that over two billion people use their products every day.

In 2010 the company launched their Sustainable Living Plan. The aim of the plan was to grow revenues to exceed $100 billion by doubling sales, and to halve environmental impact over a 10-year period. The plan included cutting the company's greenhouse gas emissions, waste, and water used in manufacturing their products but also modifying the impact of suppliers and consumers on the environment. In terms of a product life cycle, e.g. Persil, it is estimated that two-thirds of greenhouse gas emissions and half of the water used is due to consumer usage. Therefore the task was to cut the environmental footprint across the value chain of all its product offerings.

The company set about improving the nutritional quality of its food products by reducing the amount of salt, saturated fat, and sugar, along with the amount of calories, in each serve. By working with agencies such as Oxfam and the Rainforest Alliance, Unilever also wants to link more than 500,000 small farmers and small distributors in developing countries into the company's supply chain.

Other initiatives include the reduction of diarrhoea, which is the world's second biggest cause of infant mortality, by teaching consumers in Asia, Africa, and Latin America to regularly wash their hands. It also wants to make drinking water safer in developing countries with the use of a home water purifier.

The company insists that the plan is not just a PR exercise but the implementation of a new business model. Not only does the company wish to maximize financial returns but also social and environmental returns. The rationale is based on the belief that consumers make choices to buy environmentally friendly products, which over time can lead to a competitive advantage. Also, implementation of the new business model helps improve the battered image of big business.

Two years into the plan's implementation, Unilever has made solid progress by helping more than a billion people improve their health and wellbeing. The company has reached 224 million people with a programme to reduce diarrhoea disease by encouraging handwashing with soap, providing safe drinking water and promoting oral health. The handwashing campaign to persuade 71 million people in Africa and South

Asia to wash their hands before meals has resulted in sales growth of their Lifebuoy soap reaching double figures. Another campaign, which reached 49 million people, was to persuade children to brush their teeth day and night by brushing with their dad thus making it fun rather than a chore, increased the sales of Unilever's Signal toothpaste by 22%.

The plan to source 100% sustainable raw materials by 2020 is progressing well, with 36% currently being reached. The company has also helped 450,000 tea farmers to implement sustainable practices. However, the third aim of halving the environmental footprint in the value chain has been hard to accomplish. To achieve this aim the company believes there needs to be a more coordinated effort between companies, governments, NGOs, and consumers.

Changing consumer habits is the most difficult. Some change is relatively easy, like producing soap powder capsules so consumers don't over-use detergent in their washing machines. Other behaviour, however, is a little more difficult to change. For example, through consumer research Unilever found British consumers took eight minutes to shower and not the five minutes they claim in verbal responses to researchers. Despite development of a hair shampoo that was quicker to rinse, thus saving time and water, consumers still took eight minutes. Some habits are hard to change!

Questions

1. *Critique Unilever's brand promise. Is it credible?*
2. *How effective is Unilever's sustainability programme? Will it stand the test of time?*

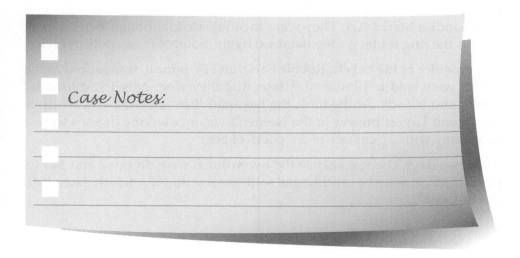

Case Notes:

Many companies decide to sponsor events or organizations for a number of reasons, such as the ability to entertain clients or to build an association between the brand and the activity, e.g. golf. Another major reason is to obtain media exposure thereby cutting through the clutter of traditional advertising mediums.

Sponsorship can be big business. For example, Heineken's deal with UEFA for the Champion League rights is $70 million per year. Recently Miller-Coors shifted its focus to ice hockey where it pays $53.5 million per year for a deal with the National Hockey League. AB InBev, the maker of Budweiser and related brands, is a big investor in sponsorship. In 2010 Bud Light paid a staggering $1 billion for a six-year deal for National Football League rights, whereas Budweiser's rights to the Major League Baseball cost only $20 million per year.

With big money changing hands, the rights of the sponsor need to be protected. Therefore, any ambush marketing activity needs to be dealt with seriously. Ambush marketing is when a company which is not an official sponsor, attempts to take advantage of an event. For example, in 1994 American Express ran ads claiming Americans did not need "Visas" to attend the Winter Olympics in Norway.

It is no surprise that Budweiser and FIFA acted quickly when they were ambushed at the FIFA World Cup in South Africa in 2010, as Budweiser had paid FIFA $25 million per year for the exclusive sponsorship rights. The ambush happened at the Netherlands versus Denmark match, where 36 blondes undressed to reveal orange (Netherland's national colour) mini skirts showing a small Bavaria beer logo. Whilst the cameras were on the young women, they were evicted and arrested under the Contravention of Merchandise Marks Act. They were then released, although two women, seen as the ring leaders, were detained by the South African police service.

The provider of the tickets, Robbie Earle, an ITV pundit, was sacked as the tickets were sold to him on the basis that they were only to be used by family and friends. At the time, the Bavarian Brewing company, which is the second largest brewer in the Netherlands, insisted the dresses were a give-away with a purchase of six-packs of beer.

After two days, charges against the two women were dropped and Bavarian Brewery reached a confidential settlement with FIFA which extends to the end of 2022.

Questions

1. *What are the pros and cons for a company to conduct ambush marketing?*
2. *What are the ethical considerations?*

Case Notes:

Ballantyne, D. (2003) A Relationship-mediated Theory of Internal marketing, *European Journal of Marketing*, 37(9): 1242–1260.

Barber, B. R. (2007) *Consumed: How Markets Corrupt Children, Infantilise Adults and Swallow Citizens Whole*. New York: WW Norton.

Berry, L. L. (1981) The Employee as Customer, *Journal of Retailing*, 3 (March): 33–40.

Bitner, M. J. (1995) Building Service Relationships: It's all about promises', *Journal of the Academy of Marketing Science*, 23(4): 246–251.

Brown, S. W. (2005) When Executives Speak, We Should Listen and Act Differently, *Journal of Marketing*, 69 (October): 2–4.

Capra, F. (1983) *The Turning Point*. London: HarperCollins.

Chonko, L. B. and Hunt, S. D. (1985) Ethics and Marketing Management: An Empirical Examination, *Journal of Business Research*, 13 (August): 339–359.

Colonius, H. (1983) *"On the promise concept"*, unpublished discussion paper, Hanken Swedish School of Economics Finland, Helsinki.

Fuller, D. (1999) *Sustainable Marketing: Managerial-Ecological Issues*. London: Sage Publications.

Gaski, John F. (1999) Does Marketing Ethics Really Have Anything to Say? – A Critical Commentary of the Literature, *Journal of Business Ethics*, 18 (February): 315–334.

Grönroos, C. (2009) Marketing as Promise Management: Regaining customer management for marketing, *Journal of Business and Industrial Marketing*, 24(5/6): 351–359.

Hirschman, A. (1970) *Exit Voice & Loyalty – Responses to Decline in Firms, Organisations and States*. Cambridge, MA: Harvard University Press.

Hunt, S. D. and Vitell, S. (1986) A General Theory of Marketing Ethics, *Journal of Macromarketing*, 6 (Spring): 5–16.

Kajzer-Mitchell, I. and Saren, M. (2000) The Living Product: A critical re-examination of the product concept' in *The Business Strategy and Environment Conference Proceeding*, University of Leeds, ERP Environment, 219–226.

Kilbourne, W., McDonagh, P. and Prothero, A. (1997) Sustainable Consumption and the Quality of Life: A macroeconomic challenge to the dominant social paradigm, *Journal of Macromarketing*, 17, 4–24.

Kotler, P. (1967) *Marketing Management: Analysis, Planning, Implementation and Control*. Englewood Cliffs, NJ: Prentice Hall Inc.

Laczniak, G.R. and Murphy, P.E. (2008) Distributive Justice: Pressing Questions, Emerging Directions and the Promise of a Rawlsian Analysis, *Journal of Macromarketing*, 18 (March): 5–11.

Levitt, T. (1981) Marketing Intangible Products and Product Intangibles, *Harvard Business Review*, 59 (May–June): 94–102.

Murphy, P. and Laczniak, G.R. (1981) Marketing Ethics: A Review with Implication for Managers, Educators and Researchers. In Enis, B. M. and Roering, K. J. (eds), *Review of Marketing*. Chicago, IL: American Marketing Association, 107–124.

Rawls, J. (1999) *A Theory of Justice*, revised edn. Cambridge, MA: Harvard University Press.

Ritzer, G. (1998) *The McDonaldization Thesis: Explorations and Extensions*. London: Sage.

Senge, P. and Carstedt, G. (2001) Innovating Our Way to the Next Industrial Revolution, MIT *Sloan Management Review*, Winter, 24–37.

Singh, J. (1990) Voice, Exit and Negative Word of Mouth Behaviour: An investigation across three service categories, *Journal of the Academy of Marketing Science*, 18(1): 1–15.

Tsui, E. (1999) *Evolutionary Architecture. Nature as a basis for design*. New York: Wiley.

Vargo, S. L. and Lusch, R. F. (2008) Service-dominant Logic: Continuing the Evolution, *Journal of the Academy of Marketing Science*, 36(1): 1–10.

Zwick, D., Bonsu, S.K. and Darmody, A. (2008) Putting Consumers to Work: "Co-creation" and new marketing govern-mentality, *Journal of Consumer Culture*, 8(2): 163–196.

Case Acknowledgements

The **Horses for Courses** case draws on information contained in:

"Aldi confirms up to 100% horsemeat in beef products", (9 February 2013), *The Guardian*, retrieved from http://www.theguardian.com/business/2013/feb/09/aldi-100-percent-horsemeat-beef-products

"Horsemeat scandal: How tastes changed", by B. Morris (14 January 2014), *BBC News*, retrieved from http://www.bbc.co.uk/news/business-25715666

"Horsemeat scandal: timeline", by F. Lawrence (10 May 2013), *The Guardian*, retrieved from http://www.theguardian.com/uk/2013/may/10/horsemeat-scandal-timeline-investigation

"Horsemeat scandal: where did the 29% horse in your Tesco burger come from?", by F. Lawrence (22 October 2013), *The Guardian*, retrieved from http://www.theguardian.com/uk-news/2013/oct/22/horsemeat-scandal-guardian-investigation-public-secrecy

The **Rise and Fall** case draws on information contained in:

"American Apparel CEO Dov Charney: A Tarnished Hero", by J. Millman, S. Ghebremedhin, and L. Effron (27 April 2012), *ABC News*, retrieved from http://abcnews.go.com/Business/american-apparel-ceo-dov-charney-tarnished-hero/story?id=16229958

"American Apparel CEO: Tattered, but Not Torn", (10 April 2012), *CNBC*, retrieved from http://www.cnbc.com/id/47007775

"The rise and fall of American Apparel", by A. Hill (25 August 2010), *The Guardian*, retrieved from http://www.guardian.co.uk/business/2010/aug/25/rise-fall-american-apparel

The **Washes Whiter** case draws on information contained in:

"Profile of a Sustainable Brand Leader, Part Two: Unilevers Sustainable Living Plan", by L. Kaye (26 November 2012), *Sustainable Brands*, retrieved from http://www.sustainablelifemedia.com/news_and_views/articles/profile-sustainable-brand-leader-part-2-unilever-sustainable-living-plan

"Unilever plans to double its turnover while halving its environmental impact", by F. Pearce (23 July 2013), *The Telegraph*, retrieved from http://www.telegraph.co.uk/earth/environment/10188164/Unilever-plans-to-double-its-turnover-while-halving-its-environmental-impact.html

"Unilever Sustainable Living Plan" retrieved from http://www.unilever.com/sustainable-living/uslp/index.aspx

OVER-PROMISING, ETHICS, AND SUSTAINABILITY

"Unilever Sustainable Living Plan: the progress made in two years", (22 April 2013), *The Guardian*, retrieved from http://www.theguardian.com/sustainable -business/unilever-sustainable-living-plan-progress

"Unilever unveils ambitious long term sustainability programme", by J. Finch (15 November 2010), *The Guardian*, retrieved from http://www.theguardian.com /business/2010/nov/15/unilever-sustainable-living-plan

The **Foul Play** case draws on information contained in:

"Beer Brand Sponsorship Strategies", *IMR Publications*, retrieved from http: //www.imrpublications.com/Free-Samples.aspx?sid=38&rid=2

"How ambush marketing ambushed sport", by J. Kelly (17 June 2010), *BBC News*, retrieved from http://news.bbc.co.uk/2/hi/8743881.stm

"World Cup 2010: Bavaria beer stunt organisers arrested", by M. Evans (16 June 2010), *The Telegraph*, retrieved from http://www.telegraph.co.uk/sport/football /world-cup/7832413/World-Cup-2010-Bavaria-beer-stunt-organisers -arrested.html

"World Cup 2020: Women arrested over 'ambush marketing' freed on bail", (16 June 2010), *The Guardian*, retrieved from http://www.theguardian.com/football /2010/jun/16/fifa-world-cup-ambush-marketing

This chapter covers the following topics:

- ▶ Strategic brand management
- ▶ Types of brands
- ▶ Semiotics
- ▶ Brand extensions
- ▶ Brand equity

**7
Successful
Brand
Building**

Brands play an important part in consumer society and over the last 20 years there has been interest from both academics and practitioners on the topic of strategic brand management. This has arisen because the brand is seen as an important asset for the firm so needs to be carefully managed. There have been a number of reasons why brand management has become a strategic issue. First, there is little growth in many markets so it becomes more important to make sure customers remain loyal to the brand. Secondly, costs to launch a new brand have increased significantly, so it makes sense to utilize existing brands in the company's portfolio.

Another reason is the short-term focus taken by managers resulting in tactical decisions being made at the expense of the brand's long-term future. Also, brands in the 1990s were used for financial reasons which forced managers' attention on equity of the brand (see the What's it Worth? section in this chapter for further discussion of brand equity). Finally, and perhaps the most important for the FMCG market, is the increased dominance of supermarket chains, with their bargaining power and the growth of own labels, which are given prominent shelf space and provide lower prices to customers. Many manufacturers are put in the situation where they have to consider manufacturing for own labels, at the expense of cannibalizing their own brand.

Whose Needs are Being Met?

There are a number of benefits which can be viewed from either the customer's point of view or from the firm's point of view (de Chernatony and McDonald, 1998). The consumer benefits from relying on a strong brand because it delivers consistent quality time after time. Second, a brand – especially with supermarket shopping – saves the consumer time as they don't have to stop and think about which brand to buy. Third, strong brands are risk reducers, and this applies especially in the electronics market. Fourth, strong brands in what can be called representation products help define the personality of the user through symbolic interactionism. Finally, strong brands develop their own personality which allows customers to easily recall them; consequently they are always in the evoked set.

From a firm's point of view, the development of a strong brand accrues many advantages. First, they are favoured by the retailer as the brand builds foot traffic. Second, a strong brand is resistant to price competition and will obtain high prices, better margins, and/or more volume. Third, strong brands enjoy a higher level of loyalty. Fourth, strong brands are forgiven by customers for their mistakes if their problem is quickly acknowledged and corrected. Finally, strong brands can be extended in other categories.

Vive la Différence

There are different types of brands, each with their own defining characteristics. High Street brands, such as Vodafone and Coca-Cola, are consumed or used by a large part of the market and have a distinct logo, style, taste, and in some cases provide a unique service. Household brands, including FMCG and consumer durables, are consumed or purchased frequently and can be found in supermarkets and large stores, for example Anchor butter or Samsung electronics. An umbrella brand is where there is a parent company with either sub-brands, for example Lever Brothers and Persil, or product brands, such as Virgin and Virgin Records. Not all brands want consumers to make the connection with the parent brand, for example Lancôme is owned by L'Oréal but the two brands are kept separate as they serve different market segments.

Luxury brands are based on exclusivity and are designed specifically for a market where status is seen as important. Such brands become fashion labels and obtain a price premium, for example, Jimmy Choo shoes. At the other end of the continuum are own label brands, sometimes called house or home brands, which are owned by the supermarket or store. They tend to be cheaper than household brands and positioned with better shelf space (eye level) and sales are generated by the use of sales promotions.

Corporate brands comprise a distinct category of brands as they help distinguish one company from another and as such they are applicable to public, private, and not-for-profit organizations, as well as trade associations and alliances. According to Gyrd-Jones et al (2013) corporate brands can be described as the sum value of an organization. Whereas a product brand uses the marketing mix with an emphasis on communications, the corporate brand utilitizes total communications, and is influenced by staff and the CEO's statements and behaviours; consequently marketing activities are a secondary influence. With a product brand the responsibility lies with the brand manager, whereas the CEO has responsibility to the corporate brand. Another contrasting dimension is that with a product brand the focus is on customers whereas the corporate brand focuses on multiple stakeholders.

A corporate brand creates awareness and recognition via the use of a logo, but they are more than just the logo as other important factors play a part. The corporate brand is CEO led and the role can influence not only customers but the other multiple stakeholders. Balmer (2001) argues that by managing the unique perception of the company a competitive advantage can be obtained. To achieve this there must be an alignment with the corporate identity.

Accordingly to Balmer (2001) corporate identity has an innate character which gives organizations their distinctiveness. The study of corporate identity has been based on many disciplines, for example, design, brand management, strategy, organizational culture, and communications, which has led to many diverse perspectives. However, from a marketing perspective, corporate identity comprises a mix of elements, both tangible and intangible, including strategy, scope, structure, staff, and culture, and as such it evolves over time. The task of the CEO is to seek alignment of these many elements. As Gyrd-Jones (2013) notes, often corporate identity is narrowly focused through maintaining visual cohesion by concentrating on logos and slogans, without realizing that staff and multiple stakeholders also contribute to the corporate identity, which can be a problem if the organization has diverse stakeholders with different agendas and also sub-cultures within the organization. If the corporate identity is imposed by management the identity is difficult to integrate throughout the organization, therefore a bottom up collaborative approach may achieve better results.

Whilst corporate identity attempts to answer the "what are we?" question, and use the answer as an attempt to communicate this to the various stakeholders, corporate image is what is perceived by the audiences after filtering the different dimensions. Obviously this can lead to a disjoint so the alignment between corporate identity and corporate image has to be continually managed.

Service brands are closely linked to corporate brands (de Chernatony and Cottam, 2008). With service brands consumers are active participants not only with respect to the technical outcome but also their involvement with the service process. Therefore a service brand has both functional and emotional values which, when combined, promise a particular experience.

What is important is the role of culture within the organization. The shared values and beliefs determine the behaviour of the service providers. This means the values of the employees are linked to the brand value. Therefore a service brand should strengthen their internal corporate culture so as to lead to an increase in employee service motivation, consequently leading to customer satisfaction. To achieve this the company may need to apply the servuction model, where touch points (where customers form impressions) are identified, service providers are trained and provided with appropriate scripts, and the process is blueprinted.

According to de Chernatony and McDonald (1998) brands have eight roles. First the brand can be a sign of ownership, signalling to the market who owns the brand. Second the role of the brand acts as a differentiating device where added values are communicated to customers, indicating the benefit being offered. The third role is where the brand acts as a functional device indicating benefits based on a rational appeal. Fourth, the brand is a symbolic device which expresses something about the user, whereby the brand personality matches the actual or desired self-concept. The fifth role is where the brand acts as a risk reducer, whether it be financial risk, service risk, or safety risk, including concerns at a personal level or concerns about harm to the environment. The sixth role is the brand being used as a shorthand device by consumers when purchasing, especially low involvement products. The brand helps consumers make decisions as the brand name is a substitute for essential information which is easy to retrieve. Another role for the brand is that of a legal device, where trademarks and registered logos protect the brand from counterfeit products. Finally, the brand can be used as a strategic device as it is recognized as an asset and over time a return on investment can be measured, which becomes an indication of brand strength.

Kotler and Keller (2012) use the notion of brand elements to describe the signs, slogans, and symbols that represent a brand. They postulate that there are six criteria to be considered when choosing a brand element:

1. Memorable – the element must be easily remembered, recognized, and recalled. This is important for the brand to be in the evoked set.

2. Meaningful – does the element link to the corresponding category? It would seem that this is not essential as successful brands do not necessarily denote their category, for example, Apple (laptops, computers, mobile phones), Orange (telecommunications), and Fonterra (global exporter of dairy products).

3. Likeable – this sign, symbol, slogan must resonate with customers.

4. Transferable – can the brand name be extended to other categories or translated into other languages without causing offence?

5. Adaptable – is it easy to modify the element over time?

6. Protectable – the legal protection of the signs, symbols, and slogans by way of trademarks etc. is important. The concept of "passing off" (does the element look like any others already in use?) should be carefully considered.

Overall it is important that the elements are meaningful and memorable for the intended audiences. However, the above approach is seen as a one-way communication process. Another approach to understand how brand names, signs, and symbols are viewed by customers is to utilize the concept of semiotics, which is the study of signs, in a generic sense, to help understand how consumers learn meanings. This is an outside-in approach with the analysis beginning with culture and not the consumer. The researcher is keen to understand the language, visual images, and signs that are used, either consciously or unconsciously, for people to communicate with each other. Therefore it is important to explore the cultural roles or codes which underpin communications.

Historically, there are two schools of semiotics (Lawes, 2002). Saussure, with an European background, based semiotics as an extension of linguistics, and thought that representation could be viewed as dyadic relationships between signified and signifier. This is in contrast to the work of the American, Pierce, who based his approach on philosophy. He claimed representation is best viewed as a triadic relationship between the object, the signifier, and the signified. In other words, a given reality is a process of representation based on the sign, the object, and the interpretant.

Marketing is divided between the two approaches. However it is thought that the triadic model is better as it broadens the scope and understanding of semiotics (de Lencastre and Corte-Real, 2010). The triadic approach avoids prescription by describing the model of the brand based on a historical-cultural-relational approach. The meaning of a sign is not universal as truth is culturally specific. The response to a sign is conditioned by lifestyle, values, way of thinking, and anything that contributes to a person's sense of self. Therefore reality is a social construction based on a system of signs, but any representation is triadic, as the sign is only one of the elements. Whilst it is tempting to see the organization as an object sending signs, it does not take into account that there are layers of signs, for example, the use of clothing generates signs, as does the use of the product. It is easy for a marketer to become "brand myopic" and treat the brand as just a label, thereby forgetting the triadic relationship. Therefore the organization does not have a brand, but the brand is supported by the organization. Managers don't determine the meaning but help customers co-create through the signs that are generated. For the marketer to understand their brand they must become familiar with the cultural landscape and how their brand is represented by the interactions of all actors – brand managers, customers, intermediaries, influencers, and other stakeholders.

To Boldly Go

A brand extension is the use of an established brand to name a product/service entering a new product category, as it can reduce the risk of launching a completely new brand. The hope is that the new brand can build on the associations of the parent brand and leverage marketing expertise, especially distribution links. However, a disadvantage of a brand extension is that the company forgoes the opportunity of building a new brand with its own equity. Also, brand dilution can occur when the associations get diminished in the minds of consumers. Another disadvantage is that the brand extension may harm the parent brand. A brand extension strategy is not guaranteed to succeed, as it has been reported that 84% of brand extensions fail (Torelli and Ahluwalia, 2012).

Aaker and Keller (1990) proposed that a brand extension works because there is a "fit" between the new brand and the parent brand. According to the authors, three factors determine the associations that are applicable to a new brand.

1. Strength of the parent brand associations: the stronger they are the more that they will carry over to the new brand.

2. Common link: if a new brand complements the parent brand either in use situations, for example, skiing and sunglasses; user type, for example skateboarders and surfers; or functional benefits, for example bank accounts and insurance, it is more likely that the brand extension will be successful.

3. Transferability: does the parent company have the technological know-how and expertise in the new category? Adidas has extended the brand name from running shoes to activewear but would customers buy an Adidas lasagne from the frozen food aisle?

However, although the concept of fit is important it is seen as being an inadequate concept to determine brand extension success. Völckner and Sattler (2006) reviewed the brand extensions literature and explored 22 brand extensions in the German FMCG market. They concluded that there are five important drivers of brand extension success. The first was fit, as described above. The second was the degree of marketing support given by the parent company to the brand extension. The third was the parent brand's strength in the market. The fourth was retailer acceptance, which was seen as critical, and finally the parent brand's experience in managing brand extensions.

What's it Worth?

In the 1980s Grand Metropolitan undertook a brand valuation of their recently acquired brands and placed the brand assets on their balance sheet. Hovis McDougall on the other hand placed their "home grown" brands on the balance sheet. By treating brands as an asset the companies decreased their debt-asset ratio thereby increasing their return on investment and allowing the company to obtain more finance. In 1990 the UK Accounting Standards Board decided that brand valuations, often carried out by consultants such as Interbrand, were unreliable so they stopped the practice. However, this has not stopped some companies continuing the evaluation exercise as an audit of their strategic management of the brand.

Brand equity is the added value that a brand contributes to a company by generating additional cash flow from customers. Feldwick (1996) makes a distinction between three types of brand equity. The first is brand value when it is either represented on the balance sheet or realized when it is sold. The second type is brand strength which is basically the consumer's attachment to the brand. Finally, brand image is the awareness and associations held by the consumer.

From a marketing perspective, in contrast to the financial perspective, the second type of brand equity, namely brand strength, is the one that is important. A strong brand increases the probability of brand choice and insulates the brand from competitive threats. Whilst giving either high profit margins and/or volume, a strong brand also gives bargaining power within distribution channels. Finally, a strong brand allows the company to undertake product line extensions as well as brand extensions (see earlier in the chapter).

There are a number of models which explore the consumer's relationship to a brand, commonly called consumer brand equity. The value of a brand is dependent upon the buyer behaviour of consumers. Aaker (2008) devised a consumer brand equity model with five components. The first is that of brand awareness, which can either be recognition (if the decision is made within the shop) or recall (if the decision is made outside the shop). Building brand awareness helps the brand into the evoked set or, at the very least, the consideration set. With low involvement products it gives customers a sense of familiarity which may be enough for them to make a selection. Perceived quality is another construct, and as has been noted in an earlier section, often equates with value for money. Brand association is the third component, followed by brand loyalty.

Brand loyalty is important as it reduces marketing costs and a loyal customer base provides a barrier to entry, as tempting customers to brand switch is costly so it may affect margins, and consequently profit potential. Also, having a large group of loyal customers allows trade leverage, for example, shelf or floor space. Fraering and Minor (2013) believe that loyalty is an evolutionary process. It begins with cognitive (reason) loyalty, followed by affective (emotional) loyalty and then conative (behavourial) loyalty where there is a commitment to purchase. The next stage of the evolutionary process is action loyalty where actions by the loyal customer overcome obstacles, such as stockouts etc. Fraering believes such an attitude is based on fortitude, where the customer rejects any other marketing overtures. The final stage is that of camaraderie where there are social ties between the customer, brand, and service provider, as well as other customers, leading to the development of brand culture, for example, the

Jaguar Car Club. The last construct of Aaker's model is that of proprietary assets, such as trademarks, technological expertise, or exclusive distribution rights.

Although Aaker's model has been criticized as it does not appear to have an underlying theory, Buil et al (2013) claim that the model is based on the hierarchy of effects model (see Chapter 9, at the section entitled Can You Hear Me Now?) so that there is a causal order among the four dimensions. The consumer learning process begins with awareness, followed by attitude, vis-à-vis perceived quality and brand associations, to the final stage of brand loyalty. Whilst the first four dimensions of the Aaker model are most widely used by marketing researchers (Buil et al, 2013), another popular model is the resonance model developed by Kelvin Keller (2001). This model is built on a series of sequential steps.

1. Identity of the brand is by building salience, that is, building brand awareness.

2. Establishing the meaning of the brand for the consumer by linking tangible and intangible offerings. The brand must meet the functional performance for the customer as well as provide the appropriate imagery to meet the customer's psychological and social needs.

3. Eliciting the appropriate customer responses to the brand, either through judgements (opinions and evaluations) or through feelings (emotional responses).

4. The consumer resonates with the brand and develops an ongoing loyal, active relationship with the brand.

In many respects the two models are similar on many dimensions, for example, awareness and loyalty. However, the main point is that the manager can use either model to build a strong brand, and in doing so build customer brand equity, which in turn will lead to a strong cash flow.

Case Study

Case 7-1 On Yer Bike

Most adults can remember their first bike and the pride that went with their newfound freedom. Chances are the bike they received as a child for Christmas or a birthday was a Raleigh. Frank Bowden, who had purchased a small bicycle company in Nottingham, England, founded the Raleigh Bicycle Company in 1890. In 1903, Sturmey-Archer became part of the group. This was an important acquisition as Sturmey-Archer had developed the three-speed gear hub.

The Raleigh Company prospered and before World War I the company produced up to one million bicycles a year. The Nottingham factory employed over 8000 staff and the factory covered 60 acres of land. The company had its own ballroom and 15 separate canteens, each catering for a different level of seniority.

In the 1950s the Tube Investment Group bought the Phillips, Hercules, Sun, Armstrong, and Norman bicycle manufacturers, and Raleigh bought BSA, which had bought the Triumph cycle division five years earlier. In 1960 Tube Investments bought Raleigh and formed TI-Raleigh, giving the company 75% of the UK market. As a vertically integrated consortium, they owned Sturmey-Archer (3-speed hubs), Reynolds (makers of steel tubing), and Brooks (saddle makers).

After World War II, Raleigh launched the lightweight sports roadster, which was lighter and quicker than other makes and superior to the balloon tyre cruiser bikes in America. In 1970 Raleigh launched the Chopper, with a small front wheel and a large back wheel, and the bike became an enormous success in Britain and America. Raleigh also sponsored cycle sport teams, especially in the Tour de France. In 1984 Team USA won medals at the Los Angeles Olympic Games riding Raleigh badged bicycles.

In 1982 Huffy bought Raleigh USA, which was then sold in 1987 to Derby Cycle, a German bicycle manufacturer. By 2000 Derby Cycle owned Raleigh in the UK, USA, Canada, and Ireland. However, in 2001, due to financial problems, there was a management buyout of all the Raleigh companies. The management paid £48 million, but in reality much less as the deal comprised mostly stock. 2002 saw the last bicycles made in the UK, with the company employing just 460 staff, working primarily on design and marketing. In 2011 the company sold 850,000 bikes, all of which were assembled overseas.

In 2012 the Raleigh Company was bought for £62 million by the Accell Group. Based in the Netherlands the company owns the Batavus and Sparta brands, and sponsors the Française des Jeux Tour de France team with its Lapierre brand.

There are two main segments in the bicycle market. One is the mass market, where bikes are sold through large merchants such as Walmart. The bikes are sold mainly on price. The second market is the enthusiast market, where bikes are sold through independent bicycle shops, sporting goods stores, and small custom bicycle builders. Within this market there are two sub-groups, namely the road cyclists and the mountain bikers, with the type of bike skewed towards leisure riders. However, there is crossover with many road cyclists also owning a mountain bike.

Nowadays there are not many bicycle manufacturers. At the top end of the market there is the Italian firm Pinarello, which makes handmade quality racing bikes. In contrast, assemblers now produce most bikes.

Since 1980 Taiwan has been the world's top frame supplier. Due to its need to export, the Taiwanese government funded the bicycle industry and initiated technological development in bicycle production. Over 95% of the bicycle manufacturers are SMEs but operate as a networked organization, sharing technological and marketing costs. However, lately Vietnam, Bangladesh, and China have entered into the bicycle frame market.

Frame manufacturers or specialized assemblers source components from multiple suppliers, and then brand their product. Therefore, bikes have become a modular product. Component manufacturing became dominant because manufacturers were not able to produce a bike at a reasonable cost so they sub-contracted certain components. Over time a limited number of component manufacturers gained economies of scale, subsequently forcing others out of the industry and only offering a limited line of standardized components.

The components connect and interact with surrounding products in a limited number of ways. International standards have been set, with some going as far back as 50 years. For instance, there are hundreds of varieties of pedals, but they all must have a defined interface into which they must screw. Each pair of pedals must have a spindle which screws into the crank. The spindle must be 9/16 inch in diameter with 20 threads per inch, and each pair must consist of a left and right thread.

A bicycle has a gear system or shifter that operates either a derailleur mechanism or an internal hub gear mechanism by a moving cable. The Japanese manufacturer, Shimano, has 70–80% of the market with other firms being Campagnolo, Suntour, Mavic, Sachs, and SRAM. Shimano achieved growth by developing quality road-racing components and developing an index shifting system, which was a technological break-through as the system allowed for easier shifting and was more efficient. This was particularly the case for mountain bikes, where a cyclist may have to shift under load. In 1990 Shimano equipped 80% of mountain bikes, which was the fastest growing segment of bicycles.

Within the component industry there are two markets. One is the OEM market, supplying assemblers, and the other is the after-market for replacements and rebuilds. There is a technical lock-in factor as parts work more efficiently with matching components from the same manufacturer. Therefore, there is a connection between the OEM market and the after-market supply.

Due to the dominance of the component manufacturers and their specialized capabilities the bicycle market has become fragmented. There has been a shift from mass production of the bicycle to "global flexibility".

Questions

1. *What were the contributing factors leading to the demise of Raleigh manufacturing bicycles?*
2. *What components of brand equity relate to the Raleigh brand?*
3. *Why did Accell buy the Raleigh brand?*

◄◄◄ Some Ideas

1. *What were the contributing factors leading to the demise of Raleigh manufacturing bicycles?*

In its heyday Raleigh was a dominant brand with 75% of the UK market. They were a traditional manufacturer, making all the necessary parts to assemble a bike. However, in the 1980s there was a power shift from traditional manufacturers to component makers, who made specialized parts to standardized specifications. With the majority of frames being supplied by Taiwan, anyone (literally anyone) can build their own bike by ordering the required frame and components, and brand it as they wish. As component makers made parts that inter-link, bike assembly is modular. With traditional manufacturers becoming assemblers, the importance of the brand takes eminence.

2. *What components of brand equity relate to the Raleigh brand?*

Using Aaker's model, the Raleigh brand still has a high level of brand awareness, especially with baby-boomers, who may be purchasers of bikes for grandchildren (see Figure 4.2). Also, there is residual knowledge of perceived quality. Consumers will have associations as Raleigh being a great British brand, so there is some nostalgia associated with the brand. A small group may associate Raleigh with bike racing. Loyalty to the brand is hard to estimate but it will depend on the geographic market. Finally, Raleigh has a proprietary asset in terms of its brand and trademark. Overall, depending on the market, it is estimated that Raleigh has reasonable consumer brand equity.

3. *Why did Accell buy the Raleigh brand?*

Accell realized Raleigh had brand equity so by adding it to their portfolio of bikes they were able to fill some segments. Also, Accell wanted access to the US market and Raleigh gave them this opportunity as the brand was well known.

▶▶▶

Case Notes:

Case 7-2 One Cool Cat

The Swallow Sidecar company adopted the name Jaguar during World War II, to avoid being associated with the "SS" of Nazi Germany. Following the war Jaguar made a number of successful sports cars, such as the XK120 (1949), the XK140, the XK150, and the iconic E-Type (1961).

In 2008 Tata Motors from India bought the Jaguar, Land Rover, and Daimler brands, as well as the Lanchester and Rover brands from the Ford Motor Company for £1.7 billion. Soon after, Tata approached the British government for an AAA-rated loan due to the credit squeeze, but the market picked up so the loan wasn't necessary. In two years Tata had created more than 8,000 jobs, and Jaguar was revitalized with the production of the F-Type, which created 1100 jobs at the plant in Castle Bromwich.

The Jaguar Land Rover (JLR) Group exports 80–85% of vehicles but the UK is still the biggest market, where sales in 2011 rose by 3.2% to 60,022. Strong overseas demand made the JLR one of Britain's top exporters. Over the same period the Russian market increased by 38.1% to 16,142, North America increased by 15.4% to 58,003, and China increased by 76% to 50,994. Jaguar and Land Rover are being seen as "trophy brands" in emerging markets such as China, and they are becoming increasingly popular in Continental Europe.

Jaguar employs 20,000 people making four different models for the premium car market. The recently designed F-Type, a two-seater coupe or convertible, is aimed to appeal to younger people. The XF model is a mid-size executive saloon and is the biggest seller. The XK is a luxury Grand Tourer, which comes as either a two-door coupe or convertible. The XJ is a full-size luxury saloon.

In 2012 Jaguar announced a brand reset. The thinking was that whilst people were aware of the brand, it lacked relevance and it was not part of their consideration set. The company wanted to emphasize the unique emotional character of the brand. The logo, the leaping Jaguar, was designed to look more three dimensional by using a chrome gradient effect and new corporate colours were introduced, along with a new font created exclusively for Jaguar.

The "Alive" campaign shot commercials, which were also available on YouTube and Facebook. The target of the campaign was a younger demographic and the aim was to synchronize with potential customers and further the brand narrative by enhancing the emotional connections. According to the CEO of the company, there was not the one customer segment any more.

Questions

1. *How important is Jaguar's heritage to its brand image?*
2. *What are the risks with the brand reset?*

Case Notes:

Case 7-3 Loyalty at the Checkout

Loyalty schemes are designed to increase the share of wallet. As most customers are "repertoire" shoppers, using a number of outlets or suppliers, a loyalty scheme is hoping to win a larger share of the customer's spend.

For the company a loyalty card creates value by getting customers to make purchases more often with the store whilst at the same time collecting data, which can be used to segment the market. From the shopping list the company can profile the customer by age, gender, and postcode, as well as determine if they are a fast food fan, a pensioner, or a family with children. The card also creates value by allowing the company to track trends and changes in behaviour, as well as giving the company the opportunity to develop mass customization of marketing communications thereby allowing a two-way flow of information. Finally, the company can stop indiscriminate sales promotions open to all, so consequently there is less junk mail generated.

The scheme can measure loyalty by the amount of recency, frequency, and value of purchases. Recency is a record of when the customer last shopped, which may indicate they have switched providers. Frequency measures how often a customer visits the shop. More often means they are more loyal. Value is an indication of the profitability of the customer base. By using recency, frequency, and value the company can identify vulnerable customers and segment the customer base, thereby differentiating their communications, and generating a comparative measure between stores.

Tesco supermarket launched Clubcard in 1995 with the campaign "Every Little Helps", allowing the company to be the dominant retailer. Customers can collect points at the checkout, at petrol pumps, and by using the Tesco credit card. Over time the customer builds up points. Every quarter the customer is sent, by direct mail, Clubcard vouchers that can be redeemed in the shop. The customer is also sent targeted coupons that can be redeemed in-store.

Currently there are 16 million active Clubcard users, but the scheme costs £500 million a year to run, so with a 10% contribution margin, Tesco would need sales of £5 billion to break even. It is estimated that Clubcard is only driving approximately 10% of sales. However, the loyalty scheme saves Tesco £350 million a year on mass advertising.

Recently shopping habits have changed. Instead of the one big weekly shop, customers are spending less but more often with convenience stores and online purchases, as well as supermarkets. For promiscuous shoppers the value of points to be collected at one retailer is not important. Also, Tesco and other supermarkets are realizing that large hypermarkets with an area of over 60,000 square feet are becoming hard to fill with products and shoppers, as it is not an inspiring shopping experience.

Over the last two years Tesco's market share has been consistently falling, due to internet purchasing becoming increasingly influential, especially with non-perishable goods, and the market share increases by other supermarkets (see Table 7-3.1). For example, the German discount chains Aldi and Lidl offer discounts across a broad range of products and are free of gimmicks. At the other end of the market is Waitrose, who offer a full service and a positive in-store experience.

Table 7-3.1 UK Supermarket market share for the 12 weeks to 17 March 2013

Supermarket	Market Share	% Change
Tesco	29.4%	+1.1%
ASDA	17.9%	−3.8%
Sainsbury's	16.9%	+6.2%
Morrisons	11.7%	−1.0%
The Co-operative	6.2%	−0.3%
Waitrose	4.8%	+12.5%
Aldi	3.3%	+30.8%
Lidl	2.9%	+10.5%
Iceland	2.1%	+8.7%

For many shoppers the loyalty card is more helpful to the company than the shopper.

Questions
1. *Does Tesco need to revamp or discard the Clubcard?*
2. *Advise a company on the merits of starting a loyalty card programme. Is this the best way to secure loyalty?*

Whisky Galore was a 1949 Ealing Studios comedy movie set during the Second World War. The movie depicts how the inhabitants of the isolated island of Todday were unaffected by the war until their supply of whisky ran out. When a shipwreck occurs containing a cargo of whisky, the inhabitants do their best to secure the windfall for themselves by outwitting the customs and excise men.

Scotch whisky is Scotland's number one export. In 2009 it exported £4.2bn of whisky, with USA being the biggest market, followed by France. However, emerging markets have been growing at a rate of 10% a year over the last five years. In markets such as Brazil, Russia, and China, Scotch whisky is seen as a status drink.

Demand is forecast to further increase so the three largest companies are in the process of increasing production by expanding distilleries, modernizing bottling facilities, and building additional warehouse space. Diageo, the world's biggest drinks company, with brands such as Johnnie Walker, Cardhu, Justerini & Brooks (J&B), Bell's, Black & White, Vat 69, Oban, Talisker, and Haig, produces 40% of Scotch whisky and is investing £1 billion in the industry. Bacardi, with the brand of Dewars Scotch Whisky, is investing £250 million and Pernod Ricard, the second biggest drinks company in the world, with whisky brands such as The Glenlivet, Chivas Regal, and Royal Salute, is investing £40 million in malt distilleries, increasing production over the next two years by 25%. These are confident moves given that it takes three years for a "new make" to be released and 10 years for malt whiskies to mature.

There are five types of Scotch whisky:

- The single malt, produced in one distillery from malted barley (without any other cereals).

- Single grain with malted barley and other cereals (note: single refers to one distillery).

- Blended Scotch whisky produced with one or more single malt whiskies and one or more single grain whiskies. The type accounts for 90% of Scotch whisky produced.

- Blended malt whisky, which is a blend of single malt whiskies from different distilleries.

- Blended grain whisky, which is a blend of different grain whiskies from different distilleries.

Scotch whisky is produced in five geographical areas. The Lowlands has only three distilleries remaining in operation. Speyside has the largest amount of distilleries with 50 in operation. The Highland region, including the islands (except Islay) has 36 operating distilleries, and Islay has nine producing distilleries.

The process of making a single malt whisky can be broken down into four main stages:

1. Malting – barley is soaked in tanks, and then dried allowing the barley to germinate, thereby making the starch in the barley soluble.

2. Mashing – the dried malt is mixed with hot water and the resulting liquid is known as wort.

3. Fermentation – the wort is poured into large vessels, where the living yeast converts the sugar in the wort to alcohol, known as wash.

4. Distillation – the wash is distilled in large copper stills, where the alcohol is separated from the fermented liquid. The alcohol, known as low wines, is fermented again. The distillation is undertaken as a batch process. The "new-made spirit" is diluted and placed into casks for maturation, usually for a period of between 10 and 18 years. During maturation natural evaporation takes place, usually losing between 1.5–2.0% per year. This loss is known as the angel's share.

The flavour of a malt whisky produced by a distillery is unique and diverse, primarily caused by the amount of peat used in malting the barley and the type of casks used to mature the malt. The casks used to mature the whisky have been previously used to make sherry or bourbon. There is an abundant supply of bourbon casks as the US authorities require bourbon to be matured in new, freshly charred oak barrels. Sometimes other varieties of cask are used, such as port, Cognac, Madeira, or beer. It is believed that two-thirds of the flavour of whisky is determined by the type of cask.

Whilst the UK Scotch whisky market accounts for only 10% of the total production of Scotch whisky, it is still an important market. Within the category, 75% of sales are of blended whisky with Bell's and Famous Grouse accounting for 50% of sales. Blended whisky drinkers skew towards low income earners, whereas malt whisky drinkers earn approximately £145,000 a year with 50% more likely to hold professional or senior management positions, enjoying pursuits such as gourmet cooking, wine drinking, and National Trust excursions. Whilst malt whisky is viewed by consumers as being of better quality, it can be three times the cost of a blended whisky.

Scotch whisky is often seen as the preserve of private detectives, who have a bottle in their top drawer, and old gentlemen sitting in leather chairs in their private club. A survey conducted in 1999 revealed that 27% of consumers purchase whisky to drink at home, either for special occasions or as a regular tipple. The marketing of Scotch whisky focuses on two channels: on-premise (bars, restaurants, nightclubs) and off-premise (grocers, specialized alcohol stores, and online spirit retailers). Both channels are important as consumers can be introduced to whisky in an on-premise environment, whereas the off-premise provides a better return.

Table 7-4.1   Taste notes of a selection of single malts

Bunnahabhain Islay produced – Sherry casks
Light, Medium-Sweet, Low Peat, with Floral, Malty Notes and Fruity, Spicy, Honey Hints

Cardhu Speyside produced – Oak casks
Light, Medium-Sweet, Low or No Peat, with Fruity, Floral, Malty Notes, and Nutty Hints

Cragganmore Highland produced – Sherry casks
Medium-Bodied, Medium-Sweet, with Nutty, Malty, Floral, Honey, and Fruity Notes

Glenfiddich Speyside produced – Bourbon/Sherry/Rum casks
Medium-Bodied, Sweet, Low Peat, and Floral Notes

Glenlivet Speyside produced – Bourbon/French oak
Medium-Bodied, Medium-Sweet, with Fruity, Floral, Honey, Malty Notes and Spicy Hints

Glenmorangie Highland produced – Bourbon American white oak casks
Medium-Bodied, Medium-Sweet, with Smoky, Fruity, Spicy Notes and Floral, Nutty Hints

Laphroaig Islay produced – American oak bourbon casks
Full-Bodied, Dry, Pungent, Peaty and Medicinal, with Spicy, Feinty Notes

Macallan Speyside produced – Sherry casks
Full-Bodied, Medium-Sweet, Pronounced Sherry with Fruity, Spicy, Malty Notes and Nutty, Smoky Hints

Springbank Campbletown produced – Bourbon/Sherry casks
Medium-Light, Dry, with Smoky, Spicy, Honey Notes and Nutty, Floral Hints

From 2005–2009 Scotch whisky in the UK market has decreased more than 23.3%, and dropped market share from 31% to 24.3%, whereas vodka has increased by 16.8% over the same period.

Unfortunately malt whisky has failed to attract the 35–54 year old market for a number of reasons. Firstly, this generation is hesitant to be seen drinking the same spirit as their parents. Secondly, given the range of malt whiskies they find making a choice intimidating, as they are unsure of the product range. Finally, consumers in this age group with enough discretionary income frequent upmarket bars and nightclubs and witness the theatre of the serve accompanying the creation of cocktails.

Questions

1. *Why is the UK market important for Scotch whisky producers?*
2. *Produce a perceptual map for the different malt whiskies as outlined in Table 7-4.1.*
3. *How can on-premise purchasers of whisky be encouraged to buy single malt whisky off-premise? Why is this difficult to achieve?*
4. *Why is the name "Scotch whisky" carefully protected?*

Case Notes:

Aaker, D. (2008) *Strategic Market Management*, 8th edn. Hoboken, NJ: Wiley.

Aaker, D. and Keller, K. (1990) Consumer Evaluations of Brand Extensions, *The Journal of Marketing*, 54(1): 27–41.

Balmer, J. (2001) Corporate Identity, Corporate Branding and Corporate Marketing – Seeing Through the Fog, *European Journal of Marketing*, 35(3/4): 248–291.

Balmer, J. (2012) Strategic Corporate Brand Alignment – Perspectives from identity based views of corporate brands', *European Journal of Marketing*, 46(7/8): 1064–1092.

Brodie, R.J. (2009) 'From Goods to Service Branding: An integrative perspective', *Marketing Theory*, 9(1): 107–111.

Brodie, R.J., Glynn, M.S. and Little, V. (2006) The Service Brand and the Service-dominant Logic: Missing fundamental premise or the need for stronger theory?, *Marketing Theory*, 6(3): 363–379.

Buil, I., Martinez, E. and de Chernatony, L. (2013) The Influence of Brand Equity on Consumer Responses', *Journal of Consumer Marketing*, 30(1): 62–74.

Dall'Olmo Riley, F. and de Chernatony, L. (2000) The Service Brand as Relationships Builder, *British Journal of Management*, 11, 137–150.

de Burgh-Woodman, H. and Brace-Govan, J. (2008) Jargon as Imagining: Barthes' semiotics and excavating subcultural communication, *Qualitative Market Research: An International Journal*, 11(1): 89–106.

de Chernatony, L. and Cottam, S. (2008) Interactions between Organisational Cultures and Corporate Brands, *Journal of Product & Brand Management*, 17(1): 13–24.

de Chernatony, L. and McDonald, M. (1998) *Creating Powerful Brands*, 2nd edn. Oxford: Butterworth-Heinemann.

de Chernatony, L. and Segan-Horn, S. (2003) The Criteria for Successful Services Brands, *European Journal of Marketing*, 37(7/8): 1095–1118.

de Lencastre, P. and Corte-Real, A. (2010) One, Two, Three: A practical brand anatomy, *Journal of Brand Management*, 17(6): 399–412.

Doyle, P. and Stern, P. (2006) *Marketing Management and Strategy*, 4th edn. Harlow, England: Prentice Hall.

Feldwick, P. (1996) What is Brand Equity Anyway, and How Do You Measure it?, *Journal of the Market Research Society*, 38(2): 85.

Fraering, M. and Minor, M.S. (2013) Beyond Loyalty; Customer satisfaction, loyalty, and fortitude, *Journal of Services Marketing*, 27(4): 334–344.

Gyrd-Jones, R., Merrilees, B. and Miller, D. (2013) Revisiting the Complexities of Corporate Branding: Issues, paradoxes, solutions, *Journal of Brand Management*, 20(7): 571–589.

Kapferer, J. (1992) *Strategic Brand Management*. London: Kogan Page.

Keller, K. (2001) Building Customer-based Brand Equity; A blueprint for creating strong brands, *Marketing Management*, 10(2): 14–19.

Kotler, P. and Keller, K. (2012) *Marketing Management*, 14th edn. Harlow, England: Pearson Education.

Lawes, R. (2002) Demystifying Semiotics: Some key questions answered, *International Journal of Market Research*, 44(3): 251–264.

Olutayo Otubanjo, B. and Melewar, T.C. (2007) Understanding the Meaning of Corporate Identity: A conceptual and semiological approach, *Corporate Communications: An International Journal*, 12(4): 414–432.

Roslender, R. and Hart, S.J. (2006) Interfunctional Cooperation in Progressing Accounting for Brands, *Journal of Accounting & Organizational Change*, 2(3): 229–247.

Santos, F.P. (2012) The Semiotic Conception of Brand and the Traditional Marketing View, *Irish Journal of Management*, 32(1): 95–108.

Schultz, M. and de Chernatony, L. (2002) Introduction: The challenges of corporate branding, *Corporate Reputation Review*, 5(2/3): 105–112.

Thoger Christensen, L. and Askegaard, S. (2001) Corporate Identity and Corporate Image Revisited – A semiotic perspective, *European Journal of Marketing*, 35(3/4): 292–315.

Torelli, C. and Ahluwalia, R. (2012) Extending Culturally Symbolic Brands: A Blessing or a Curse?, *Journal of Consumer Research*, 38(5): 933–947.

Völckner, F. and Sattler, H. (2006) Drivers of Brand Extension Success, *Journal of Marketing*, 70(2): 18–34.

Wood, L. (2000) Brands and Brand Equity: Definition and Management, *Management Decision*, 38(9): 662–669.

Case Acknowledgements

The **On Yer Bike** case draws on information contained in:

Galvin, P. and Morkel, A. (2001), The Effect of Product Modularity on Industry Structure: The Case of the World Bicycle Industry', *Industry and Innovation*, 8(1), 31–47

Isely, P. and Roelofs, M. (2004), Primary Market and Aftermarket Competition in the Bicycle Component Industry, *Applied Economics*, 36, 2097–2102

Oddy, N. (2004), Framing Production: Technology, Culture and Change in the British Bicycle Industry, *The Journal of Transport History*, 25(1), 115–117

"Raleigh Cycle sold to Accell for $100m"' by B. Harrington (26 April 2012), *The Telegraph*, retrieved from http://www.telegraph.co.uk/finance/newsbysector/retailandconsumer/9227116/Raleigh-Cycle-sold-to-Accell-for-100m.html

Wong Yue-Ming, S. (2005), 'Inter-organizational Network and Firm Performance: The Case of the Bicycle Industry in Taiwan', *Asian Business & Management*, 4(1), 67–91

The **One Cool Cat** case draws on information contained in:

"Germany and France turn to British-made Jaguar and Land Rovers", by G. Ruddick (29 May 2012), *The Telegraph*, retrieved from http://www.telegraph.co.uk/finance/newsbysector/transport/9298464/Germany-and-France-turn-to-British-made-Jaguar-and-Land-Rovers.html

Jaguar Daimler Heritage Trust website located at http://www.jaguarheritage.org/JaguarHistory_Content.aspx?TopicName=JaguarHistory_8&PageNumber=8

"Jaguar shakes up brand image with comprehensive multichannel Alive campaign", by R. Lamb (28 February 2012), *Luxury Daily*, retrieved from http://www.luxurydaily.com/jaguar-resets-image-with-multi-billion-multichannel-campaign/

"JLR chief: Car industry 'most complex on earth'", by A. Monaghan (29 September 2012), *The Telegraph*, retrieved from http://www.telegraph.co.uk/finance/newsbysector/industry/9576182/JLR-chief-Car-industry-most-complex-on-earth.html

"Tata Finally Gets Serious About Jaguar", by D. Buss (1 March 2012), *Brand Channel*, retrieved from http://www.brandchannel.com/home/post/Jaguar-Brand-Refresh-030112.aspx

The **Loyalty at the Checkout** case draws on information contained in:

"Clubcard built the Tesco of today, but it could be time to ditch it", by G. Ruddick (16 January 2014), *The Telegraph*, retrieved from http://www.telegraph.co.uk/finance/newsbysector/retailandconsumer/10577685/Clubcard-built-the-Tesco-of-today-but-it-could-be-time-to-ditch-it.html

"Clubcard couple head for checkout at Tesco", by Z. Wood (29 October 2010), *The Guardian*, retrieved from http://www.theguardian.com/business/2010/oct/29/tesco-clubcard-couple-depart

Hunt, T. (2006), *How Tesco Continues to Win Customer Loyalty*, London: Kogan

"Sainsbury's wins market share ahead of big four competitors", by K. Jefford (27 March 2013), *City Am*, retrieved from http://www.cityam.com/article/sainsbury-s-wins-market-share-ahead-big-four-competitors

"Tesco and rivals turn against huge stores as internet shopping takes over", by S. Butler (4 March 2012), *The Observer*, retrieved from http://www.theguardian.com/business/2012/mar/04/online-shopping-changes-hypermarket-strategy

"Tesco's market share slips again as customers defect", by S. Bowers (28 February 2012), *The Guardian*, retrieved from http://www.theguardian.com/business/2012/feb/28/tesco-market-share-aldi-lidl

The **Whisky Galore** case draws on information contained in:

"Diageo's £1bn shot into malt whisky", by N. Thomas (6 June 2012), *The Telegraph*, retrieved from http://www.telegraph.co.uk/finance/newsbysector/retailandconsumer/leisure/9313204/Diageos-1bn-shot-into-malt-whisky.html

"Dram fine: Diageo invests £1bn in Scotland's whisky industry", by Z. Wood (6 June 2012), *The Guardian*, retrieved from http://www.guardian.co.uk/business/2012/jun/06/diageo-invests-whisky-industry-scotland

"Value of scotch whisky exports soar 23% topping £4bn", by R. Wachman (27 March 2012), *The Guardian*, retrieved from http://guardian.co.uk/business/2012/mar/27/scotch-whiskey-exports-soar

"Vodka is the new Scotch ... ", (13 December 2010), *Key Note*, retrieved from http://www.keynote.co.uk/media-centre/in-the-news/display/vodka-is-the-new-scotch/?articleId=534

Table 7-4.1: Adapted from David Wishart (2002), *Whisky Classified: Choosing Single Malts by Flavour*, London: Pavilion Books

This chapter covers the following topics:

▶ Distribution
▶ Marketing channels
▶ Channel structures
▶ Impact of IT
▶ Role of logistics

8
Finding the Right Marketing Space

The Role of Space and Place

Distribution involves activities that make products available to customers when and where they want to purchase them. It involves a transfer of an item of exchange from one place to another, bringing it to the marketplace where customers are. Distribution channels enable goods to be brought to consumers, not the other way round. If there were no market distribution system customers would have to travel to the place of production or source of supply. Indeed, it is concern with this issue of developing optimal distribution systems that marketing as an academic discipline began in the early twentieth century. Traditional marketing models describe the exchange and distribution process in terms of movement through supply chains, distribution channels, logistics organization, transportation networks, inventories, retail outlets, delivery systems, intermediaries and agents for assortment, conveyancing, consignment, and shipment.

But the exchanges that occur in the marketing system nowadays are much more than just a process of delivery, distribution, or logistics, moving things from place to place. One reason why it is more than about transport and logistics is because it often matters enormously to customers where things come from. The "place of origin" label can provide a form of quality assurance for buyers and this may apply to raw materials (Portland stone), manufactures (Dresden china), and is particularly influential for agricultural produce (Camembert cheese, Scotch whisky). The geographical source of farm and mineral products can be the key part of the brand with the labels bearing the name of the region of origin, e.g. milk, water, wine. Indeed French wine is defined and controlled by its regional source of the grape embodying the soil, climate, history, folklore, and emotional attachment of the place where it is grown.

Another reason why distribution is much more than about the delivery of goods and services is because choosing which channels of distribution to operate in is such a major decision in the formulation of marketing strategy. This is particularly crucial nowadays as the range of traditional, social, and online retail options have expanded enormously. "Shopping is expanding into every program imaginable: airports, churches, train stations, libraries, schools universities, hospitals. Airports and malls are starting to look indistinguishable. The experience of the mall is becoming increasingly seamless with that of the department store. Even the city is being configured according to the mall" (Chung et al, 2001).

As Brennan (2006: 832) argues "firms are not simply passive victims of their environment but strive to alter competitive market conditions in their favour". But how can firms shape the markets that they engage in? Storbacka and Nenonen (2011) regard these as the key strategic questions: how firms influence the shape of the markets that they choose to engage in, and through which mechanisms these market conditions can be altered. They describe the purpose of their article as being to develop a framework for understanding how markets are formed and shaped and to use this to identify what they call "market scripting" activities that firms can engage in to actively develop markets to their advantage. They make their key assumptions about markets which reflect this proactive view of firms' roles: (1) markets consist of networks of market actors, (2) market actors co-create value by integrating their resource with the resources of other actors participating in the market, and (3) markets are social constructions co-created by market actors as they engage in market practices. Based on these core assumptions there are two important implications of this approach for our conceptualization of space and place in distribution:

1. One implication of this proactive market-shaping view for the development of a strategic approach to distribution is the necessity for a comprehensive mapping of the various "paths to market" that a firm could follow for their range of products, services, and potential customers. This spatial route map would ideally indicate the likely places where each might meet customers and the boundaries of the various spaces within the entire field of possible distribution channels.

This would then enable marketers to seek out complementary and alternative routes to market to those which they have adopted. If this mapping can be successfully accomplished, then marketers will have a better understanding of how they can develop their distribution networks – and thus shape their markets.

2. Another implication of this view for distribution follows from the three key assumptions above. These do not focus on product flows, channel structures, or transport logistics. On the contrary, they emphasize the relationships between market actors, how they deploy resources, and their type of operations or "practices". According to the market shaping approach it is through these activities and interactions that the distribution network is formed and also importantly how value is created by firms and other actors within it.

Storbacka and Nenonen's (2011) approach to shaping and making markets reflects the so-called "Nordic school" of marketing researchers whose key focus is on relationships between market actors. This is very different from the original view of distribution systems in the early days of the marketing discipline which included geography-related regional approaches to marketing distribution such as Reilly's (1931) *Law of Retail Gravitation*. Geography was an underlying influence on the development of distribution theories and, furthermore, the concept itself tended to be defined in context-specific terms of the USA where it was developed. One issue for geographically based theories is that various countries' markets and territories are significantly different in terms of market structure, transport, logistics, competition, infrastructure, etc. As Grönroos points out, the North American marketing environment is quite specific in many respects with a huge domestic market, a unique geographical structure, and a non-oligopolistic, highly competitive distribution system. "In spite of this we have, for instance, no European marketing theory or model geared to European conditions" (Grönroos, 1989: 53).

So the geographical site of the academic researchers themselves partly explains the origination of the traditional approach to distribution in marketing literature. Their location may also be important in explaining differences in relationships marketing and later developments, specifically the territorial origins of many of its early exponents like Grönroos in northern Europe, which became known as the Nordic School. Learning from Nordic appreciation of space and place, the key relationship of the future in marketing may not simply be between marketplace actors, but between marketing processes and the territories in which these occur.

The primary role of marketing channels is the performance of some basic distribution functions such as: reducing complexity, increasing value, and service delivery. These tasks are common to all types of marketing channels and the movement of physical goods is not the only type of task involved; for example promotion also flows down distribution channels, orders and payment flow back to suppliers, and negotiation and finance can flow both ways. This is illustrated in Figure 8.1 showing the product and information flows which are critical in achieving "quick response" logistics in the US garment supply. Quick response is measured by the speed at which information about changing market demands can be communicated back up the channel and products manufactured and transported down the chain in response to those demands.

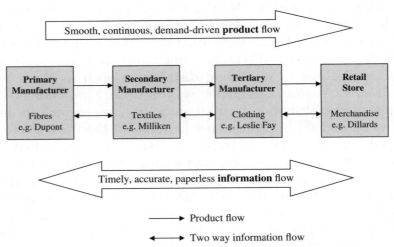

Figure 8.1 Quick response in the US garment industry. Source: Adapted from Christopher (1997)

This quick response capability is critical for the clothing textile industry in the era of "fast fashion". This is illustrated by the Spanish clothing company Zara whose core competence has been based on the implementation of rapid reaction, just-in-time principles and systems and processes which allow customer demand for up-to-date fashions to be brought to the market with lead times dramatically shorter than the industry norm.

The Zara brand was launched in May 1975 opening their first store in La Coruna with a product range incorporating women's fashion, menswear, and children's clothes. By 2004 they had 792 international stores in more than 40 countries and a commercial team at HQ comprising designers, market specialists, and buyers operating on a multi-tasking basis to ensure that design, sales, and production considerations are integrated at an early stage. Design ideas observed by company representatives on the catwalk and by co-opted scouts in "youth" arenas, such as university campuses and discos, are brought back to La Coruna and interpreted by the commercial team. The design, production, and distribution "time-to-market" has been reduced to 22–30 days in an industry where nine months was the traditional lead-time.

Zara employs a network of over 500 sub-contractors in Spain and Portugal to assemble pre-cut material sourced from a wide supplier base on a global level to reduce supplier dependency. This network of sub-contractors, allied to daily feedback from store managers on how ranges are performing, maximizes flexibility in the supply and distribution system. At the retail stores, continuous replenishment on a staggered three-day cycle and the regular introduction of new lines encourages customers to return to the stores and increases footfall. This flexibility in supply and their "fast fashion" quick response strategy also provides some protection against other suppliers copying Zara products because by the time competitors respond the item may have already been taken out of their stores and replaced by the next range.

This example illustrates how time reduction is one crucial element in the design of distribution systems. Christopher (1997) identifies three aspects of time that must be managed in the distribution system:

- Time to market: how long it takes the organization to recognize a market opportunity and to translate this into a product/service, and to bring it to the market.

- Time to serve: how long it takes to capture a customer's order and to deliver or install the product to the customer's satisfaction.

- Time to react: how long it takes to adjust the output of the business in response to volatile demand.

More aspects and key considerations regarding the design of alternative channel structures are discussed in the next section.

A channel of distribution is a set of actors, institutions, enterprises, or other types of organizations that conduct the flow of products from producers to customers. Buyers' needs and behaviour should be the most important concern of channel members. The purpose of distribution channels is to provide the best availability of products for customers at the right time, in the right places, and in the right quantities by performing key functions of logistics, transport, retailing, information, and storage.

Distribution decisions are critical because they determine a product's market presence and how and where customers buy the product. They also influence customers' overall satisfaction with the product, manufacturer, or service. There are a number of key decisions to be taken over channel design such as those concerning how many and which channels to select, the intensity and coverage required of the channel(s), and the optimal channel configuration. Their choice will be determined by many factors including the degree of flexibility, centralization, and voluntary cooperation that are best in order to reach and serve their specific markets and segments. Their options may be further limited by the extent to which the individual firm has the power to make such decisions. For example, their choice may be limited because in their sector or market it is the retailers, not the manufacturers, who have power over the channel decisions. Nevertheless, it is the service provided to final consumers that should be the key consideration in all marketing channel decisions.

One option for the distribution system is to use a direct marketing channel from the producer to the customer through courier or mail delivery, mobile download, factory outlet, or customer collection. In order to serve customers best and find the best distribution space, most channels of distribution are indirect with one or several marketing intermediaries. There are two main forms of intermediary: merchants (or agents) and functional middlemen (or brokers). The difference is that merchants buy and own the products and resell them, whereas functional middlemen do not own products, but sell them on behalf of the supplier for a fee or commission. Retailers are also intermediaries who purchase products and sell them to final consumers making their profit by a price "markup".

Whatever form or structure of the distribution system, all channel members perform distinct but complementary roles and therefore they must cooperate closely. This joint effort of all channel members to deliver products to the market quickly and efficiently is often called a "supply chain". Supply chain management (SCM) refers to long-term partnerships between channel members that aim to reduce inefficiencies, costs, and delays in a coordinated way that builds on the combined strengths of the channel members.

The key elements of SCM include: waste reduction, time saving, flexible response, unit cost reduction. Firms adopting an SCM approach seek to redesign their supply chains in ways to make them more effective and efficient, thus providing improved customer service while at the same time reducing costs and delivery time reduction often faced with fluctuating demand. The capacity for flexible response to demand changes requires the ability to "see" from one point of the supply chain to the other. Some firms specialize in providing IT software for managing and integrating total supply chain processes. This is one example of the contribution of IT to marketing channels which is the subject of the next section.

More than Just Numbers

Information is the key to finding the right marketing space. The organization and operations for supplying customers, involving distribution, transportation, logistics, materials flows, order processes, retail outlets, etc., have become more complex with the need for more and faster information to manage these processes across boundaries – national, international, organizational. In the global economy few firms do it all themselves, from source to delivery, but they have to be able to manage a complex network of processes often across great distances. Information Technology (IT) provides the capability to speed up information collection and processing enabling marketing to improve their understanding and responses to customer needs and to manage their supply processes, to move space, better and faster.

Information does more than support transactions, however; it is a product – an object of exchange – in its own right. The more information about customers, markets, and channels that is collected by the firm, the greater the need for an integration function to coordinate all the elements, analyse and interpret the mass data in order to build a complete picture. This is another key role that IT systems can perform that can help firms to better manage these functions required by the acquisition of mass information.

Marketers basically want to gather knowledge about consumers so they can make better marketing decisions in order to satisfy customers and to meet company objectives. For managers to have *knowledge* of customers, however, requires judgement and expertise as well as information, in order to select and evaluate information in their decisions. Developments in IT enable the fusing of data, its sorting, and evaluation with computer models. This is all the more important for marketers as consumers' behaviour keeps changing and therefore the most crucial pieces of information are about consumers' actual behaviour, as opposed to generic segment characteristics such as their age, income, or location. More crucially for distribution decisions, marketers need to know what consumers want to buy, how and when they want to purchase, and where they want to purchase.

It should be fairly clear to those readers who have experience of online purchasing that the Internet has had an enormous effect on consumer buying behaviour and final market delivery. When shopping, looking, or buying through company websites, the interaction between the buyer and seller is no longer dependent on the place or location of either party. The online transaction takes place in virtual cyberspace with no need for face-to-face interaction. This is not new of course; this was always the case with shopping by TV, telephone, or mail order. It is the retailing aspects online that have altered most significantly. Bricks and mortar features of shops like physical space, architecture, layout, design, store atmospherics, colour schemes, and displays, which have been found to affect customer responses, are all changed by Internet shopping where the marketplace is virtual, the customer can be anywhere, and the "shop" can be nowhere. So Internet marketing has altered the space in which market exchange takes place.

Clarke and Purvis (1994) argue that the advent of this "hyperspace" with its simulations and hyperreal shopping spaces will have radical effects on the retailing system. While it is true that the internet changes shopping space, many marketers would also point out that 90% of products and services are still exchanged in terrestrial markets and must be moved from place to place by the same transport and logistics processes. Not only do these physical distribution processes utilize new and faster means, but also they are themselves changing the use of spaces, turning more of them into retailing and shopping spaces such as gigantic retail malls with window displays, shopping arcades, and galleries all utilizing glass constructions enabling shoppers to be in and see through both the public street and the shopping space simultaneously. This is what Benjamin (Benjamin, 1955/2004) described as the "porosity" of the shopping arcades of Paris and Naples – apparently open spaces that are "harnessed" to the needs of the market. These new physical sites of consumption bring consumers into spatial presence with other consumers, sellers, commodities, and a network of buildings and supporting artefacts which also alter spaces.

Another impact of advances in IT and mobile communications has enabled companies to track and trace materials as they travel from suppliers to their final destination. IT infrastructure and the Internet have provided the framework to monitor the movement of materials instantaneously from anywhere in the world and that allows more effective management of the interwoven activities of the supply chain. Without these technological changes in the application and innovations of specialized electronics and communication systems, the effectiveness and speed of marketing channels and supply chain management would be greatly reduced.

Mission Critical

Customers' expectation that products are available anytime and everywhere is now the norm in most consumer and business markets. This demonstrates how the requirements for supplying materials have changed and constant availability is expected 24 hours a day, seven days a week. Achieving this is the role of logistics which comprises the practices and processes that physically move materials, spaces, and time in the marketplace.

The dictionary definition of logistics is the series of events required to move materials in a timely and cost effective manner. This includes the transportation and tracing of materials as they flow between the manufacturer and their customers. Logistics is also concerned with planning the steps involved in producing and moving materials including the services of documenting the processes involved in production, storage, and shipping of goods. These processes include activities such as production scheduling, determining the best method of delivering the materials, collecting customer feedback, and managing the company's website.

Logistics has always been a critical operation in order to ensure the delivery of goods to customers in a timely and cost effective manner. Nowadays logistics deals with more than the "moving of materials", encompassing the organization, tracking, and tracing of the shipments and movements involved and the entire flow of materials into and out of the company. In the global economy with multiple transportation modes and millions of such movements every day, logistics is a complex coordination and control function. It requires managing across national and company boundaries and balancing internal and external objectives. Consider the case of the motorsports marketing channels in Figure 8.2.

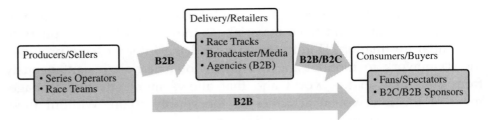

Figure 8.2 Motorsports marketing channels. Source: Adapted from Cobbs and Hylton (2012)

As we have seen the goal of marketing channels is to deliver the right items at the right time in the right market space, finding the best market niche and delivering the product to the place where the customer wants. This process does not necessarily apply quite as simply as this if we think more broadly about logistics from "moving items" to providing the best environment for the customer. In many cases the environment is as important as the actual good or service which is purchased. An example of the role of the product or service environment is in the airline business. Here there are many low-cost, "no-frills" local and national flights, which don't provide much service at all – just the seat. But if they only provide seats, then the carriers' offerings are only differentiated by price, so they are now competing with each other by providing the right environment and more optional services in addition to the minimum passenger transportation function. In the low-cost airline market these include: parking, choice of airport arrivals and departure, number of destinations, ground transportation, and purchasing tickets such as e-ticketing. They not only sell airplane tickets, but also provide a wide assortment of related travel services including car rental, hotel booking, sightseeing packages etc. These types of additional logistical services are considered essential for today's travellers. Providing a cheap seat is not enough as competitive prices can be researched on the Internet in seconds. For travellers, their purchasing decision includes all the related facilities in the air travel environment, not just the seat or the destination.

These logistics add-on services have become basic expectations in many industries. Customers are no longer expecting just the basic service from their provider – that is a given. It is the added logistical services they have come to expect that differentiate the leading companies in most industry. This is particularly the case in B2B markets where the customer's own business success is dependent on the reliability, effectiveness, and speed of their suppliers. So now freight companies, for example, are no longer being paid simply to move materials and supplies, but they are rewarded by their customers for "peace of mind" knowing that the logistics and movement of goods are being safely handled by specialists.

The customer can strengthen their core competencies and contract out the delivery, pick up, warehousing, customs brokerage etc. to their freight company. They can even use their logistics providers to help determine the appropriate price for various products by calculating and recording production schedules, shipping details, and determining the most cost efficient way of transporting the goods. As the freight couriers say in their advertising straplines, logistics providers are now offering the "complete shipping solution" customized for each of their individual customers.

So, in addition to marketers' logistic role of delivering the product to the right place, companies also need to understand the environment and context in which their products will be used in order to find the right marketing space. If the environment is not conducive to its use, then their product will be less attractive. In services marketing this is referred to as the "servicescape" (Bitner, 1992). Therefore marketers must consider all the services and facilities that make up the environment in order to enhance the logistics and delivery of their offerings.

Case 8-1 Keep on Truckin'

Eddie Stobart started making money at a young age by chopping up wood for kindling. At the age of 14 he bought a job lot of railway sleepers, chopped them up and sold them by the sack load to his teachers. In those days he was carrying around £200 in his pocket, which was a lot of money in 1968. In 1977 he took over his father's agricultural contract firm, having opened a base in Carlisle in northern England the previous year at the age of 22. Eddie worked for the next ten years running the office by day and driving trucks by night, and snatching a few hours' sleep where he could.

From 1986 to 1992 the firm grew 50% per annum, and growth has now settled to 20% per annum. Eddie made his big break in the mid-1980s during an economic recession when customers were looking for cheaper options. He built the business with an attention to detail and providing a 15-minute window on either side of the scheduled time for the delivery of goods. As there is no trade union representation on site, management decides pay rates, with drivers getting a £5 daily bonus if all jobs and staff presentation targets are met.

Trucks have distinctive lettering and are always kept clean, with each truck having a female name painted on the front of the cab, such as Twiggy, Tammy (Wynette), Dolly, and Suzi. The truck drivers wear a collar and tie, along with a company uniform, which struck a chord with customers, who equated clean and tidy staff with a quality organization, although the uniforms were meant at least partly for driver motivation. The drivers are instructed to respond with a honk when signalled by a passer-by or an "Eddie Spotter".

By 2004 Eddie Stobart Ltd had a fleet of 760 trucks generating a turnover of £120 million, and a staff of 2,000 including 1,200 truck drivers. The company had 27 depots, three of which were in Brussels, with key clients being Tesco and Nestle. The company purchased a 25-acre site in Daventry, close to the International Rail Freight Terminal with Stobart's rail service providing a round-trip to Glasgow on a daily basis, carrying loads such as pet foods, bottled water, beer, and computer goods. The £40 million investment covered warehousing, the construction of a rail siding, 75 rail wagons designed to carry 60 pallets each, and locomotives. To enable the move onto the rail network the company applied for a government grant of £20 million.

Eddie Stobart Ltd had moved from being just a trucking firm to providing fourth party logistics. Consequently the company was now in the business of supply chain management. What this means is that the company manages and runs all logistics for clients. To achieve this strategic move the

FINDING THE RIGHT MARKETING SPACE

company had to adopt information technology as an integral part of its business.

All the Stobart fleet is equipped with wireless radio-frequency equipment, GPS, along with real-time tracking and communications capability. As a result the company has the ability to trace goods down to the pallet level. Barcoding has been applied, which is key to the Tesco contract. Vital stock and location information is made available to the customer in real time through EDI, Internet, or ISDN links.

The fleet has telematics systems fitted and is a core provider of real-time data to ITIS Holdings' traffic reporting system, which allow ITIS to monitor the actual speed the vehicles are travelling at in real time. The data is one component used by ITIS in developing its real-time traffic information services. Stobart uses ITIS's sister-company Navtrack to analyse its own fleet movements. Vehicles are linked to their base via satellite, radio, and in-cab telephone, and this package allows planners to track a vehicle, re-route if necessary, and provide the customer with status reports in real time. The system also allows head office to monitor each vehicle's performance and diagnose potential problems.

However, from 2002 the firm had lost its magic, customer service standards had dropped, and the company didn't perform profitably. Eddie's brother, William, had left the business two years previously, and joined his brother-in-law at WA Developments, a firm specializing in civil engineering in the rail industry. William had played an influential part in Eddie Stobart, being intensely involved at the operational level. He had helped to maintain a strong quality and training culture among the drivers.

In February 2004 WA Developments bought control of Eddie Stobart for a reported £60 million, and William became managing director, with his brother-in-law, Andrew Tinkler, becoming chairman. He put considerable effort into winning back old contracts as well as gaining new contracts. For instance, Stobart takes waste paper to Europe and back loads with Coca-Cola and dog food. He set about re-engineering the business and applied what he had learned from the civil engineering business about detailed costing and quality systems.

He also changed the operating culture and moved from double shifting to a one-man one-truck operation with an emphasis on loaded miles. The consequence of this action was that annual miles dropped from 112,000 to 93,000 but the earnings per mile improved. There has also been a shift back to roaming trucks, including night roamers. In late 2004 he made a $6 million investment and purchased 116 new Volvo trucks. The fleet has been modified to allow 1,300 litres of diesel, compared to 800 litres on existing fleet vehicles, so that the firm can make the most of low fuel prices abroad. New livery has been adopted but it isn't painted on but rather a plastic wrap is applied on the white paint. The name on the front of the first truck of this new fleet was none other than "Paris Hilton"!

In 2007 the Stobart Group was formed through a reverse merger with Westbury Property Fund Ltd, and the Group was listed on the London Stock Exchange. The company re-positioned itself as an inter-model logistics solutions company, incorporating rail, truck, and port operations. With the Westbury takeover the Group acquired the Port of Winton in Runcorn. As part of the takeover they also acquired the O'Connor Group, with a fleet of 90 vehicles, and its "inland port" rail depot at Widnes, near Runcorn. In 2008 the Group expanded further by acquiring one of its main competitors, the James Iriam Logistics Company and also Innovate's chilled business, which expanded the Group's operation into the fresh and chilled transport business. Also in the same year the Group acquired London Southend airport and the following year the Carlisle Lake District Airport. As at August 2012 the company had 2% market share, operated 2,280 trucks and 3,500 trailers, and had 5,500 employees.

In response to the demands from their clients, the Stobart Group instigated, in conjunction with the rail giant, DB Schenker, an environmentally friendly train from Valencia, Spain to their Dagenham rail freight depot in England, carrying 30 refrigerated containers of tomatoes, oranges, lemons, and vegetables. The intention is to develop the service from once a week to five times a week. However, the management of such an enterprise is difficult as there are up to four different train networks involved. The last thing the Group wants is for a train to be shunted into a siding by mistake.

A key to the company's promotion strategy has been the development of its fan club. Mainly made up of truck spotters, the fan club now numbers over 25,000 members with a £1.5 million turnover from membership fees and merchandise, including teddy bears, sweatshirts, jackets, CDs and prints, along with a newsletter. The prize possession of the true Stobart spotter is a copy of the fleet manual, which lists all current vehicles, registration number, fleet number, make, livery, and their given name. Recently a fun ride at Blackpool was installed featuring a convoy of Eddie Stobart trucks. He has also licensed his logo to Corgi, the toy maker and Hornby trains have an Eddie Stobart locomotive and wagons set.

The naming of a truck is now the task of club members, but there is a waiting list of up to three years. However, the naming rights are sometimes auctioned to raise money for charity. For example in 2008 the company raised £20,000 by auction. Eddie Stobart truck spotting has become a quirk of British culture. To mark the 25th birthday of the firm, the Wurzels wrote a song, "I wanna be an Eddie Stobart Driver", which made the top 100.

Questions

1. *What are the critical success factors in the industry?*
2. *Why would a company use Eddie Stobart to deliver products for them?*
3. *How has the Eddie Stobart brand helped the business?*

◄◄◄ Some Ideas

1. *What are the critical success factors in the industry?*

Critical success factors are the competencies and capabilities a firm must have in order to compete in that particular market. In other words, they are the hygiene factors that are necessary to survive. Eddie Stobart is more than a trucking firm. They are providing fourth party logistics, that is, they provide a service to customers that will look after all their product distribution from supplier to buyer. A company in this market must have appropriate warehousing, which needs to be conveniently located and well organized, therefore property management is a necessary competency.

The company must have efficient IT solutions providing tracking of products so that customers can easily trace goods. As part of the IT system there needs to be the ability to monitor trucks so that they remain reliable and can navigate routes and traffic efficiently. The company needs a capable operations manager who can prioritize orders, search for backloads, and obtain work for trucks that are roaming.

2. *Why would a company use Eddie Stobart to deliver products for them?*

Companies can outsource their logistics operations to Eddie Stobart so they don't have the cost of warehousing and owning delivery vehicles. This may work better for companies with non-perishable goods. Eddie Stobart has expertise in being able to deliver products at the right place at the right time. They collect goods from suppliers, store them in appropriate warehouse facilities, and deliver them to the client, e.g. a Tesco shop, within a 15-minute window either side of the scheduled time.

3. *How has the Eddie Stobart brand helped the business?*

Eddie Stobart operates in the B2B market so a lot of work is undertaken on contract. However, before the contract is signed, the brand name gives clients an assurance of reliability and competence. Also, as some of the business is obtained by roaming trucks and securing backloads, it is essential that Eddie Stobart is top of mind for companies that need one-off or casual assignments. Finally, the brand has helped create the fan club, and through merchandising, provides the company with an additional revenue stream.

Case Notes:

Case 8-2 Easy to Spread

Limestone is a sedimentary rock and is found in several areas in both the North and South Islands of New Zealand, particularly in the Waikato, Hawkes Bay, and Otago regions. Limestone consists mainly of calcium carbonate ($CaCO_3$) and is formed from the remains of fish, coral, seashells, and other marine organisms mixed with dissolved carbon dioxide from seawater. Their remains settle on the seabed where they may be buried by other sediments over time.

Limestone is mined in a quarry and transported by truck to a crushing plant where it is reduced to the required size. Different sized limestone has different applications and different treatments produce different products. In New Zealand large quantities of lime are used in steel making and cement manufacture. For example, McDonalds Lime in Te Kuiti is jointly owned by Holcim Cement (72%) and BHP–NZ Steel (28%). In the construction industry lime is used as a soil stabilizer for roads, airfields, building foundations, and earth dams. In paper making it is used as a causticizing agent and for bleaching. Being non-toxic lime is also vitally important as an environmental clean-up material and is used for sewage treatment, water softening, as well as neutralizing sulphur oxides and industrial chimney gases.

Lime is a vital element used in New Zealand farms as a fertilizer, fungicide, and insecticide. Agricultural lime neutralizes soil acidity, increases organic matter, improves soil tilth, provides a source of trace elements, and is a direct source of plant nutrients.

Wellington businessmen who wanted to supply lime to the market gardens in the Horowhenua region started Hatuma Lime Limited in 1932. They decided that the Hatuma hills, near Waipukurau, in the Hawkes Bay, would be a good source of the product. The benefits of applying lime to increase agriculture production were recognized by the Department of Agriculture so large subsidies were given to farmers if they were to use lime as a fertilizer. After World War II, returning pilots used their skills to spread fertilizer by aerial topdressing but by 1960 the government withdrew all subsidies on lime and increased those on superphosphate.

In 1963, with sales plummeting, Hatuma Lime under the leadership of the manager, Joe Topp, developed a new product called Dicalcic Phosphate, which comprises equal parts of lime and superphosphate, mixed with water, and allowed to settle for four weeks. The rock hard material is then broken up so that it can be spread by either truck or plane. From 1977 to 1982 production of Dicalcic Phosphate increased to over one million tonnes annually so new storage sheds and mixing plants were installed and heavy machinery was purchased. In 1981 a transfer station in Marton was established alongside the railway line to service the western side of the lower North Island, particularly the Rangitikei, Manawatu, and Taranaki regions. In 1986 the government removed all farming subsidies, which meant that Hatuma Lime was able to compete on a level playing field.

Whilst superphosphate has recognizable benefits it does produce grass growth surges, and being water soluble, leads to run-off into streams, rivers, and lakes. Unfortunately superphosphate is acidic so when added to soil, the acid-hating organisms within the top layer of the soil, including earthworms, cannot thrive. Also the process of breaking down the litter layer of dead grass and manure slows, causing the soil's recycling process to shut down, consequently affecting the pasture quality and stock health. Dicalcic Phosphate, on the other hand, has a balanced pH of 6.5–7.0 (a neutral pH is 7), so the soil organisms thrive as the soil is not too acidic. As the Dicalcic Phosphate is non-water soluble the phosphate is released gradually, as needed naturally by the plants. Also, there is little run-off into streams and lakes. Other benefits include an increase in stock health, the return of clover in areas that have given up, and an improvement in soil life and humus production. Dicalcic Phosphate spreads easily after any amount of time, and it can be spread at any time of the year and at any rate.

The marketing manager of Hatuma Lime Ltd believes that the sales of Dicalcic Phosphate can be increased in the Taranaki and Manawatu regions by 10% over the coming year. He bases this belief on Taranaki being dairy country, and a large number of farms in the Manawatu area converting from sheep to dairy, coupled with the large payout from Fonterra to dairy farmers, consequently making surplus funds available for top-dressing. The marketing manager acknowledges that he has storage facilities in Marton, but it will need a good communication plan to win over farmers who have traditionally used superphosphate.

Questions

1. *What are the factors that a farmer in Taranaki will take into account before purchasing Hatuma Dicalcic Phosphate?*
2. *Outline the logistic decisions that Hatuma Lime needs to make to set up the Marton site.*
3. *What does management need to do to build the Hatuma Dicalcic Phosphate brand equity?*

Case 8-3 Cathedrals of Consumption

Shopping malls have become a ubiquitous part of the urban landscape. For some people a trip to the mall is a weekly occurrence and for others, the trip is because of the need to purchase a particular item. Whatever the reason for the visit, be it routine or planned, chances are shoppers bought more than they intended. If this is the case they have been subjected to the Gruen Transfer.

The origins of the modern mall can be attributed to Victor Gruen, with the *New Yorker* suggesting that he may be the most influential architect of the twentieth century. Born Vicktor David Grünbaum in Vienna, Austria on 18 July 1903, he studied architecture at the Vienna Academy of Fine Arts, the same school that had refused entry to Hitler several years earlier.

In 1938, with the impending annexation of Austria by the Nazis, he escaped Vienna due to being a Jew and a Social Democrat. A friend, dressed as a Nazi Storm Trooper, drove him and his wife to the airport where they were able to catch a flight to Switzerland. They then made their way to England before travelling by boat to the United States.

His first big break was when he designed a revolutionary store-front for a shop on Fifth Avenue, New York. Seen as a "customer trap" the design received rave reviews, which won him more retail architectural work. However, his most famous design is the Southdale mall in Edina, Minnesota. Gruen wanted to design a shopping complex that would change the urban landscape to reflect the architecture of Vienna. He was appalled by what he called the "avenues of horror" where a variety of shops were spread out along the street, interspersed with billboards, motels, car lots, and hot dog stands. In contrast, his utopian vision was to have the mall as the central part of the community, surrounded by apartments, houses, schools, medical centres, a park, and a lake.

Whilst most shops at the time were "extroverted", that is they faced outwards to parking lots and walkways, Gruen designed his mall with the shops being "introverted". The exterior walls were bland and had no outside windows. All the activity was to be found inside, under one roof. The mall was anchored by having one or more large stores to attract customers, e.g. Macy's or JC Penny. A single level meant shoppers had a long walk, so Gruen designed his mall on two levels, connected by elevators at each end. This meant shoppers could easily do a loop as there was two-tiered parking with multiple entry points. In the middle was a garden court, situated under a skylight. Within the court was a 20-foot birdcage with exotic birds, sculptured trees, and a café. Upon its opening, *Time* magazine described the mall as a "pleasure dome with parking".

By the mid-1970s Gruen had established the architectural firm Gruen & Associates, based in Los Angeles. The firm employed 300 staff and had designed over 50 shopping malls in the United States. Over time, with other architects becoming involved in the design of malls, an archetype has been developed. Two levels were seen as the optimum as it was difficult to get people to go to up to a third level. Nothing was to disrupt the view, including reflective glass and there were no barriers or obstacles erected between the shopper and the inside store. This was to overcome the "threshold of resistance", that is, the artificial barrier which stops the shopper from stepping inside the store. The store layout was to promote longer stays and displays were placed to entice customers to pick up an item on impulse. Temperature and humidity were controlled so the shoppers felt comfortable, no matter what the season, and the lights were on when natural light faded, as dusk is a signal to the shopper that it is time to go home.

What are the signs of a shopper who has undergone, what has been termed, the Gruen Transfer? In other words, what are the signs that they have responded to scripted disorientation cues in the environment? Chances are they display a dropped jaw and have slightly glazed eyes. They have a confused feeling and walk at a slower pace. They tend to be a little hazy and muddled, consequently losing track of their original intentions, which makes them susceptible to impulse purchases.

Unfortunately Victor Gruen's vision of a new urban landscape was never realized due to the change in the economics of mall building. In 1954 Congress changed laws on depreciation allowing malls to be written off over a 40-year period. This meant the costs of building a mall would be recouped quickly so developers built malls not as central to the community but on the fringes of cities where the land was cheap.

Gruen disowned his endeavours as he disliked the manipulation of consumers and he saw developers were only interested in profit, not in overcoming social problems through architecture and commerce. In a speech in London in 1978 he said:

> I am often called the father of the shopping mall. I would like to disclaim paternity once and for all. I refuse to pay alimony to those bastard developments. They destroyed our cities.

Questions

1. *How does the concept of servicescape impact upon mall shopping?*
2. *How can a retailer overcome the "threshold of resistance"?*
3. *How will the growth of Internet shopping impact upon the mall?*

Case Notes:

Case
Study

Case 8-4 Give Us Our Daily Bread

In 2013 the 134-year-old family baker, Warburtons, from Bolton, Lancashire became the best loved shopping basket brand in Britain, ahead of Heinz, Cadbury, and Coca-Cola. Twenty-five years ago it was only known in the North East of England and had a 2% share of the British bread market.

The British bakery market is worth £3.6 billion a year, with a total volume of just under 4 billion packs, which equates to approximately 11 million loaves being sold every single day. Bakery items are an essential part of most people's diets with 99% of British households purchasing the product. However, the bakery market is a mature product with little growth in volume sales.

Consumption changes are being affected by a number of factors. There is a growth of single and two-person households and thus there is a demand for smaller loaves. The British ethnic mix is changing, therefore there is a demand for different types of breads, e.g. pitta bread. An ageing population benefits from healthier bread products, and general health issues regarding nutrition, allergies and obesity mean that manufacturers are baking types of bread to cater for these needs. Consequently there is a move away from traditional white sliced bread to wholegrain and seeded varieties with high fibre content and less sodium.

Convenience is another factor affecting consumption, but as toast is the number one snack, the bread manufacturers are in a good position to respond. Finally, the internationalization of consumer tastes due to travel and exposure to alternative cuisines has meant an increase in the sale of bagels, wraps, pittas, etc.

The British bread market consists of four main categories. The first is wrapped sliced bread, which accounts for 89% of value of the bread category. The bread is generally pre-sliced, which consumers find convenient, and has a shelf-life of 5 to 6 days. The wrapped bread is plant manufactured and the category is branded with companies investing in advertising.

The next category is in-store baking (ISB) with most supermarket chains having their own bakery. The bread is either baked from scratch using raw materials or is made using dough, which has already been part-baked. This type of bread has a short shelf life and is often bought as a treat, especially at weekends. ISB accounts for approximately 10.7% of the bread category.

The third category is baking snacks, such as hot cross buns, crumpets, muffins, pancakes, and croissants. These products tend to be seasonal and are consumed at key events. Research indicates that shoppers start out with good healthy intentions but by the weekend the need for enjoyment takes over so indulgent snacks are purchased. In 2012 baking snacks accounted for £711 million of bread sales.

The final category is breads of the world, which accounted for £469 million of sales in 2012. Items include wraps, bagels, pittas, thin rolls (originating from America), and naan breads.

The wrapped bread market in the UK has three main companies, namely Hovis (owned by Premier Foods), Kingsmill (owned by Associated British Foods plc), and Warburtons, which is the market leader. In 2012 Warburtons sold 521 million baking items, compared to 320.7 million items by its closest rival Hovis. Plant manufactured products accounted for three quarters of all baking products.

Over the last 25 years Warburtons has started expanding gradually by entering one region at a time. They have done this by opening a depot where they would heat the bread to keep it warm. If demand for their bread proved successful they would then open a bakery. See Table 8-4.1 for their current bakeries and depots.

Table 8-4.1   Warburtons bakeries and depots

Bakeries	Depots
Bellshill (Glasgow)	Aberdeen
Bolton	Basingstoke
Bristol	Bicester
Burnley	Eurocentral (Glasgow)
Eastwood (Nottingham)	Howden (Goole)
Enfield (London)	Langley Mill (Nottingham)
Newburn (Newcastle)	Paddock Wood (Kent)
Stockton (Cleveland)	Port Talbot
Tuscany Park (Wakefield)	Runcorn
Wednesbury (West Midlands)	Squires Gate (Blackpool)
	Stone
	Thetford

During this period Warburtons engaged in brand advertising, and this is now ongoing as competition is fierce. Another initiative is Warburtons' "Families Matter" programme. For example each week 50 loaves of medium sliced bread are delivered to the Salvation Army's Easterhouse Foodbank in Glasglow.

Warburtons have modernized their bakeries utilizing technology wherever possible. For example, they have installed robots with magnetic arms that pick up and set down bread tins, which far exceeds the lifting capability of humans. Magnets are used instead of pincer arms, as tins warp due to their constant heating and cooling; consequently the tins last twice as long. This is a cost saving as the large plants have 1,200 tin sets at £60,000 per set.

At Tuscany Park, Wakefield, Europe's biggest and most modern bakery, the plant operates around the clock in a four-hour baking cycle, producing 6,500 to 8,000 loaves per hour.

Upgrading the distribution network has been an important initiative so that bread arrives as fresh as possible at each retailer. To optimize the distribution system, Navman Wireless GPS vehicle tracking along with Paragon transport routing and scheduling systems have been installed. Routes are set directly to vehicles so when the drivers arrive at work they have the sequential orders in front of them. With a fleet of 800 vehicles Warburtons deliver 2.2 million loaves of bread a day to 20,000 retailers across Britain.

Questions

1. *If Warburtons' were to expand further into Essex develop a map of the path to market.*
2. *For the above scenario, identify the market actors and indicate their relative influence.*
3. *Explore how the three aspects of time impact upon Warburtons' channel decision.*

Case Notes:

References and Further Reading

Benjamin, W. (1955/2004) The Arcades Project, *Trans H. Eiland and K. McLaughlin*. Cambridge, MA: Belknap Press, 174–175.

Bitner, M.J. (1992) Servicescapes: The impact of physical surroundings on customers and employees, *Journal of Marketing*, 56 (April): 57–71.

Brennan, R. (2006) Evolutionary Economics and the Markets-as-networks Approach, *Industrial Marketing Management*, 35(7): 829–838.

Christopher, M. (1997) *Marketing Logistics*. Oxford: Butterworth-Heinemann.

Chung, C.J, Inaba, J. and Koolhass, R. (2001) *Harvard Design School Guide to Shopping*, New York: Taschen.

Clarke, D. and Purvis, M. (1994) Dialectics, *Difference and the Geographies of Consumption, Environment and Planning A*, 26, 1091–1109.

Cobbs, J. and Hylton, M. (2012) Facilitating Sponsorship Channels in the Business Model of Motorsports, *Journal of Marketing Channels*, 19(3): 173–192.

Coyle, J., Bardl, E. and Lawley, C. (2003) *The Management of Business Logistics: A Supply Chain Perspective*. Mason, OH: Thomson Learning.

Dibb, S. (1998) Market Segmentation: Strategies for Success, *Market Intelligence and Planning*, 16(7): 394–406.

Grönroos, C. (1989) Defining Marketing: A Market-Oriented Approach, *European Journal of Marketing*, 23(1): 52–60.

Reilly, W.J. (1931) *The Law of Retail Gravitation*. Austin, TX: University of Texas Press.

Shapiro, B., Rangan, V. and Sviokla, J. (1992) Staple Yourself to an Order, *Harvard Business Review*, July–August: 113–122.

Storbacka, K. and Nenonen, S. (2011) Scripting Markets: From value propositions to market propositions, *Industrial Marketing Management*, 40: 255–266.

Case Acknowledgements

The **Keep on Truckin'** case draws on information contained in:

Anonymous (1999), "Eddie Stobart Ltd in the driving seat", *Strategic Direction*, 15(4), 11

Anonymous (2004), "Stobart back and roaming", *Motor Transport*, August 12/August 19, 8

Anonymous (2004), "The Lurve Truck", *Commercial Motor*, 3 June, 15

Batchelor, C. (1998), "Haulier set for £20m aid to establish rail terminal", *Financial Times*, 12 March, 8

Futrell, J. (2002), "New Kiddie Truck Ride Rolls Into Blackpool", *Amusement Business*, August 19, 5

Holding, D. (2002), "Driving ambition", *Supply Management*, 7(1), 39

"Keeping track at Eddie Stobart", (February–March 2003), *m.logistics*, retrieved from http://www.mlogmag.com/magazine/04/stobart.shtml

Platt, E. (2001), "Trucking hell", *New Statesman*, 10 December, 54

Semple, J. (2004), "Stobart back with passion", *Motor Transport*, July 29/August 5, 1

The **Easy to Spread** case draws on information contained in:

Lime Industries website located at http://www.limeindustries.com.au/index-2.html

"Limestone – What is limestone and how is it used?", retrieved from http://geology.com/rocks/limestone.shtml

McDonald's Lime website located at http://www.onlime.co.nz

"The Hatuma Dicalcic Phosphate® Story", retrieved from http://www.hatumadp.co.nz/about/index.htm

The **Cathedrals of Consumption** case draws on information contained in:

"The Father of the Shopping Mall, Victor Gruen as an Urbanist", by D. Fitzpatrick (13 May 2013), *Reurbanist*, retrieved from http://www.reurbanist.com/2013/05/the-gruen-effect-victor-gruen-and-the-shopping-mall/

"The Terrazzo Jungle", by M. Gladwell (15 March 2004), *The New Yorker*, retrieved from http://www.newyorker.com/archive/2004/03/15/040315fa_fact1

http://www.wisegeek.com/what-is-the-gruen-transfer.htm

"Victor Gruen (Grunbaum)", by J. Andreas (6 May 2011), *German Historical Institute*, retrieved from http://www.transatlanticperspectives.org/entry.php?rec=21

The **Give Us Our Daily Bread** case draws on information contained in:

Anonymous (2005), "RTS" magnetic robot system helps Warburtons to national success, *The Industrial Robot*, 32(5), 419

Anonymous (2013), "Baker's slice of kindness", *Evening Times*, Glasgow, 24 December, 37

Anonymous (2014), "Warburtons toasts success of joint Paragon and Navman Wireless implementation", *M2 Presswire*, January 21

Reuben, A., "A family firm that blows its own trumpet", *BBC News*, (7 March 2007), retrieved from http://news.bbc.co.uk/go/pr/fr/-/2/hi/business/6419223.stm

"The British Bakery Market", (October 2013), *The Federation of Bakers*, Factsheet No. 3

"Warburtons named Britain's best shopping brand ahead of Coca-Cola and Cadbury", by R. Sayid (2 May 2013), *Mirror*, retrieved from http://www.mirror.co.uk/money/city-news/warburtons-named-britains-best-loved-1866189

Table 8-4.1: Compiled from information located at http://www.warburtons.co.uk/corporate/our-operations

This chapter covers the following topics:

▶ Integrated marketing communications
▶ Communication objectives
▶ Communication mechanisms
▶ Media choices

9
Communi-
cation
Heaven

The role of communications plays an important part linking brand or corporate identity with brand image or corporate image. Within the marketing mix framework the "P" for promotion indicated that the task was to promote the good to the consumer, which was embedded in the "marketing to" approach. However, with the introduction of relationship marketing and the service dominant logic, promotion has been replaced with communication, indicating a two-way information flow, meaning that the approach is now "marketing with" the customer.

Obviously, if an organization did not actively promote their value proposition it would have to rely on word of mouth or customers stumbling across the brand by chance, which would have consequences with regard to sales and profit. In the twenty-first century the task of managing communications is challenging for any organization for a number of reasons. First, consumers in the post-industrial era are well educated, streetwise, and have a sophisticated appreciation of different types of media. Second, as discussed in Chapter 4, the hyper-reality allows customers to spend money creatively by exploring different themes based on the past, present, or future.

Also, fragmentation of media means that there are many different ways to reach audiences. This is especially the case with the increase in digital media. The third challenge is that whilst the market is becoming increasingly global, product offerings are being customized to suit individual needs. Consequently the task of communication becomes increasingly difficult as a mass communication strategy is unlikely to be successful. Another issue is the pervasiveness of technology in society, whereby companies can track customers' wants and desires as well as their likes and dislikes, allowing for open communication. The challenge is for an organization to capture this interaction and respond in a meaningful way.

Whilst marketing is concerned with target markets, communication concentrates on audiences. One audience is customers but they can be broken down into loyal customers who require individual messages, through a loyalty card scheme for instance; brand-switchers who need a communication strategy to convince them to try another brand; and new category users where the communication objective is to trial the product/service. Other audiences include intermediaries, influencers, general public, and other stakeholders who may require a tailored communication strategy.

Join Together

Over the past 20 years, the concept of Integrated Marketing Communications has come to the forefront (Kitchen, 2005). There are a number of reasons explaining why organizations are interested in implementing integrated marketing communications. The first is due to financial considerations. The cost of media has increased forcing companies to rethink their media spend. Second, organizations have become more sophisticated in their approach to marketing communications and are aware of the different communication channels and media, and what each can achieve. Third, following on from above, clients have become disillusioned with advertising agencies who tended to push advertising as the main channel. Some would say, cynically, that this was due to the overall agenda of agencies being one of obtaining advertising awards. However, there is evidence now to suggest that many agencies offer an integrated service, with specialists in the area of public relations and point of sale, as well as mainstream advertising. Another important reason is the power shift to retailers so having coordinated communications becomes important. Finally, the increase in technology where companies can track customers has meant that communications need to be well managed.

The goal of integrated marketing communications is to strategically coordinate all messages and media utilized to influence an organization's audiences so that a profitable relationship is built over time. Therefore by using the different mechanisms of the communication mix each specific task can be enhanced, as each mechanism affects consumers differently. By utilizing different communication channels and media a synergy is gained, which not only gives greater impact but also offsets against any weakness in the other components. By implementing an integrated marketing communications campaign the organization is attempting to affect behaviour by direct communication. This involves a good understanding of the audience's profile. By adopting a single voice and coordinating both messages and media the organization is hoping to build relationships so that repeat purchases ensure customers act as brand advocates.

Schultz and Kitchen (2000) identified four stages of integrated marketing communication development:

Stage 1 Tactical coordination of communication, led by the business but with little focus on the customer. An attempt is made to bundle together communication elements so that it appears there is one voice.

Stage 2 The organization is more focused and customers' needs are taken into account, their feedback is evaluated, and an attempt is made to align with outside agencies.

Stage 3 Investment is made in resources to build segmented databases using information technology and this information is used to organize an effective integrated communication plan.

Stage 4 Financial and strategic integration is achieved with performance measured on an ROI (return on investment) basis. The primary measurement is behavioural rather than attitudinal.

According to Schultz et al (1993) the objective is to maximize communications by balancing the different media so that there is mass advertising, interactivity (Internet sites), and addressable media (print or email). The next step is to build databases to track customer interaction as well as their likes, dislikes, and concerns, which can then be used to facilitate purposeful dialogue with the relevant audiences. Finally, it is necessary that corporate culture supports the integration and develops the organizational memory for the integration to become modus operandi.

Can You Hear Me Now?

Models of information processing have been utilized well before the foundation of the marketing discipline and have played a significant part in attempting to explain the process of marketing communications. The AIDA model, where a customer progresses from Attention to Interest to Desire then Action was developed by a sales manager for National Cash Register in the 1880s as a tool for sales staff to sell cash registers, commonly called tills. The task was to draw the customer through each stage so as to obtain a sale. This led to advertising being seen as an extension of the sales force. In other words the task of advertising was to move the customer through each identified stage in a sequential order.

Although there are numerous information processing models the most popular is the Hierarchy of Effects, where the task of marketing communications is to establish awareness of the brand, followed by knowledge. Both of these stages involve cognition, whereas the next three stages, namely liking, preference, and conviction, are based on affect (emotions). The final stage is purchase (cognitive behaviour) (Lawridge and Steiner, 1961).

The model is based on a sequential order where a customer has to go through one stage before going onto the next one. There has been a certain amount of criticism concerning information processing models. Heath and Feldwick (2008) make a number of observations concerning problems with information processing models. First, they are based on one-way communications, so the consumer does not influence the message or claim being made, whereas in the digital age a lot of communication is interactive. Second, the models assume there is active involvement of the viewer which is counter to research which indicates some messages are received subliminally. Third, cognition takes a primary role, with emotion becoming secondary; consequently the effectiveness of communication is dominated by marketing research metrics which are based on cognition, for example, advertising recall, leading to the role of emotion being discriminated against. Finally, information processing models are based on the myth that all purchases are based on rational decision making. Whilst this may be the case with high involvement products and products new to the market, it doesn't hold for all products.

In contrast, a different approach has been developed by Foote, Cone, and Belding (see Figure 9.1), where a distinction is made between products where decision making is dominated by a cognitive, rational approach and decisions where emotions and affect are predominant. In contrast to the type of decision making, the model considers the intensity of the decision making. High involvement is intense due to the financial, social, or physical risks that are a consequence of the decision, compared to low involvement purchases, which are often routine or impulse purchases with minor consequences if a mistake is made.

	THINKING	FEELING

HIGH INVOLVEMENT	1 INFORMATIVE (THINKER)
	CARE-HOUSE-FURNISHINGS –
	NEW PRODUCTS
	MODEL: LEARN-FEEL-DO
	                (Economic?)
	
	Possible Implications
	MEDIA: Long Copy Format
	              Reflective Vehicles
	CREATIVE: Specific Information
	              Demonstration
		2 AFFECTIVE (FEELER)
		JEWELLERY-COSMETICS-
		FASHION APPAREL-MOTORCYCLES
		MODEL: FEEL-LEARN-DO
		                (Psychological?)
		
		Possible Implications
		MEDIA: Large Space
		              Image Specials
		CREATIVE: Executional
		              Impact

LOW INVOLVEMENT	3 HABIT FORMATION (DOER)
	FOOD-HOUSEHOLD ITEMS
	MODEL: DO-LEARN-FEEL
	                (Responsive?)
	
	Possible Implications
	MEDIA: Small Space Ads
	              10 second IDs
	              Radio; POS
	CREATIVE: Reminder
		4 SELF-SATISFACTION (REACTOR)
		CIGARETTES-LIQUOR-CANDY
		MODEL: DO-FEEL-LEARN
		                (Social?)
		
		Possible Implications
		MEDIA: Billboards
		              Newspapers
		              POS
		CREATIVE: Attention

Figure 9.1 The Foote, Cone, and Belding Grid. Source: Adapted from Vaughn (1980)

With decisions in Quadrant 1 the model is learn-feel-do which mirrors that of the hierarchy of effects model. However, with Quadrant 2 the model changes to feel-learn-do with an emphasis on the emotional dimension of decision making. With Quadrants 3 and 4 the model emphasizes do, that is purchase, followed by either learn or feel. As can been seen, the model not only gives examples of different types of products that fit each quadrant, but also outlines different media and creative copy that can be employed. The FCB model allows for different emphasis with decision making and thus overcomes some of the criticism levelled at linear, segmented information processing models.

The FCB model allows for communication objectives to be set. For instance, for products in Quadrants 3 and 4, the communication objective would be to induce trial of the product for new category users or reminder to purchase for customers already familiar with the product. Another communication objective is to create awareness, either recall or recognition. Recall is important where decisions to purchase are made outside of the store, for example, "I have a headache, I need to buy some Nurofen", whereas recognition is important where decisions are made in the store. So with recall the brand name plays a significant role, whereas with recognition packaging details play more of a role.

Other communication objectives include reminder to use or restock the product, changing attitudes about the product, building associations, and attitude reinforcement aimed at loyal customers. Setting communication objectives is important as they facilitate the coordination of the various groups working on the campaign, and enable decision making in areas such as creative, media, budgeting, and sales promotion options. Finally, the campaign can be measured and evaluated against the communication objectives.

It is important that communication objectives are not confused with marketing objectives. Whilst the latter is focused on sales by increasing volume or market share, the communication objectives do not correlate with these objectives for a number of reasons. The campaign may be successful but sales don't eventuate due to stock-outs, competitor actions, or the carry over effect, that is, sales may occur after the campaign has ended.

Mixing it Up

The role of communications for an organization serves three different purposes. It can be to inform the public, for example to correct false impressions or to provide new information; or to persuade, e.g. changing behaviour such as road safety campaigns; or to influence a purchase decision. Finally, the purpose can be to sell by reinforcing existing attitudes or to entice new category users or brand switchers.

The communication mix refers to the different mechanisms that can be used to achieve the communication objectives. Each mechanism has its own skill set and expertise, with unique tasks that achieve different communication outcomes. The choice of the communication mechanism will depend not only on the communication objective that has been set but also the characteristics of the audience in terms of size and geographic location, the type of product in terms of technicality, complexity, level of risk, and the margins generated per sale. It is also dependent on whether the company is employing a pull strategy, that is a communication aimed at the customer so that they ask for or demand the product from the intermediary, e.g. retailer, or a push strategy whereby the manufacturer provides incentives to the intermediary so that they promote the product to the customer.

There are eight different types of communication mechanisms.

Advertising

The task is to communicate to an audience via passive, one-way communication to achieve a desired communication objective, e.g. brand awareness. There are different types of advertising such as brand, corporate, business to business (B2B), and retail. Advertising has two essential areas of expertise, namely creativity and media placement. The role of the creative department is to first develop a single minded proposition, that is, a statement that captures the essence of the product so that the audience quickly understands the message. It is the single most motivating and differentiating statement that can be said to a target audience.

The task of the creative department is to make it come alive in a compelling manner. The second task is to develop copy and execute images that appeal to the selected audience with an appropriate tone and manner. The benefit of advertising is that it has a broad reach but in a fragmented culture it can lead to wastage. It has a low cost per thousand and has the ability to create brand imagery. This is especially important for parity products, that is products that cannot be differentiated by attributes apart from their brand image, for example vodka. Without their brand image, parity products would be commodities which are only differentiated by price.

Public Relations

The task is to gain publicity for the brand or organization so that goodwill is established and a positive impact is achieved. The expertise of a public relations department centres on the ability to write journalistic copy and having contacts in the media, who have some resonance with the story and find it newsworthy. The benefits of public relations are that it is seen by the audience as being objective and independent, therefore credible, so can be trusted, and tends to have a broad audience.

Sales Promotion

The task is to facilitate trial of the product or purchase of the product. There are two main audiences of sales promotions, namely the consumer and the trade (see Push versus Pull, earlier). Sales promotions fall into two main types. Value increasing promotions change the price to increase the perceived value of the offering, e.g. discounts, coupons, multipacks, or quantity increases. Trade oriented promotions include allowances, incentives, cooperative advertising, and point of purchase displays. Value-adding sales promotions, sometimes referred to as "packaged up" promotions, offer the customer something extra, e.g. free trial, free gift, loyalty card, or a competition. For the trade it may be training programmes, trade shows, and dealer contests.

Sales promotion expertise lies in merchandising, point of purchase displays and the coordination of not only the promotion, e.g. redemption of coupons, but also the integration of communication mechanisms, e.g. advertising, PR and sponsorship, as well as related media.

The benefits of sales promotions include building inquiries, encouraging brand switching, inducing product trial, and for the trade to gain increased space allotment and offer promotional support. However, there are some inherent risks such as creating a price orientation, cannibalizing future sales, and alienating loyal customers, e.g. offering a sales promotion to new subscribers.

Sales Force

The task is to liaise with customers on a one-to-one basis to either obtain sales or provide ongoing support for a product. There are different types of sales roles which have distinct tasks. Order-takers have the task of restocking existing clients' inventory, whilst order-getters' tasks involve influencing customers to purchase the product. Problem-solvers or solutions providers have the task of solving issues or problems faced by their client, e.g. an account manager for an IT vendor. Expertise is based on staff being boundary spanners, which involves listening and being empathetic with regard to the needs of the client whilst representing the objectives of their organization. The benefit of using the sales force is that when the selling price is high, the sales force can alleviate any fears and perceived risks, build a trusted relationship, and offer technical advice before and after purchase. Depending on the product, the audience may be an Original Equipment Manufacturer (OEM), manufacturer, end user, influencer, or the trade.

Direct Marketing

The task is to communicate to the target audience via either mail or email in a personalized manner, with the aim of building a relationship.

Expertise centres on database management and the writing of personal communications. The benefit of direct marketing is that it encourages interactivity by attempting to elicit a specific response whereby the recipient is motivated to action. The campaign can be easily measured by the speed of response. By developing small scale test cases, demand can be measured and controlled growth can be managed by only contacting small sections of the audience at a time.

Sponsorship

The task is to invest in events or causes for the benefit of the brand or organization. The expertise required is in event management and the coordination of the different communication mechanisms and media to obtain the greatest impact. There are a number of benefits which are not mutually exclusive. The first is to build associations, which is an advantage in a highly competitive situation or for parity products. Second, media exposure can be obtained, which is an advantage with cluttered and fragmented media. Third, events provide opportunity for hosting select clients, and finally sponsorship can be used to gain the approval of stakeholders so that the organization is seen as a good citizen.

Design/Servicescape

The task is to communicate to the desired audience the image and quality of the brand. Expertise is required in graphic design and architecture. The benefits of a unique package design are that it draws attention to a brand and helps break through competitive clutter, as well as conveying the price/value and benefits of the product. A servicescape is concerned with the built environment, that is, the physical surroundings where the service is being offered which can either enhance or suppress customer satisfaction. Signs, symbols, and artifacts play an important part in creating first impressions and provide clues to the quality of service. Ambient conditions such as temperature, lighting, music, and scent all affect the quality of the service. The servicescape is not dependent on one single element but the configuration of all the elements.

The servicescape is an important component of the Servuction Model. Along with a service blueprint, open or closed scripts developed for contact personnel and service providers, defined touch points with a defined zone of tolerance, and the management of other customers on the premises, all contribute to the "moment of truth", that is, the perceived quality of the customer experience.

Contact Centres

The task is to handle customer enquiries either over the phone or through the company's website. Staff need expertise in understanding the company's products and empathy to deal with customers. The benefit of a contact centre is that it can be used to obtain or change orders, e.g. ticketing, provide solutions to specific customer problems and after-sales service, and deal with customer complaints.

Media Matters

Media has become increasingly fragmented, especially with the rise of digital media, including social media. A media planner is presented with a wide variety of media choices: television, newspapers, magazines, radio, billboards, Internet etc. The media mix selected for a product/service will depend on a number of factors. The media usage of the target market is an important consideration, for example, if the target audience is keen gardeners then *House and Garden* would be an appropriate placement rather than *Truckers Monthly*. Another factor is determining the required reach, that is, the number of consumers that you would like exposed to the media. Coupled to the question is one of frequency, that is, the number of times over a given time period the consumer is exposed to a communication. Also, product characteristics will determine the type of message plus the tone and manner that are required, for example, long copy format or visuals. Finally, the cost of the media, measured in cost per thousand (cpm), will be a modifying factor.

Digital media allows for interactivity where consumers can search, obtain relevant information and make bookings and purchases. It also allows for individualization as consumers have control over the type of information they seek. Whereas with traditional media consumers are passive recipients, with digital media consumers are active and in control. Digital media allows organizations to select specific Internet sites used by the target audience, with sites accessible 24/7 and without geographic restrictions. Also behavioural tracking can be monitored and patterns of behaviour identified, with sales conversions calculated. With social media customers can contribute to the strategic decision making of organizations and co-create values. Organizations can seek active involvement with buyers so that they become involved in the added value process.

Organizations can use social media to take their story to the public, thereby bypassing traditional media. The impact of customers can influence other customers and non-customers in the social network. Also, the organization can collect customer views about the product/service, especially in blogs and Facebook pages, and can correct any misinformation. The organization can receive feedback from purchasers about their buying process as well as find out why people didn't buy the product. Additionally, an organization can collect information on competitors. Organizations can have their own page on Facebook and track comments by "friends" and monitor the number of "likes". The organization can use the site for new product launches, to sell stressed inventory, or to advertise sales promotions. YouTube can be used effectively to promote brand awareness and brand associations, for example Air New Zealand's unique inflight safety videos.

Case 9-1 Departing from Platform 9

The Mallard is the world's fastest steam locomotive. Designed by Sir Nigel Gresley, the aerodynamic, garter blue, streamlined engine, which is an iconic example of British ingenuity, reached 126 miles per hour descending Stoke Bank, England on 3 July 1938. To mark the 75th anniversary the National Railway Museum York staged a two-week gala in July 2013. Billed as the "Great Gathering", the last six remaining A4 class locomotives were displayed at the Great Hall Turntable in the museum, with Hornby Model Railways (HMR) a key sponsor of the exhibition. To mark the occasion Hornby released limited editions of each six locomotives. At the same time Hornby celebrated the 150th anniversary of the birth of founder Frank Hornby, who in 1901 invented the Meccano kit set toy, which enabled children to build bridges, cranes, and trucks by bolting together interchangeable metal parts, including axles and shafts. In 1920 the first clockwork train was produced and in 1938 the first OO gauge train was sold, which became the accepted modelling standard in the UK, whereas the rest of the world uses HO gauge. Whilst both have the same track gauge, the proportions of the locomotives and rolling stock are different.

Over the years Hornby PLC has consolidated its position in the model market, now owning model train brands such as Lima and Rivarossi, Scalextric slot racing cars, Airfix kit set models, Humbrol paints, and Corgi Die-cast models (see Table 9-1.1). However, in June 2013 Hornby PLC reported that their yearly sales had dropped from £64.4 million to £57.4 million, resulting in a £3.4 million loss. Consequently no dividend was paid, whereas 3.7p had been made as a dividend the year before. According to the Chairman, two reasons accounted for the loss. The first was the disappointing sales from the models produced for the London Olympics, consisting of specially designed buses, figurines, mascot toys, and a Scalextric velodrome. The company's targets were missed by a considerable margin, resulting in their being forced to heavily discount the product. For example, a fleet of taxis, sold in a pack of 36, was reduced from the asking price of £179.64 to £53.64. The second reason was due to problems with the supply chain where 10% of the product was not delivered. Unfortunately the main supplier closed down their main factory and transferred the activity to another plant, which didn't have the expertise to assemble the product. To overcome this problem Hornby sourced other suppliers in China and India, reducing total production from the main supplier from 75% to 15%. Also, due to the mounting labour costs in China, which have increased by 15%, Hornby has repatriated approximately 10% of production back to the UK.

Table 9-1.1   Hornby PLC

Product categories	Model Trains	Slot Car Racing	Kits/Paints	Die-cast
Brands	Hornby, Electrotren, Lima, Rivarossi, Jouef, Arnold	Scalextric, Superslot	Airfix, Humbrol	Corgi, Pocher
Share of revenue	39% (2012–48%)	27% (2012–26%)	16% (2012–14%)	18% (2012–12%)
Supply source	China	China	India/UK	China
Internal product development	UK/Spain	UK	UK	UK
Routes to market	Independent toy/model stores Key accounts/major retailers 3rd party internet retailers Concession stores (UK only) Direct to consumer Internet/online			

The Hornby Model Railway (HMR) is a major division of Hornby PLC. Up until the turn of the century trains played a central part in every British boy's childhood as trains interweaved in their lives in different ways, whether it was a train trip to the seaside for holidays, a model train set in the bedroom, or train spotting at the local railway station. This love of trains is best epitomized by James May, the Top Gear presenter, who in a television series, "James May's Toy Stories", devoted an episode to model railways by attempting to build the world's largest model railway, on the Tarka trail, which is an old railway track between Barnstaple and Bideford, North Devon. To achieve his goal he recruited 400 enthusiasts to help build the track, with Hornby providing the track and a prototype of BR class 395 "Javelin". Unfortunately this attempt failed partly due to coins being dropped on the line, consequently blowing the battery, and to top it all off, the battery was stolen.

Product development is a key driver for HMR, with manufacturing being a complex and skilled process. HMR produce a variety of locomotives, such as BR class 9F, LNER class A4 Flying Scotsman, Southern Region Merchant Navy class, and Great Western Prairie tanks, as well as passenger coaches and freight wagons. Tracks and points are an important product and trackside accessories are provided through the Skaledale range. The major competitor for HMR is Bachmann Industries, with small niche players such as Peco. HMR has entered the digital era, which allows more than one train to be controlled at any one time. Recently they launched E-link and Railmaster, allowing for the control of the model railway by a personal computer or other mobile devices.

Model railway buyers can be segmented into three groups. The first group is new modellers, usually young children. They are provided with a toy range, with models like Thomas the Tank engine, and at lower price points. The second segment consists of customers who are returning to the railway model scene, and are now in position to model again, often because they have young children. The final segment are older modellers who have become enthusiasts. They have more time and more disposable income, consequently they purchase high end locomotives.

HMR sales declined by approximately 26% in the year ended June 2013, partly due to supply issues and the delays to new locomotives coming onto the market. Also, consumer confidence has waned due to the economic conditions, so retailers have been conservative with their inventory orders. Due to the tight conditions and the changing buying patterns of consumers, in August 2013 Modelzone, a toy and hobby retailer, collapsed with the consequent closing of 18 stores and the loss of 385 staff. Unfortunately, as a result Hornby PLC, a major supplier, had to write down £200,000.

> ## Questions
> 1. *What are the challenges facing Hornby PLC?*
> 2. *What does the company need to do to build the Hornby Model Railway brand image?*
> 3. *What communication strategies does Hornby Model Railway need to adopt to increase participation in the hobby?*

◀◀◀ Some Ideas

1. *What are the challenges facing Hornby PLC?*

They need to recover from the Olympic fiasco and rebuild profit. To do this they must secure supply of their models, especially the model trains, as these account for 39% of their sales. However, the biggest challenge is obtaining new customers, especially children and teenagers, as there is stiff competition from other types of entertainment, for example, computer games. The closure of model shops indicates buyers are either not interested or are buying online.

2. *What does the company need to do to build the Hornby Model Railway brand image?*

Brand image has two components, namely awareness and association. Therefore the company needs to concentrate on building awareness and creating new associations. Trainspotting in the days of steam was exciting and also there were limited distractions. Nowadays the connection with the railways is lost for most young people, especially due to the dominance of the motor car and air travel. The challenge for Hornby is to regain an interest in trains. This can be achieved using their new digital locomotives, which allow for computer programming. Model railways have become technologically more sophisticated and challenging.

3. *What communication strategies does Hornby Model Railway need to adopt to increase participation in the hobby?*

As indicated above, Hornby Model Railway needs to build brand awareness, associations, and interest. To achieve this they need to maintain a multi-channel distribution network, and also have a compelling Internet site. Hornby need to continue supporting and attending model train shows, and advertise not only in model railway magazines, but also general railway magazines. YouTube allows Hornby to display on their website tips and suggestions for building model railways, especially with digital trains, as some areas can be quite technical so receiving advice via video stream would be beneficial to modellers.

Sponsorship of the National Railway Museum should continue and closer ties should be developed with Preserved Railways. Finally, membership of the Hornby Collectors Club needs to be increased by providing activities, news items, competitions etc., to make membership attractive. The relationship between Hornby and members is important to maintain as loyal members can become advocates.

▶▶▶

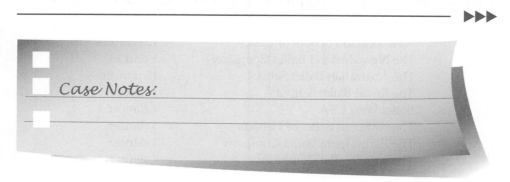

Case Notes:

Case 9-2 First Position

Angela Gendall won an AGC Young Achievers Award in 1986, which enabled her to attend the Royal Ballet School in London. Upon graduating to the Royal Ballet Company, she unfortunately sustained a back injury, but with intensive Pilates she recovered and continued to dance for the company for another four years. In 1995 she returned to New Zealand where she taught pilates whilst completing an MA in Psychology at Auckland University.

Angela revisited England in 2000, and after further training and teaching of pilates in Oxfordshire she returned to New Zealand and became a certified Polestar Pilates rehabilitation practitioner. Angela opened the Westmere Pilates studio in Auckland in 2004. Over the years a booking system was developed, allowing clients to book sessions online, as well as review their profile and record of progress. Also, clients could view their homework and review any photos and/or videos that an instructor had uploaded for them. This was not an off-the-shelf programme, but a unique system tailored for the studio. No other pilates studio had such a tailored system at the time.

Over time the studio has expanded to include two physiotherapists and six part-time pilates instructors, who all have a background in dance. Through Angela's contacts and interest the studio has concentrated on dance pilates, with 80% of the studio's 90 clients being dancers of varying age and ability. Recently the studio was extended to include a room with a sprung floor. This was designed for the Jump Training programme which focuses on giving dancers strength, control, and technique for effective jumping, and the finerPointe programme, which helps prevent injuries and improves a dancer's strength, alignment, and weight placement for pointe work. Both these programmes are available for students online to practise at their dance schools.

The success of Dance Pilates can be measured by the number of students who have been accepted into prestigious dance institutions including:

New Zealand School of Dance	12 dancers
The New Zealand Ballet Company	1 dancer
The Australian Ballet School	13 dancers
The Royal Ballet School	1 dancer
Ballet West USA	1 dancer
The National Ballet of Canada	1 dancer
The Paris Opera Ballet Company	1 dancer
The Israel Ballet Company	1 dancer

Dance, whether it be ballet, jazz, or hiphop, is an important aspect of New Zealand culture. More children participate in dance than play the national sports of rugby and netball combined. Approximately 80,000 students attend dance studios with 37% of children aged between 10 and 14 years taking part in a dance production in the past year.

Additionally there are over 14 tertiary institutions in New Zealand offering dance courses, including four offering dance degrees. Also, dance has become an examinable subject at secondary schools.

Given Angela's interest in pilates for dance, and also utilization of technology in the studio, it was a natural step for her to develop Movitae. Movitae is a web application for sharing multi-media content, like Facebook, that has been developed specifically for dancers. In particular it has been designed around privacy, so each dancer's page is protected. The system is structured to prevent the content going viral, which is an important consideration for dancers and dance teachers. A free iPhone app has been developed for easy upload but content can be uploaded and viewed from any computer or smart device. Also, the software is cloud-based allowing for easy access anywhere in the world.

Movitae is targeted at two groups, namely dancers and dance teachers, across institutions including local dance schools, secondary schools, and tertiary institutions. Dancers have the ability to upload a performance as soon as it happens. They can add it to their profile to view later and they can add the video to their timeline to show progress and achievements. The dancers can also share the video with their dance tutor to gain feedback. Dancers can also access technique and conditioning programmes with the option of personal guidance, tailored homework, and assessment from online mentors from the programme's organization.

The benefit for the dance teacher is that they can be paid online via Movitae for feedback and they can share choreography with staff, when developing a production, and with young dancers who can easily forget their steps. Teachers can also use Motivae as a noticeboard and can group their students to make the sending of content easy. Dancers can learn choreography, view progress, goal set, receive feedback from teachers and from dance professionals overseas, and can produce online CVs for audition entry.

Questions

1. *What are the communication challenges facing Movitae?*
2. *Determine the communication objectives for the selected target markets.*
3. *What channels of communication should be adopted?*

Case 9-3 Black Gold

Case Study

Are you a Vegemite or Marmite fan? Seemingly, the answer to such a question tells quite a lot about a Kiwi.

Vegemite is an Australian product made by Kraft, whereas Marmite is a New Zealand product made by Sanitarium, the makers of New Zealand's number one breakfast cereal, Weetbix. Both Vegemite and Marmite are thick, black savoury spreads, which look like axle grease, and are based on a yeast extract. New Zealand-made Marmite has a slightly different taste from the British version. Both Vegemite and Marmite form the basis of a staple Kiwi breakfast.

Sanitarium manufactured Marmite in a factory in Christchurch, producing 640,000 kg per year. Early in 2012 Sanitarium announced it would have to cease the production of Marmite due to severe damage to their factory cooling tower caused by the February Christchurch earthquake, making the building unsafe. Panic buying ended the supply at supermarkets and by March 2012, stocks had completely run out.

The company ran a TV commercial "Don't Panic", fronted by Sir Graham Henry, the former All Black Coach. The General Manager of Sanitarium suggested using the product on warm toast, as it would be easier to spread thereby conserving the amount used. Even New Zealand's Prime Minister, John Key, got involved calling for New Zealanders to ration themselves by suggesting they spread it thinner (although he himself admitted he could easily eat Vegemite in the meantime).

Within a month there were 750 jars of Marmite listed on Trade Me (New Zealand's equivalent to eBay), with a bid for a 250 g jar at $63, with proceeds going to the Cure Kids charity. The jar would normally sell for $3.50.

Initially, Sanitarium thought the product would be back on the shelves by July, but then the date was pushed back to October. Come November the company said that they had suffered snow and heavy rain, and had water coming through the factory roof, as well as having to cope with the ongoing aftershocks from the earthquake. There wouldn't be any Marmite before Christmas. They were now waiting for council approval for the newly strengthened and reconfigured factory.

In March 2014, one year on from the halt in production, the company announced that Marmite would be back on the shelves – but only the General Manager of Sanitarium and the Prime Minister knew the exact date. When Marmite did finally make it back to the shelves, some customers complained that it didn't taste the same, despite Sanitarium assuring consumers the recipe hadn't changed. Perhaps over the year consumers had become used to the taste of Vegemite?

Questions

1. *What are the communication tasks that Sanitarium needs to undertake now that Marmite is again being manufactured?*
2. *As the brand manager of Marmite, write a communication brief for the relaunch of the product. The brief should cover a six-month time frame. When allocating budget to the different activities, use a percentage figure rather than a dollar amount.*

Case Notes:

Case 9-4 Monkey Business

The chocolate division of Cadbury Schweppes was going through tough times. In 2006 it was found that some Cadbury products contained salmonella bacteria, resulting in 40 people becoming ill. The company undertook a product recall at a cost of £20 million. They were also fined £1 million for taking five months to notify the Food Standards Agency of the contamination. Unfortunately another incident occurred when the company distributed Easter eggs made on the same line which makes products with nuts in them, without an allergy warning. Then, in 2007 it was leaked that 7,500 jobs would be lost, with positions being relocated to Poland. Given these issues, the company decided to embark on a new advertising campaign to rouse brand engagement.

A new agency, Fallon London, pitched the idea of a gorilla playing drums, to the Phil Collins hit "In the Air Tonight" as they wanted watching the advertisement to be as enjoyable as eating a bar of chocolate. The Gorilla ad took three months to produce, with the suit made of knotted yak hair and the facial features made of silicon, which was able to be moved electronically. The ad was a 90-second commercial, which could be broken down into 60-second and 30-second commercials.

The 90-second TV ad was launched on Friday, 31 August 2007 during the Big Brother show. It also appeared on billboards, print newspapers, magazines, cinema, event sponsorship, and on the company website. The ad spread via viral marketing with 500,000 hits on YouTube in the first week. By November 2007 the ad had been viewed six million times on video-sharing web hosts and 70 Facebook appreciation pages had been set up. The ad had become a cult hit, with spoofs and parodies being uploaded by the public. The advertisement won many awards, including the coveted Film Grand Prix Lion at the Cannes Lions, 2008. By 2008, Dairy Milk sales, which had an annual turnover of £340 million, had increased by 9%.

Questions

1. *Watch the Cadbury's Gorilla ad on YouTube. What is it that makes the ad so appealing? How is it different from a traditional ad?*
2. *How would you "sell" the Gorilla idea to a marketing team?*
3. *How well did Cadbury use integrated marketing communications?*

References and Further Reading

Aaker, D. (2008) *Strategic Market Management*, 8th edn. Hoboken, NJ: Wiley.

Belch, G. and Belch, M. (2009) *Advertising and Promotion: An integrated marketing communications perspective*, 8th edn. Boston: McGraw-Hill Irwin.

Doyle, P. and Stern, P. (2006) *Marketing Management and Strategy*, 4th edn. Harlow, England: Prentice Hall.

Heath, R. and Feldwick, P. (2008) Fifty Years Using the Wrong Model of Advertising, *International Journal of Market Research*, 50(1): 29–59.

Kitchen, P. (2005) New Paradigm – IMC – Under Fire, *Competitiveness Review*, 15(1): 72–80.

Kitchen, P., Kim, I. and Schultz, D. (2008) *Integrated Marketing Communications: Practice Leads Theory, Journal of Advertising Research*, December, 531–546.

Kotler, P. and Keller, K. (2012) *Marketing Management*, 14th edn. Harlow, England: Pearson Education.

Lawridge, R. and Steiner, G. (1961) *A Model for Predictive Measurements of Advertising Effectiveness, Journal of Marketing*, October.

Proctor, T. and Kitchen, P. (2002) Communication in Postmodern Integrated Marketing, *Corporate Communications: An International Journal*, 7(3): 144–154.

Sashi, C. (2012) Customer Engagement, Buyer-Seller Relationships, and Social Media, *Management Decision*, 50(2): 253–272.

Schmidt, S. and Ralph, D. (2011) Social Media: More Available Marketing Tools, *The Business Review, Cambridge*, 18(2): 37–43.

Schultz, D. and Kitchen, P. (2000) *Communicating Globally: An integrated marketing approach*. London: Macmillan Press.

Schultz, D., Tannenbaum, S. and Lauterborn, R. (1993) *Integrated Marketing Communications*. Boston: McGraw Hill.

Shrimp, T. (2007) *Advertising, Promotion and Supplemental Aspects of Integrated Marketing Communications*. Mason, OH: Thomson/South-Western.

Singh, S. and Sonnenburg, S. (2012) Brand Performances in Social Media, *Journal of Interactive Marketing*, 26, 189–197.

Vaughn, R. (1980) How Advertising Works: A Planning Model, *Journal of Advertising Research*, 20(5): 27–33.

Wang, X., Yu, C., and Wei, Y. (2012) Social Media Peer Communication and Impacts on Purchase Intentions: A Consumer Socialization Framework, *Journal of Interactive Marketing*, 26, 198–208.

Case Acknowledgements

The **Departing from Platform 9** case draws on information contained in:

Hornby PLC Annual Report and Accounts 2013, retrieved from http://www.hornby.plc.uk/?page_id=4680

Hornby PLC website located at www.hornby.com

"Hornby to repatriate Airfix manufacturing from China and India", by L. Elliott (8 June 2013), *The Guardian*, retrieved from http://www.theguardian.com/business/2013/jun/08/hornby-airfix-manufacturing

COMMUNICATION HEAVEN

"Hornby to step up UK manufacturing as it battles back from Olympic slump", by G. Ruddick (7 June 2013), *The Telegraph*, retrieved from http://www.telegraph .co.uk/finance/newsbysector/retailandconsumer/10107100/Hornby-to-step -up-UK-manufacturing-as-it-battles-back-from-Olympic-slump.html

"Is the Hornby express about to hit the buffers?", by C. Middleton (26 September 2012), *The Telegraph*, retrieved from http://www.telegraph.co.uk/finance /newsbysector/retailandconsumer/9568187/Is-the-Hornby-express-about-to -hit-the-buffers.html

"James May's model railway record bid derailed by vandal attack", (26 August 2009), *The Daily Mail*, retrieved from http://www.dailymail.co.uk/news/article -1209122/James-Mays-model-railway-record-bid-derailed-vandal-attack.html

"Modelzone toy retailer collapses after failure to find buyer", by S. Neville (28 August 2013), *The Guardian*, retrieved from http://www.theguardian.com /business/2013/aug/28/modelzone-collapses-deloitte-fails-buyer

"Model maker Hornby reports loss", (7 June 2013), *BBC News*, retrieved from http://www.bbc.co.uk/news/business-22810510

Table 9-1.1: Compiled from Hornby Annual Report and Accounts 2012 > Corporate Governance Report, Business Model and Strategy, p. 16

The **First Position** case draws on information contained in:

Movitae website, located at https://movitae.com

Westmere Pilates website, located at www.westmerepilates.co.nz

Angela Gendall was interviewed by David Stewart for this case.

The **Black Gold** case draws on information contained in:

"Marmageddon! New Zealand Faces Shortage of Marmite Spread", by T. Newcomb (20 March 2012), *Time,* retrieved from http://newsfeed.time.com/2012/03 /20/marmageddon-new-zealand-faces-shortage-of-marmite-spread/

"Marmite back from March 20", by D. Williams (12 February 2013), *The National Business Review*, retrieved from http://www.nbr.co.nz/article/marmite-maker -stays-mum-comeback-dw-p-132443

"Marmite back in production – Sanitarium", by S. Kirk (12 February 2013), *Dominion Post*, retrieved from http://www.stuff.co.nz/life-style/food-wine/8293575 /Marmite-back-in-production-Sanitarium

"Marmite shortage spurs 'Marmageddon' fears", (19 March 2012), *The New Zealand Herald*, retrieved from http://www.nzherald.co.nz/business/news/article.cfm ?c_id=3&objectid=10793070

"No end in sight for Marmite shortage", by S. Kirk (28 May 2012), *Dominion Post*, retrieved from http://www.stuff.co.nz/life-style/food-wine/7000981/No-end -in-sight-for-Marmite-shortage

"Not all old fans happy with 'the new' Marmite", by C. King (21 March 2013), *Dominion Post,* retrieved from http://www.stuff.co.nz/life-style/food-wine/8452459/Not-all-old-fans-happy-with-the-new-Marmite

The **Monkey Business** case draws on information contained in:

"Cadbury issues Easter egg recall", (10 February 2007), *BBC News,* retrieved from http://news.bbc.co.uk/go/pr/fr/-/2/hi/uk_news/6349199.stm

"Cadbury's reorganisation", by R. Peston (19 June 2007), *BBC News,* retrieved from http://www.bbc.co.uk/blogs/thereporters/robertpeston/2007/06/cadburys_reorganisation.html

"Face to face with Cadbury's drumzilla", *Daily Mail,* retrieved from http://www.dailymail.co.uk/news/article-490094/Face-face-Cadburys-drumzilla.html

"Fallon and MPC 'Go Ape' for Cadbury's Dairy Milk", (24 January 2008), *The Moving Picture Company,* retrieved from http://archive.today/5NHSn

"Net fans go ape over gorilla ad", by W. Oliphant (2 November 2007), *Birmingham Mail,* retrieved from http://icbirmingham.icnetwork.co.uk/mail/news/tm_headline=net-fans-go-ape-over-gorilla-ad&method=full&objectid=20052125&siteid=50002-name_page.html

"Product recall costs Cadbury £20m", by F. Walsh (2 August 2006), *The Guardian,* retrieved from http://www.theguardian.com/business/2006/aug/02/food.foodanddrink

This chapter covers the following topics:

▶ Marketing mavericks
▶ Marketing as practice
▶ Marketing as service
▶ Digital marketing

10
Maverick Marketing

Why Marketing Needs Mavericks

Marketing is an important subject with enormous impact on modern life. More and more people are studying marketing and all kinds of enterprises, authorities, and organizations seek to employ staff with marketing expertise, skills, and knowledge. Business schools and universities have undergone a thorough marketization process and students have been redefined as customers who demand the latest useful theories and knowledge from their instructors. Yet paradoxically from an academic and theoretical perspective, there is no universal agreement about what marketing knowledge is or what are the appropriate methods for discovering it.

Despite the fact that marketing knowledge is the foundation of the discipline and it underpins all of its theories and practices this current state of academic disagreement is not new. Many of the earliest debates in academic marketing concerned which methodologies were most suitable and the theoretical underpinnings of academic marketing research itself. One major debate, which filled the marketing journals from the 1940s until the 1960s, is often summarized under the heading "marketing as science versus art" (see Alderson and Cox, 1948; Bartels, 1951; Buzzell, 1963). What Alderson and Cox meant by the development of marketing theory was the generation of general or abstract principles that enable us to better understand and predict marketing related phenomenon. This focus on prediction and control represented a particularly restrictive view of marketing theory which limits its application primarily to managerial issues.

Anderson's later paper in the *Journal of Marketing* (1983) provided the first formal, critical examination of these established marketing research assumptions from an alternative philosophical position. He questioned whether all knowledge about markets and marketing could be discovered via a single scientific method. Scientific inquiry, Anderson proposed, was a social and historical exercise which is "affected as much by sociological factors as by purely 'cognitive' or empirical considerations" (Anderson, 1986: 156). The implication for the production of knowledge in marketing was that researchers should embrace multiple philosophical positions and methods, each one possessing advantages and limitations and which should be explicitly recognized.

In the UK and Europe there were attempts to take a more critical approach to the subject in the 1990s though publications such as the conference and publications on "Rethinking Marketing: Towards Critical Marketing Accountings". Through an edited collection of contributions from leading and emerging new scholars it aimed to offer "a bigger picture of the social space which marketing occupies and the taken-for-granted ideas which occupy it" (Brownlie et al, 1999: 15). The radical philosophies and methodologies which they discussed were presented under the portmanteau label as "critical" in marketing, but the approaches which this comprised did not always sit comfortably together. What they all have in common, however, is that they embraced distinctly alternative objectives in their analysis and critique of marketing theory and practice.

In 2005 in a special editorial of the *Journal of Marketing* (see Bolton, 2005) leading US academics argued that much of the classical body of marketing knowledge has flaws and limitations and that we urgently need to rethink and re-examine the purpose, scope, and contribution that marketing science can and should be making. The outgoing JM editor at the time, Ruth Bolton, explains her purpose as being to urge marketers – both scientists and practitioners – to "expand their horizontal vision" using a quotation from *The Great Influenza* by Barry (2004) to illustrate what she means by horizontal vision. In this book Barry describes a characterization of the "genius" that produces major scientific achievements including his depiction of William Welch, who, although he was a very influential medical researcher in the early twentieth century, failed to generate any important findings.

> The research he did was first-rate. But it was only first-rate – thorough, rounded, and even irrefutable, but not deep enough or provocative enough or profound enough to set himself or others down new paths, to show the world in a new way, to make sense out of great mysteries... To do this requires

a certain kind of genius, one that probes vertically and sees horizontally. Horizontal vision allows someone to assimilate and weave together seemingly unconnected bits of information. It allows an investigator to see what others do not see and to make leaps of connectivity and creativity. Probing vertically, going deeper and deeper into something creates new information. (Barry, 2004: 60)

Meanwhile other academics in the same edition of JM voice the concern of marketing practitioners with elevating the status and authority of marketers in organizations. For example, Frederick Webster sees the tasks as "Rebuilding the influence and integrity of Marketing … Because marketing has been downsized or eliminated as a corporate function in many firms, marketing competence has waned in those organizations" (Webster, 2005: 4).

In a commentary entitled "When executives speak, we should listen and act differently" Brown (2005) mentions that several of the essays note:

> The weak linkage between marketing scholarship and marketing practice. Further contributing to this scholarship–practice gap is the diminished role and influence of marketing in companies. Sheth and Sisodia indicate (p. 11) that "many strategically important aspects of marketing … are being taken away by other functions in the organisation." The authors also note that at many companies, marketing has become a form of sales support. (Brown, 2005: 3)

Other marketing academics have responded to these concerns about the state of the discipline by seeking to find out what knowledge is useful, relevant, and valid for marketing today and developing new tools, different approaches, and alternative perspectives that offer new insights on particular or general issues. Each of these offers a different way to look at and understand marketing phenomena from alternative methodological and theoretical perspectives with different underlying assumptions.

Möller et al (2010) observe this transition as follows:

> From a fairly monolithic theoretical position in the 1960s we have traveled to a world of differentiated and specialised research scene involving metatheoretically disparate research traditions. From an initial functional view of marketing our focus has extended in various directions including the aspects of services marketing, political dimensions of channel management, and interaction in business networks, relationship marketing, and a service-logic informed theory development. As marketing academics we should not mind this, the current flux is an indication of the progress of the discipline. (Möller et al (2010))

The variety of new approaches reflects this recognition that marketing is no longer, if it ever was, "a homogenous universally applicable concept, transcending cultures and contexts" (Cannon, 1980: 140). This is caused in part by the dramatic wide ranging shifts in the work in which marketing occurs such as globalization, technology, migration, digital economy, virtuality, market deregulation, climate change, consumerism, and many others of which marketing is part.

> This presents a continual challenge for academics in an applied discipline like marketing operating in a fast-moving world because existing models and theories may tie them into particular ways of thinking, skewing their perspectives in ways that often go unquestioned and unrecognised. The building blocks of theory are its underlying concepts and definitions, the unstated assumptions that are often normative and shared amongst a particular group of individuals. *That is why we also need academics who are able and willing to question, interrogate and when necessary overthrow existing theory.* (Maclaran et al, 2009)

So this is why marketing needs mavericks who are willing to stand out from the crowd, often at first alone. In the remainder of this chapter we review and briefly assess three new approaches and debates which – although not exactly maverick now because they each have many adherents – each originally stood out from the mainstream and set out to create afresh the building blocks for marketing theories of the future. These new approaches concern (i) performativity of markets, (ii) service dominant logic, and (iii) the impact of IT on marketing.

The Ways Things Are Done Around Here

The term 'marketing as practice' encompasses a number of approaches which explicitly focus on role of wider cultural practices, including marketing activities and processes, in the construction of markets. As Araujo (2007) neatly explains, these reject the assumptions inherent in most economics and marketing theories where markets appear as "a natural given" as exemplified by Williamson's (1975: 20) dictum: "In the beginning there were markets". On the contrary, Araujo addresses the role of marketing in the construction and operation of markets by taking a perspective based on recent contributions in economic sociology that had previously been largely ignored in marketing academics' conceptualization of the exchange process.

Araujo's approach is influenced by the work of Callon (1998) and others to focus on the calculating agencies that enable the creation and operation of markets. Rather than regarding marketing practices as operating within pre-defined markets, Araujo argues that marketing practices have *a performative role* in helping to create the market and consumption phenomena they describe. The central notion of "performativity" goes beyond issues such as how theoretical frameworks permeate market participants' language and behavioural assumptions to the relationship between theories and practice in general.

Kjellberg and Helgesson (2006) develop a practice-based framework that comprises multiple theoretical influences that can play a part in the shaping of markets. They apply a broad definition performativity to take account of these multiple theoretical influences and their conjecture that the issues facing market actors are likely to be dynamic and multiple in character rather than static and dual.

They approach this issue by examining the practices that constitute markets by inquiring into how theories shape such practices, e.g. through being embedded in mundane tools that assist in regulating exchanges or in producing images of markets. The multitude of practices that constitute markets suggests the simultaneous presence of many efforts to shape markets.

Other researchers use "practice theory" to attempt to bridge the perceived theory–practice divide and explain the way marketing phenomena occur in practice. In particular it focuses on the practices - i.e. routinized types of behaviour that include both doing and saying – around which individuals express and share meanings and construct identities. Practice theory can be applied to study how such meanings are produced and reproduced in the ongoing interplay between everyday life and wider cultural forces in and around marketing.

For example, Warde (2005) notes that the wider practices in which the consumption process is integrated have often been ignored by consumer researches. This is an important omission, he argues, because people consume to support the particular conventions of the practice in which they are engaged such as eating, skiing, motoring etc. The similarities and differences between people in terms of their possessions can then be seen less as an outcome of personal choice, and more as an outcome of the way in which the practice is organized. Similarly Svensson (2007) argues that it is important to explore the human side of marketing in order to counter the mainstream marketing managerial oriented approach and better match the lifeworlds of marketing practitioners. Accordingly, he draws attention to the social and discursive nature of doing marketing work and the practices involved.

Cova and Cova (2012) use this approach to examine how marketing discourses help shape consumers. They employ a performative or practice-based approach to examine and critique the notion of the so-called "new consumer" who is supposed to be "active, knowledge-able, demanding, channel-hopping and, above all, experience seeking" (Stuart-Menteth, Wilson, and Baker, 2006: 415). Far from possessing such agency they find that there is a role for marketing ideas that perform, shape, and format the structure of consumer competencies. The paper concludes that marketing discourse comprises a governmental process that pressurizes citizens to see themselves primarily as consumers.

A Call to Service

Previously most theory assumed marketing to be about tangible goods and products, reflecting previous economic conditions. In mainstream marketing theory services were regarded as the exception and marketing tangible, physical goods the norm. The services marketing specialist field itself highlighted the "unique characteristics of services" which set them, and the study of them, apart from the "normal" marketing, i.e. of physical goods. Hypothetical differences between goods and services were stressed and distilled into the four characteristics of inseparability of production and consumption, heterogeneity, intangibility, and perishability (Zeithaml et al, 1985). These generic characteristics vis-à-vis mainstream marketing also function as a raison d'être for service marketing (Lovelock and Gummesson, 2004: 22).

Service Dominant Logic

Vargo and Lusch (2004, 2008) challenged this view of the key differentiators of services versus goods and argued for a shift in marketing theory towards services as "the norm". They propose a complete "service dominant logic" (SDL) for all marketing that constitutes a general theory of marketing. They present a wider more abstract definition of "service", as the application of specific skills and knowledge (i.e. competences) with beneficial consequences for someone. This definition goes far beyond service as an object of exchange and makes it applicable to *all* marketing practice and theoretically encompasses everything in advanced society. They are not modest in their ambitions for SDL, which they posit as the primary organizational principle of society.

> [We] have also suggested that S-D logic could provide the foundation for a revised theory of the firm, a theory of service systems, and *a revised theory of economics and society*. (Vargo and Lusch, 2008: 3)

Although Vargo and Lusch's arguments for the predominance of service in marketing are primarily theoretical, there are additional reasons to support this view based on the nature and changing structure of modern economies within which marketing occurs. Compared to previous centuries, fewer economic and business activities produce or exchange physical goods and more now market services, produce services, or consume services. Therefore most markets exchange services in one form or another, not material products.

In advanced economies the proportion of economic activity in the service sector is expanding and now far exceeds that of manufacturing or agriculture according to all relevant measures such as percentage of total output or employment. The evidence clearly shows that all developed economies are de-industrializing, with a consequent shift in economic activity away from manufacturing towards service. In some countries more than 75% of economic output (GDP) in developed countries now centres on services (OECD 2013).

As a new contender for dominance in marketing theory, in a short time SDL has stimulated much renewed interest and discussion about theory development in marketing. The focus of SDL is on marketing as a value co-creation process that is service-based. According to this view marketers do not sell physical products or create value. They can only provide value propositions, embedded in offerings, and their value depends entirely on the experiential evaluation of customers. Service, not goods, is the fundamental basis of exchange and goods are merely "distribution mechanisms for service provision". Another key aspect is the role of know-how, capabilities, and competencies that are the key "operant resources" for both creating value propositions and extracting value from them as the primary source of competitive advantage. The corollary is that the role of tangible, finite "operand resources" is to provide the raw material inputs.

Central to the SDL approach is its distinction from that referred to by Vargo and Lusch as the historical, still prevailing goods dominant logic, (GDL) based on tangible goods and the activities associated with their delivery:

Since at least the time of Smith's (1776) declaration that "productive" meant the creation of surplus tangible goods that could be exported to enhance national wealth, the lexicon of economics, business, and society in general (in its discussion of business) has developed around a logic of tangible goods. The goods-centric nature of the language of commerce can be seen in the core lexicon: "product", "production", "goods", "supplier", "supply chain", "value added", "distribution", "producer", "consumer", etc. This foundational lexicon reflects more than just words available to talk about goods; it reflects an underlying paradigm for thinking about commerce, marketing, and exchange in general. (Vargo and Lusch, 2008: 2)

Thus GDL is presented as the antithesis to the SDL, which provides a "shift in thinking" and is advocated as the basis of a new unified theory of marketing. It is based on ten foundational premises (FPs) which are presented with various conceptual and empirical justifications. These are summarized below with verbatim explanations from Vargo and Lusch (2008: 7).

The Foundational Premises of SDL

FP1   Service is the fundamental basis of exchange
Explanation: The application of operant resources (knowledge and skills), "service," as defined in S-D logic, is the basis for all exchange. Service is exchanged for service.

FP2   Indirect exchange masks the fundamental basis of exchange
Explanation: Because service is provided through complex combinations of goods, money, and institutions, the service basis of exchange is not always apparent.

FP3   Goods are a distribution mechanism for service provision
Explanation: Goods (both durable and non-durable) derive their value through use – the service they provide.

FP4   Operant resources are the fundamental source of competitive advantage
Explanation: The comparative ability to cause desired change drives competition.

FP5   All economies are service economies
Explanation: Service (singular) is only now becoming more apparent with increased specialization and outsourcing.

FP6   The customer is always a co-creator of value
Explanation: Implies value creation is interactional.

(continued overleaf)

FP7 The enterprise cannot deliver value, but only offer value propositions
Explanation: Enterprises can offer their applied resources for value creation and collaboratively (interactively) create value following acceptance of value propositions, but cannot create and/or deliver value independently.

FP8 A service-centred view is inherently customer oriented and relational
Explanation: Because service is defined in terms of customer-determined benefit and co-created it is inherently customer oriented and relational.

FP9 All social and economic actors are resource integrators
Explanation: Implies the context of value creation is networks of networks (resource integrators).

FP10 Value is always uniquely and phenomenologically determined by the beneficiary
Explanation: Value is idiosyncratic, experiential, contextual, and meaning laden.

Together these ten propositions form the basis for SDL. There is a very broad range of assertions and themes addressed by the FPs and the scope of socio-economic theory and practice which they encompass is very wide. Taken together it is not an overstatement to suggest that *everything is a service*.

> All of this may sound like we are suggesting that everything is a service. In a very *real sense we are*; we are suggesting that economic exchange is fundamentally about service provision. (Vargo and Lusch, 2004: 326)

We do not have space here to discuss and evaluate all these aspects of SDL adequately. We recommend readers to consult one of Varo and Lusch's original works (2004, 2005, 2006, 2008) in order to explore their ideas further.

The New Frontier

The so-called digital revolution of the Internet, e-commerce, computer-mediated markets, and the mobile economy is built on a technology that essentially removes distance as a barrier between buyer and seller. Many implications for marketing follow from this. In the view of many marketing authors the most important implications are for consumer behaviour, communications, traditional channels, marketing relationships, and negotiations.

Today, the effects of the digital age are felt throughout marketing practice in all organizations, impacting all the core operations areas, including market analysis and decision making, monitoring and control, communications, distribution channels, product development, service management and delivery, etc. Although modern marketing practice requires that marketers have a clear understanding and ability to use information technology even the basic technical capabilities of IT have far outstripped most marketers' knowledge and capability to utilize it (Brady et al, 2002).

One topical example which illustrates the potentially transformative effects of digitization on marketing is the value-added opportunities that can be created and delivered in the developing mobile economy. The current mobile market is developing rapidly as the availability and choice of mobile application services are offered to customers independently of the network supporting these services. Traditionally, much of the control of the value chain and delivery process has remained with the seller, which has been a top-down approach based upon some long-term service subscription. However, the customer is now able to control the configuration for network access so the degree of customer empowerment is greater. The specification of the device's function is set by the user or by software acting on the user's behalf. Users, through their customized intelligent mobile terminals, will interact with numerous networks in search of various services at prices acceptable to them.

The shape and characteristics of the mobile information future will depend on the behaviour and interaction of four key actors, service providers, customers, competitors, and regulation bodies. This digital business model has a huge potential for realizing richer communication, information, and entertainment services, anywhere and anytime. Generally, the more vertically integrated the mobile service, the easier it is to use but the less flexibility it provides to users. Multiple business models can co-exist to serve groups of consumers differentiated by the relative weighting of these two attributes (ease of use vs flexibility). However, the more disaggregated the business model, the stronger the innovation engine of the mobile economy. In other words, there is a fundamental tension between truly fixed functionality and the user-customized approach for diversity and constant change. So the implications for marketing in this single example are potentially transformational for the marketing function in many types of organizations beyond the mobile service industry.

Furthermore, it is as yet unclear what will be the impact on the customer, e.g. how they will respond when faced with so much more choice. Also, the key dimensions influencing customer behaviour in this new infoscape are not clear, e.g. technology, knowledge, use, functionality, etc. The dynamic and intertwined effects of any technology are notoriously difficult to determine; therefore, the impact of the digital on marketing is always going to be a moving target. Despite a considerable amount of research in this fast-moving area many basic questions such as these remain unanswered.

Case Study

Case 10-1 Brave New World

Are you a surfer? Searchable? Both? The Internet has permeated our lives, to the extent that the world has gone digital. This has given marketers the opportunity to reach people in different ways, but these ways are ever changing.

Digital has affected the growth of billboards. Once seen as a dull industry, the advent of low-cost flat screens has meant that billboards can now have advertisements to rival television commercials. Advertisers can change their message based on the time of day, or change the advertisement quickly to reflect a major event, like an FA Cup score. Billboards offer interaction via smartphones, where consumers take a photo of the billboard via an app that provides production information, the nearest retail location, and discount vouchers.

Mobile advertising has started to grow with advertisers targeting consumers on their smartphones via Google, Facebook, etc. Consumers now spend more time with their smartphones and tablets than they do on their computers.

Smartphones are becoming like a "Swiss army knife", as they are used for texting, emailing, gaming, media viewing, browsing, and purchasing. Shoppers can use their smartphones to scan bar codes to see if they can get a better deal. Mobile phones are an important device in a customer's shopping journey, along with using PCs and going to the store.

An app has been developed so that when your smartphone is close to a store or café chain that you like, a message will alert you to the location and offer you a discount on a certain purchase, e.g. a muffin.

Vocalink, which runs UK's payments infrastructure and is owned by 18 banks and building societies, has developed a smartphone app known as Zapp. The system, which can be used by the 18 million current account holders with HSBC, First Direct, Nationwide, Santander, and Metro Bank, will at first be used for online payments, but it is expected that by 2015, the app will be able to be used in one in five stores. Zapp is deemed to be more secure than a credit card as card numbers are not shared with a third party.

Soon, shoppers will be able to leave their wallets at home.

Questions

1. *How does the growth of digital change marketing?*
2. *Is digital marketing a revolution or an evolution?*

MAVERICK MARKETING

Case 10-2 Power by the Hour

On 4 November 2010, shortly after take-off from Singapore, passengers on a Qantas flight heard a loud bang, indicating a mid-air failure in one of its Rolls-Royce Trent 900 engines. Due to an oil leak, a fire had exploded in the engine, causing the disintegration of the turbine discs, which blasted through the plane's wing. The flight landed safely and subsequently Qantas grounded its entire fleet of Airbus A380 planes, pending further investigation. In June 2013 the final report of the incident concluded that several pipes in the engine were too thin and needed modification. Rolls-Royce admitted that they had fallen short of safety standards and in response they overhauled their quality management systems and implemented further safety features that would shut the engine down if a future incident occurred.

The aircraft manufacturing industry is strong and it remains resilient to incidents such as the one above. For the period 2012–2033 Airbus Industrie forecast that 27,300 passenger aircraft, with capacity of 100 seats or more, would be ordered, as well as 900 new freighter aircraft. They predict in the same period there will be a doubling of passenger aircraft inventory from 15,500 to 32,500 planes. At the Paris Air Show in June 2013, airline operators placed 677 new orders with manufacturers, consisting of 340 from low-cost airlines and 337 from full service airlines, whilst Rolls-Royce received close to £5 billion for new engine orders, boosted by the fact that they were appointed the dedicated provider of engines for the new Airbus A350, which is Airbus Industrie's answer to the Boeing 787 Dreamliner. Consequently Rolls-Royce' order book is now close to £61.4 billion.

Part of Rolls-Royce' success is the Trent engine. When the company emerged from state ownership in 1980 they set the goal of building a jet engine for every type of aircraft. At that stage they had approximately an 8% share of the civil turbo fan market, compared to Pratt and Whitney, the dominant leader, who had 90% of the market in the 1960s. There are huge development costs with building a new jet engine, so the strategy was to build a family of engines based on a common core. The product of this strategy was the Trent, which is a three spool, high bypass turbofan engine that can be scaled to meet performance and thrust requirements (see Table 10-2.1).

The engine has 10,000 parts, with titanium fan blades at the front which suck in air that is then compacted by a smaller set of blades and is funnelled into a combustion chamber where it is ignited by kerosene, causing an explosion to produce the power to turn the fan blades, thus causing a loop. However, approximately 80% of the engine's thrust derives from air that

Table 10-2.1 Trent engine types

Date Introduced	Model	Aircraft	Early Adopters
1989	Trent 700	Airbus 330	Cathay Pacific Trans World Airlines
1993	Trent 800	Boeing 777	Cathay Pacific Singapore Airlines
1999	Trent 500	Airbus 340	Virgin Atlantic Airways
2000	Trent 900	Airbus 380	Singapore Airlines Qantas
2004	Trent 1000	Boeing 787	All Nippon Airways Air New Zealand
2007	Trent XWB	Airbus 350	Qatar Airways Emirates Airline

bypasses the combustion chamber. Rolls-Royce is still developing the high performance engine to make it more efficient and more compact. To achieve this the company is linked with 28 universities in the UK by providing research funds. Due to the breadth of intellectual property and its history of research and development, Rolls-Royce has created high barriers to entry, but competition between the three engine manufacturers is intense. The company now has 40% of the market behind the market leader, General Electric (GE).

A jet engine has a life of 20 to 25 years, with full overhauls necessary every five years. All jet engines need ongoing maintenance and traditionally this was provided by service agreements between the Original Equipment Manufacturer (OEM) and the airline. Jet engines were bought or leased and a transaction fee was paid for every single maintenance event based on spare parts and labour costs. Therefore the OEM profited when the equipment failed and maintenance was required. This meant the OEM made money when the aircraft was not flying in contrast to the airline that made money when the plane was in the air.

Rolls-Royce decided to change the model by aligning the two goals of being a service provider and keeping the aircraft flying, that is, Rolls-Royce would be paid for continuous up time, rather being paid by the old model of continuous down time. Therefore the new model was to move from a transaction-based maintenance provider to a service provider where performance outcomes became the goal. This strategy would let airlines worry about the core business of flying instead of worrying about down time. In essence the incentive for Rolls-Royce was to reduce engine down time by improving engine on-wing life by increasing engine reliability and undertaking preventive maintenance. In pursuit of the goal to minimize disruptions Rolls-Royce actively manages the engine through the life cycle.

Termed "power by the hour" customers pay a fixed fee for every flying hour. To implement this strategy the company instigated a collaborative approach with their customers so that they could fully understand the customer's operation. This approach required Rolls-Royce to build a partnership with the airlines, which meant a culture change from being an OEM jet engine manufacturer to being a customer-centred service provider. The product developed, TotalCare, has three basic elements, namely operational support, repair and maintenance, and information management with optional services that an airline can purchase. For instance, in Derby, the headquarters of Rolls-Royce, staff monitor the performance of 3500 engines flying at any one time as the engines are equipped with sensors. This enables them to spot potential issues, thus negating the need to strip the engine down, as this can be costly if the engine fails in a remote location and has to be removed and shipped to a site where the overhaul can take place.

TotalCare is a single source solution that allows airlines to transfer technical and financial risks associated with engine maintenance to Rolls-Royce, thereby from the airline's point of view there are no surprises as costs are predictable allowing for financial planning by agreeing on a fixed dollar rate per hour flying. It also allows the airline to gain improvement in efficiency by minimizing operational disruptions. Rolls-Royce reports that 92% of Trent engines sold have TotalCare agreements representing half the revenue for the company and providing 70% profit.

Rolls-Royce has been able to exploit synergies by selling the Trent engine and TotalCare package in other applications where turbines are used, such as in the Queen Elizabeth ship, aircraft carriers, and electricity generators. A subsidiary company, Tidal Generation, is developing underwater power turbines where the tide is used to generate electricity. It is believed that this technology has the potential to provide 7.5% of the UK's electricity.

Questions

1. *Evaluate Rolls-Royce's response to market demand.*
2. *Apply the principles of service dominant logic to the TotalCare programme.*
3. *Does the TotalCare programme provide Rolls-Royce with a competitive advantage?*

Case Study

Case 10-3 Organized Chaos

Guerilla marketing is the breaking of marketing methods by avoiding traditional media channels to reach people with a marketing message. Unlike traditional media, where the ad can be shown over a long period of time, with Guerilla marketing the idea is to make a big impression before disappearing. There are many types of Guerilla marketing, as it is a loosely applied term. For instance, viral marketing, when a message is sent via social media, connects people in a personal and memorable way. Viral marketing can be seen as digital word of mouth.

Flash mobs are another example of Guerilla marketing. In this case a group of people infiltrate a public area, blend with the public, then perform a song or dance to promote a marketing message. A well-known example of flash mobs is people having a mass pillow fight.

Flash mobs are popular due to the ease of communication via the internet, phone, or text messaging. However, labour costs can be high and other expenses may be incurred due to the need to hire the necessary signs, vehicle, and props to support the event. A flash mob was used to create the TVC "Dance", created by Saatchi & Saatchi London for T-Mobile (now EE) as part of their "Life's for Sharing" campaign.

At 11.00 am on Thursday, 15 January 2009 at Liverpool Street Station a troupe of 350 dancers, including tourists and underground staff, performed to music such as Lulu's "Shout", Kool & the Gang, the Viennese Waltz, and Millie Small's "My Boy Lollipop". Hidden cameras filmed the spontaneous reactions of commuters.

The three-minute TVC was shown as a news item for the entire break on "Celebrity Big Brother", 48 hours after being filmed. Extra footage showing the making of the ad could be viewed by people hitting the red button on their TV remote controls. The ad was placed on YouTube and went viral. In March 2010 the T-Mobile ad won the television commercial of the year at the British Television Advertising Awards.

Questions

1. What was the purpose of the TVC and was it successful?
2. What other types of Guerilla marketing exist?
3. Why do companies adopt it as a strategy?

Case 10-4 Different to the Core

Can 60 seconds make a difference? In 1984 one company ran one television ad just once to announce its new product. The placement was the commercial spot during the third quarter of the Super Bowl; the company was Apple Computer and the product was the Macintosh personal computer. Decades later it is still talked about and, according to *Forbes* magazine, it rates as the best Super Bowl ad ever.

Apple (dropping the "Computer" from its name in 2007) had positioned itself as doing things differently to the status quo. The company was viewed as creative, innovative, and counter-culture following the "1984" debut. However, during the 1990s the company languished – co-founder Steve Jobs had left the business and its advertising became much more conventional, relying on product features and price points more than brand. Jobs returned to the company late in 1996 and is said to have been struck by the lack of innovation shown by the product development and marketing teams.

He set about seeking new ideas from advertising agencies and re-appointed Chiat/Day, the agency which had delivered "1984" so successfully. The new concept was "Think Different". The ads did not include any product information, and instead featured images of famous people. Payment for the use of the images was in the form of donations of money and computer equipment to charities and not-for-profit organizations. Print advertising was placed in magazines other than computing, e.g. fashion and popular culture, and billboards – use of which was practically unheard of in the computer industry at the time – were secured in major New York and Los Angeles sites. It was a clear re-establishment of Apple's counter-culture image that it had discarded in the 1990s.

The "Think Different" ads won a large number of awards and Apple went on to send complimentary posters to public schools across the US for them to hang the different portraits of celebrities in classrooms. It was a message of inspiration and a dedication to those who dared to make a difference. The campaign ran until 2002 and acted as a turning point for Apple.

Questions
1. *In what ways can Steve Jobs be considered a maverick marketer?*
2. *Can his influence be replicated, and would Apple want this to happen?*

Alderson, W. and Cox, R. (1948) Towards a Theory of Marketing, *Journal of Marketing*, 13(2): 137–152.

Anderson, P. (1983) Marketing, Scientific Progress, and the Scientific Method, *Journal of Marketing* 47(4): 18–31.

Anderson, P. (1986) On Method in Consumer Research: A Critical Relativist Perspective, *Journal of Consumer Research*, 13(2): 155–173.

Araujo, L. (2007) Markets, Market-making and Marketing, *Marketing Theory*, 7(3): 211–226.

Barry, J.M. (2004) *The Great Influenza: The Epic Story of the Deadliest Plague in History*. New York: Viking Penguin.

Bartels, R. (1951) Can Marketing be a Science?, *The Journal of Marketing*, 51(1): 319–328.

Bolton, R. (2005) Marketing Renaissance: Opportunities and Imperatives for Improving Marketing Thought, Practice, and Infrastructure, *Journal of Marketing*, October: 1–24.

Brady, M., Saren, M. and Tzokas, N. (2002) Integrating Information Technology into Marketing Practice, *Journal of Marketing Management*, 18(6): 555–578.

Brown, S.W. (2005) When Executives Speak, We Should Listen and Act Differently, *Journal of Marketing*, October, 3.

Brownlie, D., Saren, M., Wensley, R. and Whittington, R. (eds) (1999) *Rethinking Marketing: Towards Critical Marketing Accountings*. London: Sage.

Buzzell, R.D. (1963) Is Marketing a Science?, *Harvard Business Review*, 41(1): 32–40.

Callon, M. (1998) (ed.) *The Laws of the Market*. Oxford: Basil Blackwell.

Cannon, T. (1980) Marketing: The state of the art (or science), *Management Learning* 11, 138–144.

Cova, B. and Cova, V. (2012) On the Road to Prosumption: Marketing discourse and the development of consumer competencies, *Consumption Markets & Culture*, 15(2): 149–168.

Kjellberg, H. and Helgesson, C. (2006) Multiple Versions of Markets: Multiplicity and Performativity in Market Practice, *Industrial Marketing Management*, 35(7): 839–855.

Lovelock, C. and Gummesson, E. (2004) Whither Service Marketing? In search of a new paradigm and fresh perspectives, *Journal of Service Research*, 7(1): 20–41.

MacLaran P., Saren, M., Goulding, C. and Stevens, L. (2009) Rethinking Theory Building and Theorizing in Marketing, 38th *European Marketing Academy Conference*, University of Nantes, France, May 2009.

Möller, K., Pels, J. and Saren, M. (2010) "The Marketing Theory or Theories into Marketing? Plurality of Research Traditions and Paradigms". In *The SAGE Handbook of Marketing Theory*, MacLaran, P., Saren, M., Stern, B. and Tadajewski, M. (eds), London: Sage, 151–173.

OECD. Statistics 2013 http://stats.oecd.org/data.

Smith, A. (1776/1961) *The Wealth of Nations*. Edwin Cannan (ed), London: Methuen.

Stuart-Menteth, H., Wilson, H. and Baker, S. (2006) Escaping the Channel Silo: Researching the New Consumer, *International Journal of Market Research*, 48(4): 415–438.

Svensson, P. (2007) Producing Marketing: Towards a Social-Phenomenology of Marketing Work, *Marketing Theory*, 7(3): 271–290.

Vargo, S. L. and Lusch, R. F. (2004) Evolving to a New Dominant Logic for Marketing, *Journal of Marketing*, 68 (January): 1–17.

Vargo, S.L. and Lusch, R.F. (2006) Service-Dominant Logic: What It Is, What It Is Not, What It Might Be. In *The Service-Dominant Logic of Marketing: Dialog, Debate, and Directions*, Lusch, R.F. and Vargo, S.L. (eds), Armonk, NY: M.E. Sharpe, 43–56.

Vargo, S.L. and Lusch, R.F. (2008) Service-dominant Logic: Continuing the evolution, *Journal of the Academy of Marketing Science*, 36(1): 1–10.

Vargo, S.L. and Morgan, F.W. (2005) Services in Society and Academic Thought: An Historical Analysis, *Journal of Macromarketing*, 25(1): 42–53.

Warde, A. (2005) Consumption and Theories of Practice, *Journal of Consumer Culture*, 5(2): 131–153.

Webster, F.E. (2005) Rebuilding the Influence and Integrity of Marketing, *Journal of Marketing*, October, 4.

Williamson, O.E. (1975) *Markets and Hierarchies: Analysis and Antitrust Implications*. New York: Free Press.

Zeithaml, V., Parasuraman, A. and Berry, L. (1985) Problems and Strategies in Services Marketing, *Journal of Marketing*, 49(2): 33–48.

Case Acknowledgements

The **Brave New World** case draws on information contained in:

"Britain takes the lead in mobile advertising", by C. Williams (12 December 2013), *The Telegraph*, retrieved from http://www.telegraph.co.uk/finance /newsbysector/mediatechnologyandtelecoms/digital-media/10512003 /Britain-takes-the-lead-in-mobile-advertising.html

"Building with big data", by Schumpeter (28 May 2011), *The Economist*, retrieved from http://www.economist.com/node/18741392

"Out-of-home advertising Billboard boom", (23 April 2011), *The Economist*, retrieved from http://www.economist.com/node/18587305

"Zapp app to enable millions more shoppers to pay by smartphone", by H. Meyer, *The Guardian*, retrieved from http://www.theguardian.com/business/2014/jan /15/zapp-app-millions-shoppers-pay-smartphone

The **Power by the Hour** case draws on information contained in

Coates, D. (2013), "Rolls-Royce", *Growth Champions*, September, retrieved from http://growthchampions.org/growth-champions/rollsroyce/

"Customising services packages: Why TotalCare works", (6 December 2006), *Air Transport News*, retrieved from http://www.atn.aero/article.pl?&id=713&keys =rolls%20royce

"Questor share tip: Rolls-Royce is a real growth engine", by G. White (10 June 2012), *The Telegraph*, retrieved from http://www.telegraph.co.uk/finance/markets /questor/9321043/Questor-share-tip-Rolls-Royce-is-a-real-growth-engine.html

"Questor share tip: Rolls-Royce orders fly after Paris Air Show", by G. White (28 June 2013), *The Telegraph*, retrieved from http://www.telegraph.co.uk/finance /markets/questor/10146670/Questor-share-tip-Rolls-Royce-orders-fly-after -Paris-Air-Show.html

"Rolls-Royce Engine Support", (1 June 2006), *Aviation Today*, retrieved from http://www.aviationtoday.com/regions/china/Rolls-Royce-Engine-Support _345.html#.UwK1hf3u7wI

Rolls-Royce Holdings plc website located at www.rolls-royce.com

"Rolls-Royce jet engine which exploded on Qantas A380 superjumbo flight failed due to a 'poorly built oil pipe'", by O. Williams (27 June 2013), *Daily Mail*, retrieved from http://www.dailymail.co.uk/news/article-2349454/Rolls -Royce-jet-engine-exploded-Qantas-A380-superjumbo-flight-failed-poorly-built -oil-pipe.html

Ryals, L. (2010), 'Rolls-Royce Totalcare: Meeting the Needs of Key Customers', *Cranfield Executive Briefing*, March

"The Rolls-Royce Of Effective Performance-Based Collaboration", by K. Vitasek (11 June 2012), *Maintenance Technology*, retrieved from http://www.mt-online.com /june2012/the-rolls-royce-of-effective-performancea-based-collaboration

"Why Rolls-Royce is one British manufacturer flying high in a downturn", (Summer 2009), *Design Council Magazine*, Issue 6

"Why Rolls-Royce is seen as engine of recovery for UK economy", by D. Milmo (11 November 2011), *The Guardian*, retrieved from http://www.theguardian.com /business/2011/nov/11/rolls-royce-engine-recovery-economy

Table 10-2.1: Compiled from information located at http://www.rolls-royce.com /civil/products/largeaircraft/

The **Organized Chaos** case draws on information contained in:

"Guerrilla Marketing Vs. Viral Marketing", by D. Ingram, *Houston Chronicle*, retrieved from http://smallbusiness.chron.com/guerrilla-marketing-vs-viral -marketing-11786.html

"T-Mobile flashmob wins TV ad of the year", by M. Sweney (11 March 2010), *The Guardian*, retrieved from http://www.theguardian.com/media/2010/mar/11 /tmobile-flashmob-ad-of-year

"T-Mobile unleashes guerilla dance routine at Liverpool Street", by J. Bowser (15 January 2009), *Brand Republic*, retrieved from http://www.brandrepublic .com/news/873942/T-Mobile-unleashes-guerilla-dance-routine-Liverpool -Street/

The **Different to the Core** case draws on information contained in:

"Experts and Viewers Agree: Apple's '1984' Is the Best Super Bowl Ad Of All Time", by J. Smith (30 January 2012), *Forbes*, retrieved from http://www.forbes .com/sites/jacquelynsmith/2012/01/30/experts-and-viewers-agree-apples -1984-is-the-best-super-bowl-ad-of-all-time/

"Microsoft falls behind Apple for first time in 20 years", by C. Arthur (28 April 2011), *The Guardian,* retrieved from http://www.theguardian.com/technology /2011/apr/28/microsoft-falls-behind-apple

"Think Different: The Ad Campaign that Restored Apple's Reputation", by T. Hormby (10 August 2013) http://lowendmac.com/2013/think-different-ad -campaign-restored-apples-reputation/

Glossary

Adoption rate   The relative speed consumers adopt a new technology or idea. The adoption rate will be influenced by the type of innovation, time, communication channels used, and the social system.

Advertising   A non-personal form of communication used to persuade people to buy a product or service, or to undertake a certain action, e.g. drive safely.

Advertising media   The different types of media used to reach target audiences, e.g. newspaper, radio, website, etc. Often referred to as the media mix.

Advertising reach   The number of people exposed to a media schedule over a given time period. This can be compared to frequency, which is the amount of times a person has been exposed to the specific media.

Barrier to entry   The obstacles that need to be overcome by a new entrant into a market.

Boundary-spanners   The people who link the organization with external networks, e.g. customer service representatives.

Brand   A brand is a name, term, sign, symbol, or design used to identify and distinguish one product/service in the marketplace from the competition.

Brand extension   The use of an existing brand name used on a new product in a different category. The belief is that positive associations of the parent brand will be transferred to the new brand.

Brand switching   This occurs when consumers change their buying behaviour from one brand to a competitor's brand. Often consumers have within a category a portfolio of brands they choose so will switch depending on circumstances. Switching behaviour may also occur when there are line extensions, e.g. cherry coke to diet coke.

Buyer Power   A situation where the buyer has dominance over the seller.

Capabilities   Unique activities or attributes that enable a company to pursue their marketing strategy.

Category   A category is a group of products or services that fulfil the same customer need, e.g. fast food.

Competitive advantage   A company can gain a competitive advantage by either providing the same value as competitors at a lower price, or charging a higher price than the competitors by sustaining increased added value.

Consumer durables   Products bought by consumers for long-term use, e.g. washing machine.

Costing   A calculation that is used to determine the value of something that has been produced.

Cost-plus pricing   A pricing strategy that determines the selling price of a product by calculating the cost then adding a percentage markup.

Critical marketing   Involves the exploration of marketing beyond business and the market exchange process to broader societal issues, including a criticism of marketing and its role in consumer society.

Critical success factors   Factors or activities that are necessary for a business to be successful within a given industry at a particular point in time.

Crowdsourcing   The process of obtaining work, ideas, or funding from members of the public, often via the Internet.

Debt:equity ratio   Indicates the leverage of a company and is calculated by dividing the company's total liabilities by stockholders' equity. A high ratio would indicate the company is using debt to finance its assets.

Demand backward pricing   A pricing method where costs are deducted from the price consumers are willing to pay, thereby calculating likely profitability of a product or service.

Differentiation   A strategy to offer unique benefits compared to the competition that are valued by the customer.

Diffusion of innovation   A theory that explains how innovation spreads through a community by five distinct stages.

Disposable income   The amount of income a household has after tax has been paid. Disposable income is used to pay essentials, such as food, transport, and housing. Any money left over is discretionary income, which can be used on non-essential items.

Distribution channels   The path(s) used to get goods from the manufacturer to the consumer.

Economies of scale   The average cost decreases as output increases, thereby leading to a cost advantage.

Economies of scope   The average cost decreases when spread over a number of products.

Environmental scanning   The task of monitoring the external environment for opportunities and threats.

Experience curve   The more a task is performed the more the unit cost decreases due to increase from experience of learning and increase in experience from economies of scale.

First movers   Often termed pioneer brands, first movers can quickly build market share and shape the market, including setting customer preferences.

Five Forces framework   Developed by Michael Porter, the framework outlines five forces that influence industry attractiveness and profitability.

Forecasting   A planning activity to determine the future demand for a product/service by selecting the influential variables, based on management's experience, knowledge, and market research.

Form   A subset of a category.

Hierarchy of effects   A model outlining the five stages of successful advertising.

Innovation   A process where new products, services, or ideas are generated to meet the needs and expectations of the customer.

Internal marketing   The process of communicating to employees as if they are the customers, thereby enabling them to understand their role in the marketing programme.

Macro environment   The external factors that affect the performance of the organization, e.g. the economy.

Marginal pricing   Selling an additional product at the variable cost plus a margin, assuming that the current output is priced at full cost.

Market penetration   The number of people in a target market who consume a product or service, often expressed as a percentage.

Market research   The process of obtaining information in an organized way to determine customers' needs, wants, and product/service experiences.

Market share   The percentage of the penetrated market for a product/service held by one company at a specific time.

Marketer   A person who organizes the relational exchange between the organization and the customer.

Marketing mix   A framework used by marketers to organize their endeavour. Often referred to as the 4Ps, representing Product, Price, Promotion, and Place. To include the increased interest in the service economy an additional 3Ps have been added, namely Personnel, Process, and Physical Evidence.

Marketing strategy   The long-term allocation of resources within a market to enhance the company's relational exchange so that a sustainable competitive advantage is obtained.

Micro environment   Factors in the immediate area of operation that influence a business's performance.

Modular manufacturing   A process whereby modules are produced which are interchangeable so can be used on different models.

Moment of truth   A point in the interaction between the organization and customer, where an impression of the quality of the service is obtained.

Network marketing   A system of long-term collaboration between organizations, suppliers, and customers.

Perceptual map   Technique used to plot customers' perceptions of the different products or brands in a category in relation to each other. Two or more defining attributes are used as the x and y axes. Perceptual maps are a visual representation of products' or brands' position within the category.

Physical evidence   The physical cues that consumers use as a substitute to gauge the quality of an intangible service offering.

Planning   The task of developing a plan to manage the demand of a company's offering by identifying the activities to satisfy customers' needs and wants.

Positioning   The task of influencing the customer's perception of a brand relative to the competition within a given market.

Pricing   The task of setting the selling price of a product/service in a market.

Relational exchange   The arrangement between a buyer and seller based on the long-term benefit for both parties. This can be compared with transactional exchange, which is a short-term, one-off arrangement.

Relationship marketing   Activities that build trusting and long-term relationships with customers, thereby building loyalty.

Reverse engineering   The task of disassembling a product or system to see how it has been constructed, so as to improve the design.

Sales management   The task of managing the sales force and related activities to meet the company's sales objectives.

Segmentation   The grouping of homogenous customers into different groups based on their distinct needs and wants.

Service Dominant Logic   Notion proposed by Vargo and Lusch (2004) that all marketing is about service as opposed to physical goods.

Servicescape   The physical environment, including ambience, where a service is delivered.

Switching costs   The cost that may be incurred by buyers when moving from one brand to another.

SWOT   An analysis of a firm's internal strengths and weaknesses compared to the opportunities and threats in the external environment.

Synergy   The combined total effect and performance of combined activities that is greater than the sum of the individual parts, e.g. 2+2=5.

Target market   The segment of a population that a company can serve that is definable, accessible, actionable, and profitable.

Target ROI   A method of setting the selling price based on a profit percentage of the investment required to produce the product. The company calculates the unit cost to produce a product then adds the required amount to recoup a return on the initial investment.

Value chain   The distinct but linked processes that a firm undertakes to add value to a product.

Value creation   The activities that a firm uses to generate the perceived value of a product/service.

Value proposition   An implicit promise a company makes to deliver a particular combination of values to the benefit of the customers.

Acronyms Used

4Ps   Product, Price, Promotion, Place

7Ps   Product, Price, Promotion, Place, Personnel, Process, Physical Evidence

AIDA   Attention, Interest, Desire, Action

B2B   Business to Business

B2C   Business to Consumer

C2C   Consumer to Consumer

CCT   Consumer Culture Theory

CEO   Chief Executive Officer

CRM   Customer Relationship Management

FMA   First Mover Advantage

FMCG   Fast Moving Consumer Goods

GDL   Goods Dominant Logic

GDP   Gross Domestic Product

IMC   Integrated Marketing Communications

IT   Information Technology

JM   Journal of Marketing

MIS   Marketing Information System

NCU   New Category User

NPD   New Product Development

OEM   Original Equipment Manufacturer

PIMS   Profit Impact of Market Strategy

PLC   Product Life Cycle

PR	Public Relations
R&D	Research and Development
RM	Relationship marketing
ROI	Return on Investment
SBM	Strategic Brand Management
SBU	Strategic Business Unit
SCM	Supply Chain Management
SDL	Service Dominant Logic
SWOT	Strengths, Weaknesses, Opportunities, Threats
TM	Transactional marketing

Index

Index compiled by Annette Musker